Virtual Ethnography

Virtual Ethnography

CHRISTINE HINE

SAGE Publications
London • Thousand Oaks • New Delhi

First published 2000, Reprinted 2001, 2003

 SAGE Publications Ltd
6 Bonhill Street
London EC2A 4PU

SAGE Publications Inc
2455 Teller Road
Thousand Oaks, California 91320

SAGE Publications India Pvt Ltd
32, M-Block Market
Greater Kailash – I
New Delhi 110 048

British Library Cataloguing in Publication data

A catalogue record for this book is available
from the British Library

ISBN 0 7619 5895 9
ISBN 0 7619 5896 7 (pbk)

Library of Congress catalog record available

Typeset by Mayhew Typesetting, Rhayader, Powys
Printed in Great Britain by The Cromwell Press Ltd,
Trowbridge, Wiltshire

Contents

Acknowledgements

This book is about the ways in which use of the Internet is made meaningful in local contexts. It is therefore appropriate, as well as necessary, that I should start by acknowledging the local context which made production of this book possible. Since 1991 I have been a member of the Centre for Research into Innovation, Culture and Technology (CRICT) at Brunel University. The intellectual environment provided by CRICT, the people I have met and the ideas I have encountered there have been central to the development of the perspective explored here. I owe a huge debt accumulated over the years to Steve Woolgar, Mike Lynch, Alan Irwin, Geoff Cooper, Eric Hirsch, Janet Rachel, Stuart Shapiro, Janet Vaux, David Oswell, Julian Petley, Chris Carne, Clare Fisher, Liz Ackroyd, Debbie Chagouri and Donna Page. Supervising PhD students has also been a source of insight and inspiration, and I thank Linda Hitchin, Andrea Buchholz, Tilly Blyth, Nathan Blau, Robert Pain and Dan Neyland. Teaching a course on the Social Dynamics of Communications Technologies has helped me to formulate and clarify my ideas, and I am grateful to the Communications and Media Studies and MA Communications and Technology students who have taken that course over the years and helped to make it a stimulating and enjoyable experience. Teaching Communications and Media Studies students to develop web pages has been an opportunity to combine theory and practice, and to participate in the learning processes through which web pages are made to make sense. More widely, I have benefited hugely from the opportunity to present and discuss portions of this work at conferences and workshops, particularly the Society for Social Studies of Science, European Association for Studies of Science and Technology, Internet Research and Information for Social Scientists (IRISS '98) and the Technology, Speed and Society meeting organized by Cambridge anthropologists.

Brunel University made the award which enabled me to employ a research assistant, Allegra Catolfi Salvoni, for the project which turned into this one. Allegra made a major contribution to the gathering of both literature and data for the project and was a joy to work with. The Department of Human Sciences at Brunel granted me a teaching-free semester to devote to the production of the manuscript. Great thanks are due to Chris Rojek at Sage who encouraged me to turn *Virtual Ethnography* into a book. Physiotherapist Ann McLaughlin is to be thanked for helping to maintain and restore my ability to sit at a keyboard during the latter stages of web surfing and manuscript preparation. For their support, tolerance and encouragement, I must thank Simon Manze, the Hine and Manze families, and many friends. Finally, I owe a great debt to the producers of web pages and contributors to newsgroups who gave up their time to help in the research and share with me their own local understandings of the Internet.

1 Introduction

The Human Race, to which so many of my readers belong, has been playing at children's games from the beginning, and will probably do it till the end, which is a nuisance for the few people who grow up. And one of the games to which it is most attached is called, 'Keep tomorrow dark', and which is also named (by the rustics in Shropshire I have no doubt) 'Cheat the Prophet'. The players listen very carefully and respectfully to all that the clever men have to say about what is to happen in the next generation. The players then wait until all the clever men are dead, and bury them nicely. They then go and do something else. That is all. For a race of simple tastes, however, it is great fun.

(Chesterton, 1904: 1)

We take issue with [the] implicit assumption that some inherent property or characteristic of technology accounts for the impact of technology on our lives. We propose instead that myriad other aspects of our relation with technology must be taken into account if we are to achieve a useful understanding of its consequences. These other aspects include: our attitudes towards technology, our conceptions of what technology can and cannot do, our expectations and assumptions about the possibilities of technological change, and the various ways in which technology is represented, in the media and in organizations. We aim to provide a critical exploration of the view that these latter aspects of the technology are preeminently consequential for the ways in which we organize our work, institutions, leisure and learning activities. This approach requires us to understand different ways of thinking about and representing technology at least as much as differences in the technology itself. Indeed, in what follows we argue for the need to treat the very idea of 'the technology itself' with considerable caution.

(Grint and Woolgar, 1997: 6)

Extreme futures and everyday uses

Chesterton in 1904 has a cautionary tale for those who wish to predict the future. The sheer abundance, diversity and originality of predictions in 1904 make it seem impossible for all of them to be wrong, but all of them do turn out to be wrong. The mistake which the futurologists had been making was that they took isolated events that were going on in their time, and extrapolated from there to extraordinary futures. The sole thing that they failed to predict was that the future would be very like the present. Only more dull.

Despite Chesterton's critique, the business of futurology is very much alive today and is still based on extremes. One particularly persuasive current format is the foretelling of strange new futures based around the advent and widespread use of computer-based communication, with Negroponte (1995) and Gates (1996) among the most prominent in a legion of futurologists. To date, far more effort has been expended on predicting the revolutionary futures of the Internet than has been put into finding out in detail how it is being used and the ways in which it is being incorporated into people's daily lives. This book is a contribution to the ongoing debate about the significance of recent developments in communications technologies. In the book I develop a methodology for investigating the Internet in order to conduct an empirically based exploration of its current uses. The focus in this book is on finding out what the players of 'Cheat the Prophet' are up to this time: a task for which an ethnographic methodology is ideally suited.

At the most basic level, the Internet is a way of transmitting bits of information from one computer to another. The architecture of the Internet provides for ways of addressing the information that is sent, so that it can be split up into packets, sent out across the network and recombined by the recipient. All kinds of information are in theory equal: bits are transmitted in the same way whether they represent text, audio, images or video. The meaning of the bits comes from the patterns which they make, from the software which is used to interpret them, and of course from the users who send and receive them. The capacity to send information from one computer to another can therefore be used to provide many different ways of communicating. Communication can be synchronous or asynchronous, it can consist of private messages between known individuals or discussion among large numbers in relatively public forums, and it can be textual or audio or visual. Talking about 'the Internet' encompasses electronic mail (email), the World Wide Web (WWW), Usenet newsgroups, bulletin boards, Internet Relay Chat (IRC), Multi-User Domains (MUDs) and many other applications (Kollock and Smith, 1999). All depend on the ability of the Internet to transmit information between computers. This view of the Internet as a distribution system for information has been used extensively in predictions of its future impact. It forms the starting point for an extrapolation to revolutionary effects. Here I will demonstrate how one of these projections of radical change works, to illustrate some of the tricks and omissions which it entails.

One of the future effects which has been predicted in the way described above is the end of the book. Books seem an old-fashioned way of disseminating information, when viewed in the light of advances in information and communication technologies. How much more straightforward to store the information electronically and transfer it to the point of use instantaneously, copy after copy, on demand. The sheer force of logic seems unassailable: all we need is the technologies and systems to make it possible, the necessary arrangements for everyone involved to be paid their due amount, and little can then stand in its way. Negroponte puts this point forcefully:

The methodical movement of recorded music as pieces of plastic, like the slow human handling of most information in the form of books, magazines, newspapers, and videocassettes, is about to become the instantaneous and inexpensive transfer of electronic data that move at the speed of light . . . The change from atoms to bits is irrevocable and unstoppable. (1995: 4)

Small wonder that Negroponte feels the need to apologize to his readers for having written a book. Mitchell (1996) also discusses the implications of electronic communications technologies for the book publishing and retailing industries, as a part of his examination of the role of electronic communications in redefining urban space. Mitchell describes possible future scenarios for transferring packages of information from originator through retailer to user, with information stored centrally, downloaded to a bookstore or even the home, and only then printed out to provide a physical object. Distribution of information instead of printed texts also opens up new possibilities for personalized products based on individual preferences. A similar argument is played out in many different fields. The recipe is simple: take something with a material form; then argue that the same function can be carried out in virtual form; assume that the virtual form will (by force of its own logic) displace the material form; propose a dire threat to the industry that produces the material form and radical changes for the users of the old material form and the new virtual form. The trick depends upon stripping the material form of social significance and imbuing it with purely technical qualities. The equivalence of material and virtual form can then be declared, and the revolutionary prospects appear.

Based on this logic the book is undoubtedly under threat from a development like the Internet. It seems ironic, then, that in 2000, books should be one of the most popular commodities traded on the Internet. It is debatable whether Internet bookshops are making money from their book sales, but certainly book selling is one of the more successful forms of Internet commerce in terms of volume of sales. Rather than displacing the sale of books, the Internet is helping their distribution to thrive, and the revolution of the Internet has turned, for the time being, into a new kind of mail order. There are some obvious reasons why buying books might be a popular use of the Internet. Internet bookshops have certainly attempted to lure customers with financial incentives, but it is unlikely that the appeal of Internet bookshops is based wholly on economic advantages. The convenience of ordering a book online and having it arrive in the post, too, has some appeal provided you do not need to see the book before you buy. Why books in particular should be appealing probably depends also on levels of trust. Electronic commerce has been slow to take off, with high levels of suspicion of electronic systems for handling money and of previously unknown electronic retailers. In circumstances of low trust, it seems quite plausible that a packaged product like the book or a CD, considered always the same no matter whom you buy it from, should be an acceptable thing to buy. The book is traditionally thought of as separate from the retailer: the author is the brand (Lash and Urry, 1994). For now, the packaged nature of the book and its material form may make it the ideal Internet commodity. This casts some doubt on the apparently unassailable logic by which digital information was going to displace the material form. The material form has a long history supporting its claims to be a trustworthy source of information and encouraging its users to think of it and use it in particular ways (Johns, 1998). Virtual forms of information do not have the same cultural understandings to support them.

The equation of the Internet with the end of the book is therefore not as straightforward as extreme predictions make it seem. In the future, electronic systems of information distribution may well become more important and might threaten the economic viability of conventional bookshops and publishers. The rush to get online in the publishing industry certainly signals some fears that their position is uncertain. The material manifestations of information may well alter, bringing consequences for the spatial, temporal and economic circumstances of information distribution. But if this does happen, it will involve much more than the compelling logic of a different way of distributing information. It will involve a shift in the mundane lived experience of buying, owning and reading information. For believers in the extreme predictions of radically altered future societies, people using the technology in mundane ways can easily be sidelined as lacking in imagination or missing the point. Writing in 1978, Hiltz and Turoff predicted of computer conferencing that 'by the mid-1990s it will be as widely used in society as the telephone today' (1993: xxv). Reflecting in the mid 1990s on their previous misplaced optimism, they advance an explanation: they had underestimated the importance of 'social inertia' (1993: xxix). The explanation retains the technological capacity for revolution, but shifts the effects a little further forward into the future. This book focuses precisely on what Hiltz and Turoff call social inertia: the practices through which the technology is used and understood in everyday settings. These lived experiences will need to alter if radical future predictions are going to be realized.

This argument suggests that, rather than technology itself being an agent of change, uses and understandings of the technology are central. This is the point which Grint and Woolgar (1997) make in the quotation with which this chapter began. There is a place for a study of the everyday practices around the Internet, as a means to question the assumptions inherent in the prediction of radically different futures. Ethnography is an ideal methodological starting point for such a study. It can be used to explore the complex links between the claims which are made for the new technologies in different arenas: the home, the workplace, the mass media and the academic journal and monograph. An ethnography of the Internet can look in detail at the ways in which the technology is experienced in use. In its basic form ethnography consists of a researcher spending an extended period of time immersed in a field setting, taking account of the relationships, activities and understandings of those in the setting and participating in those processes. The aim is to make explicit the taken-for-granted and often tacit ways in which people make sense of their lives. The ethnographer inhabits a kind of in-between world, simultaneously native and stranger. They must become close enough to the culture being studied to understand how it works, and yet be able to detach from it sufficiently to be able to report on it. This book explores the ways in which an ethnographic perspective can be adapted to cast light on the construction of the Internet in use. Ethnography allows us to focus on what Knorr-Cetina (1983) calls the 'locally situated, occasioned character' of Internet use. The aim is to study how the status of the Internet is negotiated in the local context of its use.

Foreshadowed problems

It is always useful for ethnographers to consider and attempt to articulate the assumptions which they take with them into the field. Growing familiarity with the setting may either reinforce these foreshadowed problems (Hammersley and Atkinson, 1995: 24) or prompt their wholesale rejection. A continuing examination of the starting assumptions forms one way of learning about the field setting in a way which remains relevant to theoretical debates. The ethnography which is described here takes as its starting point the background of extreme predictions about the significance of the Internet. I have set the scene above for a sceptical approach to these claims. A further set of questions is raised by the work of academic commentators on the Internet, or cyberspace as it is often termed. Kitchin (1998) summarizes proposed effects of cyberspace into three categories: changes to the role of time and space; changes to communication and the role of mass communication; and a questioning of dualisms such as the real and the virtual, truth and fiction, the authentic and the fabricated, technology and nature, and representation and reality. These predictions have been made against a backdrop of wider debates in social theory about the significance of recent social and technical change. The brief and selective survey given here should serve to map the intellectual territory that the Internet inhabits, even if it does not do justice to the complexity of debates. Internet theorizing occurs in a context of disagreements over the most apt characterization of current modes of social organization. It is beyond the scope of this book to intervene in these debates. This is an ethnographic text, and as such its sympathies are thoroughly with the micro-level of analysis rather than the macro-level of such theories, and with understanding the present rather than dissecting the parameters of social change. Periodization debates are used here as a backdrop for statements made about the implications of the Internet and its predecessors and to provide some useful pointers to ways of interpreting the Internet.

The dominant characterization distinguishes between premodern or traditional, modern, and postmodern conditions of social organization. For some, the new communications technologies are a logical upshot of the preoccupations of modern society with rationality and control. For others, the new communications technologies are distinctive in their emphasis on uncertainty, and thus are the embodiments of a postmodern mode of (dis)organization characterized by the fragmentation of concepts such as science, religion, culture, society and the self. Finally, for some, the new information and communication technologies are the agents of such radical changes in social organization that they deserve a period all to themselves: the information society. Thrift (1996b) describes a 'virus of new era thinking' which tends to hail technological developments as revolutionary without attending to the history of such claims. Webster (1995) also takes a sceptical approach to claims that the role of information in society demands a distinct periodization. Working through technological, economic, occupational, spatial and cultural definitions of the information society, he finds each potential dimension of change to be insufficient to constitute a radical discontinuity. In those who argue for radical discontinuity, among whom he includes Daniel Bell, Mark Poster and Manuel Castells, Webster finds an underlying, often unstated, reliance on the capacities of the technology to induce social change. Webster's (1995) sympathies are undoubtedly with the theorists of the modern who stress continuity of social organization.

Theorists of modernity provide a specific framework for understanding the development of communications technologies. Modernity, to summarize crudely, is characterized by a stress on rationality and control, by organization through surveillance and by a stress on the nation state as a means of controlling social life. It is also characterized by the importance of expert knowledges such as science. Modernity has had some key technologies: the clock, the calendar, the map, the computer. For Giddens (1990) the clock and the calendar contribute towards the formation of 'empty' dimensions of time and space. Time becomes a universal concept, allowing for coordination across distance. Space is separated from the physical locations known as place. The separation of time and space and their transformation as factors in social ordering is referred to as time–space distanciation. This process is enabled by disembedding mechanisms: systems of exchange and knowledge which are independent of particular locations in time or space. In this way of thinking, the new information and communication technologies are an extension of an existing concern with greater control through greater knowledge and coordination across time and space. The new technologies form part of the trend towards abstraction and are extensions to the capacity to organize and know which is a part of modern life. The Internet has yet to be explicitly addressed by theorists of modernity like Giddens (1990; 1991) and Thompson (1995). However, the general framework of a relationship between mediated interaction, social organization and space–time is thought-provoking. History suggests that technological developments can have far-reaching cultural implications for the lived experience of space and time (Kern, 1983). The Internet might be seen to augment possibilities for restructuring social relations across time and space, but as a part of modern preoccupations with social control rather than a threat to them. A study of the everyday uses of the Internet might therefore do well to look at the time–space relationships which are enacted in its use.

Postmodern theorists have it that the foundations of modernity are increasingly in crisis, and that the bases for organizing social life are undergoing a radical shift. A fragmentation of such modern concepts as the self, society and culture accompanies a loss of faith in the 'grand narratives' of science and religion (Lyotard, 1984). Social relations in space–time are also implicated in postmodern thought, though here the increasing compression is thought to lead to fragmentation rather than potential for rationalization and control (Harvey, 1989). For postmodernity, the new communications technologies are part of a process where doubt is cast on authenticity, representation and reality, the unitary self and the distinction between self and society. Poster (1990; 1995) identifies in the new media the provision of new conditions for subject formation, which amount to a decentring and dispersal of the subject. He also identifies the blurring of the boundaries between human and machine and between reality and virtuality as postmodern phenomena. In the Internet postmodernity seems to have found its object, in an 'anything goes' world where people and machines, truth and fiction, self and other seem to merge in a glorious blurring of boundaries. For some, cyberspace signals the breakdown of modernity (Nguyen and Alexander, 1996), is a postmodern context for playing with the self (Turkle, 1996), or is intrinsically a playful medium (Danet et al., 1997). For a study of everyday usage, this raises some obvious questions about the ways in which issues of authenticity and identity arise and are managed and about the ways in which the boundary between the real and the virtual is experienced, if indeed there is any idea left of 'the real' (Baudrillard, 1983).

Webster (1995) advocates social theory as an antidote to the simple social impacts view of information technologies, which proceeds largely from a straightforward technologically determinist view that technologies have particular social effects. Webster sets up social theory as an enriched way of thinking about the complexities of the relationship between technologies and societies. Even Webster, in advocating social theory, does however acknowledge that less obvious forms of technological determinism are present in the works of some of the social theorists he reviews (1995: 215). Many theorists say that technological developments 'support', 'facilitate' or 'encourage' social developments in particular directions, while they hesitate to say that the technology directly causes social developments. A final but crucial set of foreshadowed problems are provided by the challenges to technological determinism which sociology of science and technology provides. Grint and Woolgar (1997) argue for a recognition that what we perceive as the impact of technology accrues not in virtue of some intrinsic quality of the technology itself, but as a result of contingent sets of social processes. The so-called inherent qualities of technology are built in during the design process as the upshot of negotiations about the nature of users.

The apparent impacts of the technology depend on users being taught to use the technology in appropriate ways. This process is contingent on the successful performance of sets of social relations between designers and users through and around the machine. It is indeterminate: users are in principle free to understand the technology in quite different ways from those that the designers intended. The shorthand for this argument is the 'technology as text' metaphor (Woolgar, 1991a; Grint and Woolgar, 1997). Chapter 2 returns to the issues raised by attempting to apply this framework to the Internet. For now, it serves as a suggestion that it would be valuable to incorporate into an ethnography of the Internet a sceptical approach to the inherent qualities which are proposed for the technology, in particular the qualities which are supposed to make the Internet a force of social transformation. A study of everyday uses should pay detailed attention to the understandings which users have of what the Internet is for.

An ethnographic approach to the Internet

As an analytic starting point it is unproductive to take any features of the technology as taken for granted and simply the way things are. Our beliefs about the Internet and what its properties are can be opened up to enquiry just like Azande beliefs about witchcraft (Evans-Pritchard, 1937), English beliefs about kinship (Strathern, 1992), American understandings of the immune system (Martin, 1994) or any other ethnographic topic. Beliefs about the Internet may have important consequences for the ways in which we relate to the technology and one another through it. Ethnography can therefore be used to develop an enriched sense of the meanings of the technology and the cultures which enable it and are enabled by it. This book takes a starting point which is in dialogue with the theoretical projections of the Internet's significance, using them as the foreshadowed problems for an ethnography of the Internet in use. The specific research questions raised by the theoretical review are:

- How do the users of the Internet understand its capacities? What significance does its use have for them? How do they understand its capabilities as a medium of communication, and whom do they perceive their audience to be?
- How does the Internet affect the organization of social relationships in time and space? Is this different to the ways in which 'real life' is organized, and if so, how do users reconcile the two?
- What are the implications of the Internet for authenticity and authority? How are identities performed and experienced, and how is authenticity judged?
- Is 'the virtual' experienced as radically different from and separate from 'the real'? Is there a boundary between online and offline?

I set out to explore these questions through an ethnographic study of a particular instance of Internet use. The questions form the motivation for carrying out the ethnography and an organizing principle for discussing the findings. In the rest of this introductory chapter I will briefly introduce the argument of the book as a whole. The book broadly divides into two parts. Chapters 2 and 3 are the methodological preamble which argues the case for a distinctive methodological approach to understanding the Internet. Chapter 4 then describes the design and conduct of an ethnography based on these principles. Chapters 5, 6 and 7 constitute the main body of the ethnography which explores the questions listed above.

Given that the foreshadowed questions provide a pointer towards what is going to be studied, the question then is where to go to conduct the study. When the object of study is the Internet, finding a place to go to is by no means straightforward. This problem forms the basis of Chapter 2. I argue that there are two distinct ways of viewing the Internet, each with its own analytic advantages and each of which suggests a different idea of the appropriate field site. The first view of the Internet is that it represents a place, cyberspace, where culture is formed and reformed. Early approaches to computer-mediated communication (CMC), conducted largely in experimental mode, suggested that it was an impoverished medium of communication. Aggression and misunderstandings could be expected where people were limited to text-based communications, and the transmission of the social cues vital to communication would be constrained. The possibilities for widespread use of text-based CMC at that stage seemed limited by the narrow bandwidth of communication which it provided. As the precursors to the Internet gained currency outside experimental settings, this viewpoint was increasingly challenged. Rheingold (1993) was notable in arguing that CMC could provide for a far richer form of interaction than had previously been envisaged and that it provided a space for community formation. More systematic studies drew on ethnographic methodology to establish CMC as a site for rich and sustained interactions which could be viewed as constituting cultures in their own right. Ethnographic studies of online settings made a major contribution to the establishment of a view of the Internet as a culture where the uses people make of the technology available to them could be studied. These approaches established cyberspace as a plausible ethnographic field site.

The second way of viewing the Internet introduced in Chapter 2 is that it is a cultural artefact (Woolgar, 1996). This approach sees the Internet as a product of culture: a technology that was produced by particular people with contextually situated goals and priorities. It is also a technology which is shaped by the ways in which it is marketed, taught and used. To speak of the Internet as a cultural artefact is to suggest that it could have been otherwise, and that what it is and what it does are the product of culturally produced understandings that can vary. The ethnographic approach provides some pointers here too. Drawing on research in the sociology of science and technology and in media sociology, it is suggested that we can usefully think of technologies and media as having interpretive flexibility: ideas of their sensible use are developed in context. Local contexts of interpretation and use therefore form the ethnographic field. Studies of the Internet to date have focused on its status as a culture and consequently largely neglected it as a cultural artefact. Combining the two approaches to the Internet raises some methodological difficulties. This is due to problems in translating an approach traditionally applied in specific bounded social settings to a communications technology which seems to disrupt the notion of boundaries. Ethnographers have often settled for studying either online or offline contexts. To combine the two requires a rethinking of the relationship between ethnography and space, to take account of the Internet as both culture and cultural artefact.

The methodological problem with which Chapter 2 ends forms the basis for Chapter 3. Recent thinking on the relationship between the experience of the ethnographer and the ethnography as a written product, on the reflexive shaping of the ethnographic project, and on the construction of the ethnographic object provides some useful hints for ways in which ethnography could be creatively appropriated for the Internet. Face-to-face interaction, and the rhetoric of having travelled to a remote field site, have played a major part in the presentation of ethnographic descriptions as authentic. A limited medium like CMC seems to pose problems for ethnography's claims to test knowledge through experience and interaction. The position changes somewhat if we recognize that the ethnographer could instead be construed as needing to have similar experiences to those of informants, however those experiences are mediated. Conducting an ethnographic enquiry through the use of CMC opens up the possibility of gaining a reflexive understanding of what it is to be a part of the Internet. This provides a symmetry to the ethnography, as the ethnographer learns through using the same media as informants. Developments in mobile and multi-sited ethnographies provide some pointers for exploring the making of ethnographic objects which cross geographic spaces along with informants. These developments open up a space for thinking about ethnography as an experientially based way of knowing that need not aspire to produce a holistic study of a bounded culture. This presents an opportunity for rethinking the shaping of the ethnographic object and reformulating the grounds for ethnographic engagement with the field. The chapter ends by proposing some principles for the conduct of a virtual ethnography. An ethnography of, in and through the Internet can be conceived of as an adaptive and wholeheartedly partial approach which draws on connection rather than location in defining its object.

The first part of the book therefore lays the ground for a particular approach to ethnography which is almost but not quite like the real thing: a virtual ethnography. In Chapters 4, 5 and 6 the methodological propositions in the early part of the book are put into practice in an investigation of the Internet. The case study chosen to explore the Internet as both culture and cultural object is a media event: the case of Louise Woodward.

The trial of Louise in a Boston court for the murder of a child in her care received much media attention and stimulated a large amount of activity on the Internet. Supporters of Louise who had watched the trial produced their own web sites to argue for her release and to campaign on her behalf. In the aftermath of the trial, web users could read up on the trial, register their support, lobby the judge and review the evidence. News reports, video and sound files were all available online. Using the web, people could read the results of a polygraph test or listen to Louise's cry as she heard the jury's guilty verdict. In discussion groups the rights and wrongs of the case were hotly debated. People positioned themselves for and against Louise, using a variety of resources to try to convince one another. The case therefore provided rich and varied material for an ethnographer to explore. Media coverage of the case provided a further dimension to the ethnography. The Internet role in the case received media attention, particularly when the judge announced his decision to release his verdict through a web site. The case therefore provides an interesting setting in which to consider the state of the Internet at the time. Chapter 4 sets out the scene for rendering the Louise Woodward case on the Internet as an ethnography. The ethnography is based upon analysis of the emergence of Internet activity related to the case over time, and engagement with the producers of this activity, in both newsgroups and web sites.

Chapters 5, 6 and 7 contain the main body of the ethnography, organized around themes which stem from the foreshadowed problems discussed earlier in this chapter. Chapter 5 takes as its starting point the question of the capacities of the Internet to restructure social relations in time and space. A discussion of the understandings which designers of web pages and users of newsgroups have of the technology sets the scene for an exploration of the temporal and spatial relationships which emerged. Users of the Internet make their practices meaningful through the shared understandings which render the production of a web page or a contribution to a newsgroup as a form of social action. This involves a complex understanding of the relationship between the technology of the Internet and social relations in time and space. Web page authors make their pages meaningful largely through their understandings of the audience for their pages and their understanding of visits to their pages as a form of recognition. They are therefore concerned to produce timely web pages which are well connected, in order to maximize visitors. Newsgroups are a highly differentiated form of social space which is collaboratively maintained by users performing their postings as temporally and situationally relevant to the group. Rather than transcending time and space, the Internet can be shown to have multiple temporal and spatial orderings which criss-cross the online/offline boundary.

Chapter 6 explores the 'problem of authenticity' which is often associated with the Internet. Reliance on mediated communication is often thought of as posing a problem in determining the reliability of statements and the identity of authors. The use of the Internet for identity play has been much documented. This chapter explores the extent to which the authenticity problem is experienced by users of the Internet, and the ways in which concerns with authenticity are managed. Authenticity is construed as a discursive performance, in which accounts are organized to promote perceptions of their authenticity. Newsgroup discussions are a particularly testing ground for authenticity performance, since it is routine for posters to challenge previous messages. The grounds for these challenges vary widely between newsgroups. Challenges based on identity are, however, rare in the newsgroups studied here. It appears that authenticity of identity is largely unquestioned where it is not directly pertinent to the topic of discussion. Web pages too can be interpreted as performances oriented to promoting authenticity. Two contrasting strategies were identified: the ethnographic mode, where the author performs an identity to promote their knowledge as experientially based; and the scientific mode, in which the author's identity is erased to present the page as objective knowledge. Far from embracing play, it can be seen that those using the Internet to share views on the Louise Woodward case were frequently concerned to promote the authenticity of their position and drew on a variety of resources to do so.

Chapter 7 reviews the implications of the ethnography for understandings of the Internet. The Louise Woodward case provides a basis to consider the interpretive flexibility of the Internet. Online activity can be seen to enact and make available understandings of the technology. On the one hand, we can see that there are some quite stable and widely accepted ways of using the Internet, as displayed by the collaborative social space of the newsgroup. The Internet shows a low degree of interpretive flexibility for the users of particular spaces. The diversity of spaces provided by different newsgroups, however, suggests high levels of freedom for users to develop different understandings of the technology. Newsgroups are locally stable but also diverse. The perception of web pages as individual territory encourages web designers to experiment with the technology and allows for a diversity of web pages to develop. As a part of this process, however, web producers reflexively monitor the way in which their own pages compare with other pages that they see. This monitoring tends to stabilize the WWW around a set of commonly understood appropriate uses. Web pages too, then, are potentially diverse, but are locally stabilized by monitoring the interpretations of others. The Internet has routinely been employed by its users to monitor their own interpretations in the light of other users' interpretations. It has been treated as a performative space in which users need to act appropriately. Through this, the technology is stabilized by users themselves. The social relations which form on the Internet stabilize the technology and encourage its users to understand it in particular ways. The Internet has been proposed as a transcendent technology which is used to bypass dualisms like self/other, real/virtual, nature/culture and truth/fiction. It turns out to have a more complex relationship to these distinctions than straightforward transcendence or erasure. As Robins says: 'We must demythologize virtual culture if we are to assess the serious implications it has for our personal and collective lives' (1995: 153). The everyday uses of the Internet are more interesting, more nuanced, more differentiated and more dull than the ✓ futurologists would have us believe and promise to provide many future areas of research. The final section of the chapter explores some omissions occasioned by the design of the ethnography reported here, and proposes some promising avenues of future study.

On one level this is a methodological text: the aim is to develop an approach to the study of mediated interaction and to demonstrate through example the procedures, problems and benefits which the approach brings. It is not, however, straightforwardly a 'how to do it' guide. I hope that the book will contain some provocative and useful ideas for anyone starting out to conduct an ethnography involving computer-mediated interaction. I hope that it will provide some intriguing possibilities for taking an ethnographic approach to the Internet. Part of my argument, however, is that ethnography is strengthened by the lack of recipes for doing it. From the first, ethnographers have resisted giving guidelines for how it should be done. Ethnography is a lived craft rather than a protocol which can be separated from the particular study or the person carrying it out (Rachel, 1996). The methodology of an ethnography is inseparable from the contexts in which it is employed and it is an adaptive approach which thrives on reflexivity about method. The approach to ethnography which is described here is intended to do justice to the richness and complexity of the Internet and also to advocate experimentation within the genre as a response to novel situations.

If this is not a straightforward methodological text, neither is it an introduction to the use of the Internet, a technical manual or user guide. I have assumed to a large extent, in this introduction and throughout the book, that readers will be familiar with concepts such as newsgroup, web page and search engine, making some assumptions about the currency of the Internet as a familiar object to readers. I have therefore not included detailed technical descriptions or instructions in the main body of the text. I considered that these might be boring and intrusive to readers who already knew, and would detract from the broader points which I wished to make. However, I hope that the book will also raise some intriguing issues for readers to whom the Internet is still strange and puzzling. For their purposes I have included a technical glossary. These descriptions may be insufficient for use as instructions for using the Internet, but should serve to explain the kinds of interaction which are discussed in the main text. I hope that some readers will feel inspired to explore uses of the Internet which are new to them, and to treat the experience in an ethnographic spirit.

2 Internet as Culture and Cultural Artefact

Chapter 1 introduced the idea that the Internet could be understood in two quite different ways: as a culture in its own right, and as a cultural artefact. This chapter takes these two perspectives as a starting point to discuss how we might develop an ethnographic approach to understanding the Internet. It has been suggested that developments in cyberspace provide a variety of new ethnographic field sites (Escobar, 1996). Here, the models of culture and cultural artefact are used to provide a structure for thinking about two aspects of cyberspace which can be seen as field sites for an ethnographer. Each view of the Internet suggests different methodological approaches and distinctive sets of problems and advantages. The first section reviews the approaches that have established the Internet as a culture and discusses some methodological dilemmas and innovations that this view has entailed. The second section then reviews the basis for viewing the Internet as a cultural object that is socially shaped in production and use. In the final section, the problems and opportunities provided by bringing together Internet as culture and Internet as cultural object are explored.

Internet as culture

The concern with the effects that CMC might have on communication processes is almost as well established as the technology itself. Early approaches to the study of CMC were far from acknowledging it as a site for rich cultural interchange. In comparison with other communication media and particularly in comparison with face-to-face interaction, email seemed limited. It seemed that computers could not support the same richness of communication as offered by face-to-face situations (Baym, 1998). Much of the early work on CMC considered its use in organizational contexts, often from a social psychological perspective. This research has been influential in establishing an understanding of the qualities of CMC. In this section I draw heavily on the work of Rudy (1994; 1996) in mapping and characterizing the organizational research on CMC. One strand of research which Rudy describes concerned itself with the criteria used to make a selection of the communication medium for a given task (media choice). Researchers differed in the extent to which they attributed choices to inherent qualities of the media that people could use to make rational decisions. Ideas about the particular qualities that CMC provided were however largely established by the other main body of research on CMC in organizational settings, focusing on media effects. In the consideration of the Internet as culture, the types of communication that CMC affords are more pertinent, and this area will therefore be the focus of interest in the first part of this section.

Much of the media effects research was motivated by concerns with the problems of management: what would be the best way of setting up systems for CMC within organizations, and what might be the benefits and potential pitfalls? These general concerns were translated into some more specific questions: what kinds of tasks could be achieved by groups using electronic communication; how did the different communication media compare in their effects on communication; and what effect did different media have on groups working together? The issue of group working in particular became a focus of considerable interest. This question was also fed by a long-standing interest within social psychology on group processes. The new communications medium provided by CMC also afforded a new experimental setting in which to consider some more general hypotheses concerning processes within groups. Experimental methods were employed to establish consistent features distinguishing communications using one medium from those using another. Experiments were designed on the basis that differences between the functioning of groups using different communications media would demonstrate inherent differences between those media.

The 'reduced social cues' model for understanding CMC is probably the best-known and most influential of the technology-based approaches. This position was established through experimental studies on group decision making (e.g. Kiesler, Siegel and McGuire, 1984; Sproull and Kiesler, 1986; 1991). Typically a group of people would be given a task to perform via a computer-conferencing system, and their performance would be compared with that of groups performing the same task via face-to-face meetings. The resulting process would be analysed by measuring a selection of variables and comparing them between the computer-mediated and the face-to-face groups. Typical measurements might include equality of participation between genders or between members of different status, time or number of interactions taken to complete a task, and levels of aggression. The variables consisted of a mixture of assessments of the content of messages (e.g. level of aggression) and straightforward counting procedures (e.g. level of contribution). A social psychological approach to analysing these results suggested that computer-mediated communication was lacking in social context cues, with a resulting disinhibiting effect on participants. The text-based medium of electronic mail stripped out social context cues (features such as gender, age, race, social status, facial expression and intonation) routinely used in understanding face-to-face interaction. The lack of social cues could be used to explain both the equality of participation and the high levels of aggression perceived in the computer-mediated groups. Flaming (markedly aggressive tones in electronic communications) can be explained as a disinhibition in the light of the lack of social context cues, leading participants to focus more on themselves than on other participants. Increased equality of participation can be explained as a disinhibition in the absence of visual and aural reminders of the status of other participants, leading again to a tendency to focus on self rather than others (Sproull and Kiesler, 1986; 1991).

The 'reduced social cues' model for understanding CMC and its effects has come under attack from more context-based approaches. Authors in this field are prone to stress the differences between use of CMC in different contexts. Spears et al. (1990) and Lea and Spears (1991) pointed out that previous work had focused on comparing CMC with face-to-face settings. An alternative approach was proposed which compared use of the same technology under different experimental conditions. This alternative approach suggested that the effects of CMC on group decision making processes could be varied depending on the extent to which participants thought of themselves as part of a group. In effect, they argued that what the 'reduced social cues' model attributed to the technology could be understood as a function of the ways in which the experimental groups had been organized. The upshot of this approach was that researchers should focus more on the context in which the technology was used, including the influence of social identity (orientation towards a group) and deindividuation (operationalized as visual anonymity of participants to one another) on group processes.

Mantovani (1994) also disputes the dominant 'reduced social cues' model. Mantovani assembles a review of observation-based studies that demonstrate that rather than overcoming spatial and hierarchical barriers in organizations as the 'reduced social cues' model suggests, CMC tends to reinforce them. There is thus little basis for maintaining that the technology has specific social effects independent of its context of use. Mantovani also questions the basis for some of the quantitative measures used to establish equality of participation. As he points out, even if a low-status member of the group contributes equally, this does not mean that their contributions have been given equal weight to those of high-status group members. Unlike the experimental settings where participants are usually either anonymous to one another or at least previously unknown, users of CMC within organizations are often thoroughly aware of status differentials. Mantovani suggests that rather than asking what social effects CMC produces, the opposite question deserves attention: how does the context shape the use and effects of CMC? This point will be revisited in the final section of this chapter.

The understanding of CMC as a technology with particular social effects has also proved controversial in other quarters. It has been observed that outside the strictly controlled experimental setting, rather than providing a limited and constraining medium for communication, CMC has provided rich and complex social experience. Rheingold (1993) was particularly influential in establishing a view of CMC as providing a community in its own right. Rheingold's descriptions of his experiences with the WELL (Whole Earth 'Lectronic Link) portray a committed group of people who offer one another support and advice, who enter into close relationships and who conduct intense arguments. His account is the highly personal one of someone convinced by the potential offered by the technologies of CMC for bringing people together, for reforming the connections threatened by modern life, and for enhancing democratic participation. The term 'virtual community' was used by Rheingold to portray the level of commitment and connection experienced by users. His definition stresses the use of CMC to form sustained relationships:

> Virtual communities are social aggregations that emerge from the Net when enough people carry on those public discussions long enough, with sufficient human feeling, to form webs of personal relationships in cyberspace. (1993: 5)

Curtis (1992) and Bruckman (1992) were among the developers of MUDs who wrote about the social structures that emerged in these settings. Their observations added to the accumulating evidence that CMC was far from inimical to the formation of social relationships (Parks and Floyd, 1996). Following on from early work on the WELL and on MUDs, claims have frequently been made that online environments can form virtual communities. Newsgroups, bulletin boards, IRC and role-playing environments such as MUDs have all been described in these terms. By the early 1990s a counter-current of work that stressed the communicative possibilities rather than the inherent constraints of CMC was established. This work proved highly influential in shaping the development of research agendas focused on the actual uses of the technology rather than its hypothetical potential or its effects in experimental settings. Researchers moved on from the observation that CMC felt like a community to its participants and began to pay detailed attention to the ways in which that perception was created and sustained (Jones, 1995; McLaughlin et al., 1995; Kollock and Smith, 1999). The relationship between CMC and social science was reconceptualized: in arguing that meaningful social relations existed in cyberspace, researchers effected a move towards CMC as a context of social relations in its own right, rather than a medium used to good or bad effect within other contexts. Between the poster of one newsgroup message and the author of a response, a space opened, and that space was a cultural context.

The introduction to the ground-breaking edited collection *Cybersociety* proposed that new ways of doing research were needed to study the 'non-traditional social formations' found online (Jones, 1995: 11). The context of CMC was subsequently colonized by a range of social science methodologies and approaches. Once CMC was conceptualized as culture it became the business of anthropology, cultural studies, political science, communication and media studies, psychology and sociology. Researchers entered cyberspace to study the social, cultural and political formations they found there. Stone observes that cyberspace is now crowded with 'researchers swarming over the virtual landscape, peering around at virtual natives and writing busily in their virtual field notes' (1995: 243). Each discipline employed its own range of methods, adapting them to the online setting as seemed fit. Quantitative analysis provided a way of exploring the uses to which the Internet was put, by counting and correlating the occurrence of various features of messages posted. The ambitious ProjectH (Rafaeli et al., 1994) was a particularly notable attempt to map the emerging social structures of newsgroups, as well as allowing its researchers to reflect on the experience of using CMC to coordinate the project (Sudweeks and Rafaeli, 1996). This large scale study involved content analysis of a large corpus of newsgroup postings, allowing the exploration of themes across a range of newsgroups. Mark Smith (1999) has developed methods for producing a systematic mapping of the social structure of Usenet, including levels of activity and links via cross-posting between newsgroups. Quantitative studies have an important role in providing for a structured analysis and comparison across settings. Qualitative and interpretive studies are however particularly well placed to study a cultural context in its own terms and have been influential in establishing the features of CMC.

The Internet and similar networks provide a naturally occurring field site for studying what people do while they are online unconstrained by experimental designs. Naturalistic studies of online settings take observations of the rich and complex uses of CMC as a starting point for the analysis of situated behaviour (Wynn and Katz, 1997). Many studies of this kind have been explicitly positioned against the experimental studies that established CMC as a limited medium (Baym, 1995a; 1995b; 1998; Paccagnella, 1997). Their aim is to do justice to the socially rich and often innovative uses to which CMC is put outside the experimental settings. A form of naturalistic enquiry is proposed as a way of focusing on the uses and interpretations of the technology in action. Qualitative approaches to CMC have, not surprisingly, focused on the linguistic resources which participants create and use. Drawing on perspectives from discourse analysis (Baym, 1995a; McLaughlin et al., 1995) and ethnomethodology (Correll, 1995; Thomsen et al., 1998), researchers have made a case for studying the practices through which meanings are made in context, through the interaction of participants. In online settings the apparent absence of a pre-discursive reality encourages the application of constructivist frameworks.

A discursive and practice-oriented approach to online community offers up the possibility of seeing online phenomena as functional in a social sense. Rather than seeing flaming as destructive or as a direct response to the limitations of the medium, as the experimental studies have it, discursive approaches stress the ways in which conflict can have social functions (A.D. Smith, 1999). Through identification of insiders and outsiders and through the assertion of community values, episodes of conflict can be seen as strengthening community rather than posing a threat (Franco et al., 1995; Phillips, 1996). Hierarchies can be formed, patterns of power can emerge (Reid, 1999) and standards of conduct can become set (McLaughlin et al., 1995). The organization of newsgroup postings can be seen as functional, as header information, signature files and styles of message nurture the development of separate and often stable identities for participants (Baym, 1995b; Donath, 1999). The practice of quoting sections of the previous message in a response to that message reinforces the sense of an ongoing discussion rather than isolated utterances. Linguistic devices such as emoticons, in-jokes and local codes and abbreviations contribute to the formation of a community with shared practices, shared knowledge and language and collective goods (Kollock and Smith, 1994; Baym, 1995c; Fernback, 1997; Kollock, 1999). Similarly, Reid (1995) argues that MUDs can develop a common culture through the sharing of language and the development of ways in which participants can make themselves and their environment meaningfully present to one another through textual means. The crucial step in all of these observations is to see features of Internet interactions as functional in a social sense, enabling the achievement of a distinct culture.

The perspective that newsgroups constitute communities in their own right has been influential in shaping a generation of studies. Studies of online communities have been proposed as promoting a new definition of community, which relies more upon shared social practices than on physical boundaries (Jones, 1995; Watson, 1997). There are, however, critics who suggest that these formations are far from constituting a community as generally understood. Their concern is with the level of commitment and responsibility which participants associate with online social formations. It is suggested that online formations cannot be considered communities when participants can simply log out or turn off when they choose. The level of connection and intimacy is insufficient to make participants members of a community, although they may feel as if they are. This type of social formation is a pseudocommunity (Beniger, 1987). Advocates and critics of the idea of online communities tend to end up arguing about the authenticity of online social formations in relation to their real counterparts, in a way which often harks back to a romanticized view of traditional communities (Wellman and Gulia, 1999). There is, however, a wider dimension to this debate. Watson (1997) points out that although to speak of newsgroups as communities often 'feels right' to ethnographers and to participants, the term itself carries a considerable amount of cultural baggage. To say that something is or is not a community is to perform political work. Arguing over whether online social formations map directly on to those that occur either ideally or actually in offline settings may be a distraction from the study of whatever develops online in its own terms.

Along with virtual community, another prominent topic in the study of online social environments has been identity play. This interest stems from observations that people using text-based environments have often exploited the potential for representing themselves in ways quite different from their offline personae. This tendency is particularly apparent in role-playing environments such as MUDs, where participants actively select a gender for their character and input a description often couched in physical terms. There is no guarantee that the gender and description will have any correspondence with the offline persona. Role-playing MUDs, with their emphasis on fantasy, offer up the possibility of experimentation with social interaction in a quite different role from that played in offline life (Turkle, 1995; Bromberg, 1996). Interest has also been focused on the ways in which people represent themselves on IRC channels through techniques such as the creative use of nicknames (Danet, 1998). Although identity play is less to the fore in many newsgroups and bulletin boards, the idea of identity play has been prominent in some notorious cases of deception (Van Gelder, 1991; Stone, 1996). There is considerable variation in the importance given to online identities. Identity play might simply be viewed as people exploiting the potential of the medium to try out a different role, or it might be seen as a fundamental threat to the idea of a unified self (Poster, 1995; Turkle, 1995). Whether there was ever a unified self to be threatened is a topic for some debate (Wynn and Katz, 1997).

It is a short move from observing that people play with identity in online settings, to suggesting that the technologies themselves are causing a change in conceptions of identity. It is worth reviewing the status of the technology in depictions of online community and identity. From an experimental mode in which the technology acquired the inherent quality of impoverished communication, we appear to have moved to an opposing but equally determined view of the technology as leading to rich social formations and fragmented identities. More recently, authors have taken pains to stress that the development of online community is not inevitable: virtual communities may fail (Kolko and Reid, 1998) or be places of tension and fragmentation rather than cohesion (Mitra, 1997). Identities may be multiple, fragmented and playful (Turkle, 1995; Stone, 1991), but may also be stable and sustained (Baym, 1995a; 1995b; 1995c; 1998). Far from conventional identity categories like gender, race and sexuality being erased, there is considerable evidence that these are still important ways in which some users of the Internet organize their understandings (Savicki et al., 1996; Dietrich, 1997; Shaw, 1997; Zickmund, 1997; Danet, 1998; Poster, 1998; Burkhalter, 1999; O'Brien, 1999).This observation increases the importance of critical analysis of the social processes and social formations that develop online, without assuming that communities will automatically form or that identities will intrinsically be fluid. The properties of the Internet are differentially socially constructed in the multiple social settings that develop online. While individual settings in the CMC context may be highly socially organized, the technology does not necessitate this kind of organization. The technology of CMC appears to lead to a widely varying array of different kinds of social organization, and community is only one metaphor for understanding online social formations. Recently authors have suggested narrative as an alternative framework for understanding online social phenomena, with virtual community just one of many different kinds of narrative (Jones, 1998; Poster, 1995).

As mentioned above, methodological approaches to the study of CMC contexts have varied widely. Ethnography holds particular appeal for studying 'what people actually do' with the technology. Once we think of cyberspace as a place where people do things, we can start to study just exactly what it is they do and why, in their terms, they do it. However, as with all methodologies, moving ethnography to an online setting has involved some re-examinations of what the methodology entails. In an offline setting we might expect an ethnographer to have spent a prolonged period living or working in their field site. We would expect them to have observed, asked questions, interviewed people, drawn maps and taken photographs, learnt techniques and done what they could to find out how life was lived from the point of view of participants. Moving this approach to an online setting poses some interesting problems: how can you live in an online setting? Do you have to be logged on 24 hours a day, or can you visit the setting at periodic intervals? Can you analyse newsgroup archives without participating and call that ethnography? Snapshot approaches (Mitra, 1997), restricted samples (Phillips, 1996) and retrospective analyses (Aycock and Buchignani, 1995) have undoubtedly provided some thought-provoking analyses of online phenomena. These selective approaches allow researchers to focus on a specific topic of interest and to follow it through in detail without being overwhelmed by the sheer mass of words that some newsgroups produce. Cross-newsgroup samples (McLaughlin et al., 1995; Parks and Floyd, 1996) have similarly contributed to the systematic analysis of a given topic across settings. The temporal organization of these studies and their focus on restricted topics would usually be seen to prohibit their identification as ethnographic studies, and Lindlof and Shatzer (1998) caution against making excessive generalizations about community processes from a small sample. The selectivity of these approaches goes against the ethnographic ethos of engagement with events as they happen in the field, and of a holistic attention to all practices as constitutive of a distinct culture.

Two researchers whose studies fit the more generally accepted model of ethnography are Baym and Correll. Baym (1995a; 1995b; 1995c; 1998) and Correll (1995) undertook studies in which real-time engagement with discussions as they developed was combined with other kinds of interaction: email exchanges with participants, electronic or face-to-face interviews and the posing of general questions to the group. The distinctive nature of the claim to being ethnographic in these studies is that their authors aim to study enduring practices through which the community becomes meaningful and perceptible to participants. In this way, the ethnographic approach becomes a way of studying the achievement of a meaningful cultural context for participants. Ethnography is a way of seeing through participants' eyes: a grounded approach that aims for a deep understanding of the cultural foundations of the group. The use of different ways of observing and communicating with participants provides a kind of triangulation through which observations can be cross-checked. It is particularly important that both Baym and Correll use two-way interaction, allowing the ethnographer to ask questions of informants and explore developing ideas. In their holistic approach, interactive and multi-channel communication, and long-term engagement, these ethnographies are markedly different from the more selective approaches to the study of online settings.

Reliance on electronic interactions can raise some problems for ethnographic analysis. Traditionally, the validity of the ethnographer's observations relies upon the breadth of observations and participations that have contributed to the findings. Given the ethnographer's sustained and involved presence, it seems unlikely that informants could keep up a false or fabricated identity. Margaret Mead may have been fooled by her informants, but her failing is held to be that she did not sufficiently engage with the field (Freeman, 1996). When we move from face-to-face interaction to electronically mediated contact, the possibilities for informants to fool the ethnographer seem to multiply. Identity play is acknowledged almost as a norm in certain online settings, such as MUDs. In this context, to take statements made by participants as having any relation to their offline lives is problematic. Turkle (1995: 324) discusses the dilemma in the context of her own study of the relationship between experiences of virtual environments and understandings of real life. Turkle chose not to report on online interactions unless she had also met face-to-face the person involved, considering that for her purposes this level of verification of online identities was required. She acknowledges that this 'real-life bias' is appropriate for her own study, while it may not be so for others. The decision to privilege certain modes of interaction is a situated one. If the aim is to study online settings as contexts in their own right, the question of offline identities need not arise. This point will be revisited in Chapter 3.

The popularity of the ethnographic approach to online phenomena probably owes something to the accessibility of the field site to increasingly desk-bound academics. In the current academic climate, time for prolonged immersion in a physically located ethnographic field site is hard to come by. The Internet is available from the researcher's desktop, and can be accessed whenever there is time. Newsgroups are often archived, so that the discussions can be retrieved long after they first arose. The potential to go back in time to review events poses some intriguing possibilities for the ethnographer. Field notes, recordings and photographs have a long history as records of events that allow the ethnographer to review data and to reconsider and refine observations. They also have an important function in allowing the ethnographer to show an apparently unmediated portrayal of the field to audiences. Methods of recording data are, however, necessarily selective. It is common to feel anxiety at not writing down or recording 'the right things' during an ethnography. The ethnographer knows that what is written and recorded in the heat of the moment in the field can later assume greater significance as it comes to stand in for the field experience itself. In contrast, the record of a newsgroup's discussions in an archive seems non-selective: the 'ultimate field recorder' as Stone (1995: 243) suggests. The whole of the discussion is laid out, as it happened, and reviewing events in the field is no longer mediated by the technologies of data recording. It appears that ethnography can be time-shifted so that the ethnographer's engagement can occur after the events with which they engage happened for participants. Ethnographer and participants no longer need to share the same time frame. In some important ways this depends on how the ethnographic project is conceived. If the aim is to recapture the participants' experience, then time-shifted ethnography falls short. Part of following a newsgroup in real time is making sense out of the arrival of messages in the wrong order, waiting for responses to messages, and experiencing periods of high and low activity in the newsgroup. With a collapsed ethnographic time frame these features of participant experience are less accessible. In a similar vein, Reid (1995) argues that printouts from MUD interactions lose their ethnographic meaning when read after the event. The utterances of participants might be preserved, but the experience of participating is not.

A more active form of ethnographic engagement in the field also requires the ethnographer, rather than lurking or downloading archives, to engage with participants. Making this shift from an analysis of passive discourse to being an active participant in its creation allows for a deeper sense of understanding of meaning creation. Instead of being a detached and invisible analyst, the ethnographer becomes visible and active within the field setting. Questions can be asked and emerging analytic concepts tested and refined, with the cooperation of informants. This kind of engagement also allows for a reflexive understanding of what it is to be a user of CMC. Being a participant in a newsgroup entails reading, interpreting and replying to messages as they arrive, which according to the vagaries of news distribution mechanisms can be very different for users at different locations. The ethnographer cannot stand in for *every* user and recreate the circumstances in which they access the newsgroup, but she can at least experience what it is like to be *a* user. Reflexive engagement with the medium brings the interpretive problems of being a user of the medium to the fore, and in this way provides new angles on the experience of being a user for exploration (Markham, 1998). A reflexive understanding of the medium, if critically examined, can provide for insights not accessible from the analysis of archives.

Being actively engaged in a newsgroup poses some challenges to the ethnographer, not least of which is the negotiation of access and the requirement to self-present in ways acceptable to potential informants (Lindlof and Shatzer, 1998; Thomsen et al., 1998). To participate in a newsgroup without revealing one's role as a researcher would, as in all cases of covert ethnography, pose a considerable ethical problem. Arguing that online interactions are sufficiently real to provide a context for an ethnographic study has an ethical corollary: online interactions are sufficiently real for participants to feel they have been harmed or their privacy infringed by researchers. The ethical dimensions of research in online settings have been much debated. The status of messages posted to a newsgroup or events in a MUD is controversial: it is questionable whether they are best seen as public statements and therefore fair game for the researcher, or as the property of their authors and not to be appropriated for academic purposes without permission (King, 1996; Waskul and Douglass, 1996). In offline settings it is rare for a researcher to reveal the name of an informant, for fear of causing embarrassment or harm. By extrapolation, researchers in online settings have often treated user names as similarly sensitive and changed identifying details to avoid the possibility of adverse consequence. This move is in accord with an approach that treats online interactions in their own terms as real to participants. To do otherwise would be to treat online identities as if they did not matter to participants, whereas in many settings they patently do matter.

While an important move, focusing only on user names is potentially insufficient: the availability of newsgroup search engines such as dejanews (http://www.dejanews.com) raises the possibility of a sufficiently committed reader being able to trace the source of any verbatim quotation. If the ethical commitment is to severing traceable links between the ethnographic text and a context that readers could identify, changing the user name is not enough. Refraining from making verbatim quotations would pose a considerable challenge to the reporting conventions of discourse-based research. Focusing on changing identifiers is not a total solution, but a situated compromise. Online settings are heterogeneous, as are the disciplines which study them, and no single ethical code is likely to do justice to all (Herring, 1996). It is the ethnographer's task to find out during the ethnography what is considered sensitive, not as an additional task but as a part of the ethnography itself. The researcher needs to apply an ethnographic sensitivity to the recognition of potential ethical problems and the development of solutions that are appropriate in context (Reid, 1996). This in turn provides more insight into the extent to which participants see their online interactions as real. Negotiation of consent can be seen as an ongoing process throughout the ethnography, rather than an isolated initial event (Allen, 1996). In online settings this can, however, pose some problems. The difficulties of negotiating consent with informants whose identities are unstable and whose presence may be ephemeral pose some problems for conventional notions of informed consent (Lindlof and Shatzer, 1998). The interactions involved in negotiating consent may affect the research setting or presuppose the topic of investigation (Jones, 1994). There is no quick fix to ethical problems and ultimately responses by informants to the written ethnographies are unpredictable (Brettell, 1993; Hine, 1995).

Active engagement with a newsgroup might be seen to make the ethnographer's observations more authentic, in the sense of being more like the experience of participants. However, this argument only works for the active participants, who may be only a minority of those following the newsgroup. The status of lurkers, who read newsgroups but do not post messages, has always been problematic for ethnographic studies of CMC. Ethnography relies on observable features of interaction and the reading-based activity of the lurker is simply invisible to the observer of a newsgroup. Even direct appeals to newsgroups addressed to all participants including lurkers may receive little response: lurkers by definition lurk, and do not respond to the postings of participants even when the participant is an ethnographer. From a discursive point of view, the silent are difficult to incorporate into the analysis. Lurkers are known to be present and their presence may be confirmed by records of accesses to the newsgroup, but for the ethnographer of the newsgroup they leave no observable traces. From a community-based perspective lurkers can be seen as important only in as far as they eventually become active in the group (Correll, 1995) or are acknowledged by the active members of the newsgroup as an audience (Franco et al., 1995). Alternatively, they may be simply viewed as not a part of the community (Paccagnella, 1997): community becomes an elective phenomenon in which some who could participate choose not to, for whatever reason. What is not observable is simply defined out of the purview of the ethnographer, who then concentrates on those for whom the newsgroup is a community. Similarly, from an identity-based perspective lurkers have no online personae, and so are not present in any meaningful way (MacKinnon, 1995; 1997) or not 'part of the social' (Jones, 1997a: 13). While lurkers are not important or meaningful to ethnographers except in so far as they are part of the awareness context (Glaser and Strauss, 1964) of active participants, assuming that this is also the case for the lurkers themselves seems glib.

In newsgroups, sidelining the lurkers and focusing on active participants for the purposes of ethnographic study has been relatively easy. In their unobservability, lurkers are rendered as unimportant to the ethnographer as they appear to be to the newsgroup. The absence of the lurker in the ethnographic text enhances the perception of the newsgroup as a coherent bounded entity. Ethnographic approaches to CMC as a context have concentrated on bounded settings such as MUDs, IRC channels and newsgroups. The boundaries of the group being studied are symbolically enacted (by active participants) through the discourse of the group and through the devices which control access such as MUD addresses and passwords, IRC channel names and newsgroup hierarchies. The socially constructed and maintained boundaries coincide with the (socially constructed) technical devices that carve out a bounded space. This might not be a conventional, physical notion of place, but it is analogous in its focus on bounded social contexts. On the WWW observability becomes even more of a problem for the ethnographer, since little of the interpretive work that goes into producing and reading a web page is readily apparent, apart from through a textual analysis of the pages themselves. The rich social interaction that characterizes the MUD or the newsgroup seems absent, or at least lost to ethnographic observation. The appropriate unit of analysis is also less clear. By contrast to the newsgroup or the MUD, the WWW is less easily rendered as bounded social space and the would-be ethnographer of the WWW is left in doubt whether to focus on the construction of an individual page, on the relationship between the author of a page and an audience, or on the hypertextual relationships between interlinked pages.

Individual web pages are developed by designers who may have little direct social contact with one another, virtually or face-to-face, except by viewing and making links to one another's pages. Each has their own domestic or institutional context that shapes the development of the site and could form the object of an ethnographic study. The relationships between pages are largely enacted through the hypertext links that allow a visitor to move from one page to another. The links themselves are observable through the source code of the page. Whether anyone in practice follows the links is less clear to the ethnographer, although individual web developers may track the paths that visitors to their pages take. The hypertextual form of the WWW seems more suited to a view of social organization as networks rather than as segmented social spaces like communities (Jackson, 1997), although these approaches too may be restricted to studying links in principle rather than links followed in practice. Social network analyses focus on the interconnectivity and patterns of connection rather than the content connected, and therefore only portray one aspect of the structure of the WWW. Web pages were at first relatively static representations, in which the same text and images were presented to whoever visited until the developer chose to update the page. Latterly more interactive features have been incorporated into some sites, including dynamic updates, guest books, chat forums, interactive virtual environments and experiments in web pages as social space (McLaughlin et al., 1995). In any of these interactive settings the problem of observability is temporarily solved and the ethnographer has again a bounded social setting upon which to focus. It is less obvious that an ethnographic approach can be applied to the WWW itself, rather than the bounded social settings of specific pages.

The most prevalent framework to date for understanding web pages has been to focus on personal home pages developed by individuals and to view them as a form of self-presentation, or construction of self (Turkle, 1995). The web page becomes a managed site for portraying oneself and one's connections (H. Miller, 1995). This approach misses several important features of web pages: the conception of the web audience and the technology's capabilities; the social and institutional location of the web designer; and the relationships between web pages. While the view of the web page as a form of self-presentation focuses attention on the detail of the web page itself, a broader view might also incorporate a recognition of both the context in which the page was produced and the web context into which it is inserted. This approach includes interaction with web site designers and real-time engagement in the developing web landscape. Only by including the features which surround and enable the production of a web page can we have a view of web production as a meaningful social act that incorporates a view of the emergence of relationships on the web over time. Chapters 4, 5 and 6 of this book consider how we might incorporate a view of the WWW page as a social act into the design of an ethnographic study of CMC. To do so requires a reconceptualization of the relationship between ethnography and bounded social space, discussed in Chapter 3.

In this section I have shown how naturalistic studies overall, and ethnography in particular, have posed a challenge to the limited view of CMC provided by experimental studies. In highlighting the rich and complex social interactions that CMC can provide, researchers have established CMC as a cultural context. In so doing, researchers have drawn upon frameworks that focus on the construction of reality through discourse and practice. A style of ethnography that involves real-time engagement with the field site and multiple ways of interacting with informants has proved key in highlighting the processes through which online interaction comes to be socially meaningful to participants. In claiming a new field site for ethnography and focusing on the construction of bounded social space, the proponents of online culture have, however, overplayed the separateness of the offline and the online. A focus on community formation and identity play has exacerbated the tendency to see Internet spaces as self-contained cultures, as has the reliance on observable features of social organization. The interactions between the various social spaces both online and offline remain to be explored, although this is a task that cannot easily be accomplished from within the online setting. Observing online phenomena in isolation discounts social processes offline which contribute to an understanding of use of the Internet as a meaningful thing to do. Some pointers towards this approach may be drawn from the studies of CMC in organizations that suggest that perceptions of CMC, its success and the uses to which it is put depend heavily on the context in which it is used rather than on inherent features of the medium itself (Mantovani, 1994). For this dimension I turn to a review of the grounds for considering the Internet as a cultural artefact.

Internet as cultural artefact

The Internet, strictly speaking, is no more than the sum of the computers that can communicate using its language, the protocol TCP/IP. More loosely, the term 'Internet' is used to denote a set of application programs that enable particular kinds of communication and sharing of information. The applications that are available at any one time have a large part in shaping what the Internet is understood to be. Since the early electronic mail applications, which work best for asynchronous one-to-one communication, new applications such as bulletin boards, Usenet, IRC, MUDs and MOOs, video conferencing and the World Wide Web have extended the possibilities for communication into the synchronous and the one-to-many or many-to-many. There are now a multitude of different ways of accessing what is in principle the same network of computers, and through the new applications the network comes to look very different. The World Wide Web in particular, with its user-friendly clickable hyperlink structure, is credited with bringing the Internet to a wider audience with a low tolerance for learning new technical skills. In contrast to many technologies which take a material form, it is harder to say where the Internet begins and ends and what is meant when the term is used: computers, a protocol, applications programs, content or domain names and email addresses. Both its production and its consumption are dispersed among multiple locations, institutions and individuals. The Internet is as much a discursively created object as a single, given artefact. In this section, I explore some discourses that make up the Internet as an object, and review approaches that provide analytic purchase on the constructed nature of technologies.

An NOP (1999) survey calculated that the proportion of the UK population with access to the Internet at home was 14%. The numbers of these potential users who use the Internet regularly may be much fewer. On this basis, the Internet is still a minority technology. Numbers online might be growing, but the Internet is far from saturation even among those who could afford access. Yet if we turn away from user surveys, and conduct a more informal cultural survey, we find a somewhat different picture. The Internet is everywhere (within an 'everywhere' limited to places where the mass media are readily available). Reviews of web sites regularly appear in newspapers and magazines outside the market niche for net-related magazines. Several broadsheet newspapers and the occasional tabloid newspaper in the UK have weekly supplements devoted to the Internet, computing and related developments. The zeal with which the online world is promoted might be related to commercial interests and cross-ownership or the attraction of journalists to the new and fashionable. However, the permeation of the Internet into the news media marks it out as a topic of general concern or interest, not restricted to a technical elite. On television too, the Internet is widely commented upon and brought into general magazine programmes besides the series devoted entirely to computing. The Internet has been embraced by television, and is promoted as a supplement to the viewing experience, allowing access to further information, the sending of feedback (for example, Newhagen et al., 1995) and occasional opportunities to interact with stars and experts from the shows. The permeation of the Internet spreads outside even the mass media targeted at the young and the male. It is not just regularity of appearance in the mass media that makes the Internet a mainstream technology, but also the matter-of-factness of those appearances in a wide range of settings.

The web site address on the cornflakes box signifies the Internet as a mainstream object with meanings outside a restricted technical elite. Few people in the developed nations at the end of the twentieth century can be unaware of the Internet, although many may still be baffled as to what it is and what precisely they might do with it. In just a few years, the giving of email addresses and web page addresses (Uniform Resource Locators, or URLs) has become routine. Not all of us may actually have easy access to the Internet, and certainly few of us will take up the invitation to 'Visit our web site' on the advertisement, television programme or cornflakes packet, but we are expected to understand that we could. URLs and email addresses do not come with instructions for use: we no longer say more than 'This is a web site address' when we exchange URLs. Advertisements for Internet service providers even outside the technical press seem rarely to explain patiently what the Internet is for and what can be done with it. Increasingly they seem to cut straight to the differentiating factors: how fast are their connections; how much does it cost; how easy is their software to install and use; how good is their support? These statements suggest a confidence that the Internet is available as a cultural object to at least a significant audience.

This is not to say that those who have access to the Internet automatically know what to do with it. The central heating engineer working in my home tells me that his wife has the Internet at home, but does not yet know what to do with it. His cousin, who set it up for her, does know what to do with it because he works with computers and has a friend who knows about the Internet. We talk about the possibility that he could use the Internet link at home to avoid driving to the central office to collect job specifications by having them emailed or faxed via a modem. Notable in this short anecdote are several features common to many new technologies (Silverstone and Hirsch, 1994). The capacities of the technology are not readily apparent and available in advance to those who acquire them. Rather, they are worked out in a process of negotiations and interpretations, which happen in the specific context in which the technology is bought and used. Working out what the Internet is for is a process involving social networks such as cousins who have friends who know what to do with it, media representations that convince us that this is a desirable commodity, and finding uses for the technology that fit in with and transform local contexts. Vehviläinen (1998), Wakeford (1997) and Morse (1997) have shown how women in particular have been able to appropriate the technology in ways which are meaningful within their lives. The meaningfulness of the technology does not exist before the uses themselves, but is worked out at the time of use. At the same time, making the use of the Internet meaningful involves representing it to others as valuable in recognizable ways. At this point the abstract 'Internet' becomes meaningful in a concrete and contextual fashion. To say that the Internet is a mainstream object is not to imply that it is the same object to all. To paraphrase Ang (1996: 80), the Internet is everywhere but it is not everywhere in the same way.

Clearly, while we might be comfortable talking about 'the Internet' as if it were one object, it is going to mean very different things to different people. The technology is going to have very different cultural meanings in different contexts. This point would benefit from a more detailed empirical investigation. Here I draw again on anecdotal evidence. In teaching a course on the social dynamics of the Internet, I ask students to bring in cuttings from newspapers, whether articles or advertisements, which refer to the Internet. We use these to talk through the images of the Internet and the Internet user that they portray. The class often consists of students from a wide range of backgrounds and countries of origin. Newspaper stories that the group used in the 1998 session portrayed the Internet as a dangerous place, where pornography was rife, paedophiles networked and neo-Nazis found a safe haven. One student from Brazil found these stories particularly puzzling: 'We just don't have this picture.' This is a reminder that in thinking of the Internet we should not necessarily expect it to mean the same thing to everyone. It could be said that ideas about what the Internet is are socially shaped, in that they arise in contexts of use in which different ways of viewing the technology are meaningful and acceptable:

> It is essential to treat telecommunications and computer-mediated communications networks as *local* phenomena, as well as global networks. Embedded within locally specific routines of daily schedules and the 'place ballets' of individuals, Internet has been shaped by its users. (Shields, 1996: 3)

The Internet could therefore usefully be viewed as shaped by the social context. As with media choice within organizations, perceptions of what a medium is for and what it symbolizes can be influential in determining when it is used (Trevino et al., 1987).

In another way, access to the Internet is shaped and the applications developed for it are shaped by the expectations of what it is for and how it ought to be used. Stefik (1997) argues that our metaphors for thinking about the Internet have been crucial in influencing the ways in which the Internet has developed and may be similarly influential in shaping its future. Metaphors can certainly be influential in suggesting certain moves and precluding others (Lakoff and Johnson, 1980). Stefik is particularly concerned that the options of policy makers and technology producers are closed off by the metaphors they use. Within the dominant metaphor of the information superhighway or I-way, Stefik identifies the digital library, electronic mail, electronic marketplace and digital worlds to represent the ways in which the Internet is and has been conceived of as a store of knowledge, a communications medium, a commercial forum and a place for experience. Stefik argues that these different conceptions of what the Internet is for deserve closer examination if the Internet is to be actively shaped to maximize benefits and imaginative uses of the technology. It has also been argued that metaphors for understanding the Internet, particularly the 'electronic frontier', are gendered and have implications for acceptable online roles and uses (L. Miller, 1995).

In becoming an object of the mainstream the Internet has come a long way from its origins. The commonly accepted and often-told myth of the origins of the Internet has it that it first came about as a military technology. Within the US Department of Defense's Advanced Research Projects Agency (ARPA), the urge to connect computers was conceived to allow computing power to be shared between remote sites. The intention might be a collaborative one, but the way in which it was enacted was according to military principles of resisting damage from enemy assault. The architecture that resulted was designed to be resistant to attack, with routing of data between remote machines able to adapt to the loss of parts of the network. This 'bombproof' system was enabled by a protocol for message packaging and addressing which was independent of the architecture of any one machine, and allowed very different computers to communicate. The close relationship between the military and the research activities of the universities enabled a gradual spread of ARPANET beyond the original network. Stories of the spread of the Internet present it as a technology that found a natural appeal. It simply grew, because it was too good not to. Along with this growth came a change of emphasis. Communication, although only a minor part of the original plan, became a major focus and emphasis on the use of networks for sharing access to processing power dwindled in comparison:

> The romance of the Net came not from how it was built or how it worked but from how it was used. By 1980 the Net was far more than a collection of computers and leased lines. It was a place to share work and build friendships and a more open method of communication. (Hafner and Lyon, 1998: 218)

The brief outline of the Internet's history told above is no doubt a distorted version of the events as they might be told by the protagonists. Hafner and Lyon (1998) bring this simplistic version of the origins of the Internet into question. Rather than a straightforward translation of a particular ethos into a corresponding design, Hafner and Lyon portray a complex set of interactions between computer scientists, politicians and research funders that together resulted in a network that could have been otherwise, and that could have foundered at many stages in its development. In particular, Hafner and Lyon counter the claim that the aim to build a bombproof network was a major drive in developing the network. Abbate (1998) shows how the development of ARPANET was shaped by particular policy contexts, of which Cold War military concerns were only one component. The intentions and experiences of the developers of the early networks might differ from the prevailing myth, but it is not the intention here to judge between them. It is for that reason that the story was described as a myth rather than a history. This is the story that users of the Internet tell each other about what kind of technology the Internet is and what kind of people they are.

The story of the origins and development of the Internet contains some key themes: the appropriation of a militaristic technology for humanitarian and libertarian purposes; the assertion of the natural human desire to communicate; the reclaiming of a weapon of destruction for the good of the people. Similar stories are told about the development of Minitel in France as a source of information, and its appropriation by users as a way of communicating (Lemos, 1996). The expansion of the Internet from the military research establishments to universities more widely allows the technology to be reshaped, or possibly, to reveal its true nature. This theme permeated much of the early use of the Internet: its proclaimed anarchic nature, the counter-cultural attitude of the hackers and cyberpunks, and the emphasis on shared responsibility of early netiquette. Early theorizing about the Internet emphasized identity play, the development of online community and the discovery of new ways of communicating and sharing. A major shift in the Internet's identity occurred with the commodification of Internet access and its availability to people outside the universities on a fee-paying basis. Internet service providers (ISPs) package and sell Internet access to members of the public. The early influx of people accessing the Internet on a commercial basis was controversial to those who had shaped its culture. Newcomers who were unaware of the norms and values shaped in the early days were seen as threatening the culture or simply being rude (Herz, 1995).

From its early restricted origins, the Internet has become a commodity in principle, although not in practice, open to all. As a commodity, it needs to be sold to its purchasers, and considerable financial gains may be there for a company that can create and cater to demand. ISPs both feed on and contribute to the cultural trend. A complicated relationship with the original values of the Internet is the result. Many new users may be completely unaware of what it symbolized to its early enthusiasts. Its users now have arrived through varied routes of access and paths to understanding what it means for them. They have been exposed to a myriad of different messages about what to expect from the technology, themselves and their fellow users before they even begin to interact with others online. They use the Internet for work, for leisure, for information and for shopping. They explore new relationships and sustain existing ones. They assess what they see online in relation to what they know to be sensible and appropriate using interpretive codes both learned online and imported from offline settings.

The Internet can therefore be seen as thoroughly socially shaped both in the history of its development and in the moments of its use. The ways in which the Internet is currently understood and used are the upshot of historical (as an embodiment of Cold War military ideals or as a triumph of humanitarian values over said military ideals), cultural (through mass media in differing national contexts), situational (in institutional and domestic contexts within which the technology acquires symbolic meaning), and metaphorical (through the concepts available for thinking about the technology) shaping. This social shaping produces the object we know as the Internet, although the object that each of us knows is likely to be subtly and sometimes radically different. This way of thinking about technology owes its origins to the field of science and technology studies, and in particular the social construction of technology (SCOT) approach (Pinch and Bijker, 1987). A range of related approaches (including MacKenzie and Wajcman, 1985; Bijker et al., 1987; Bijker and Law, 1992; Bijker, 1995) has established that rather than being seen as the result of an independent technical logic, the technologies that we end up with could always have been otherwise.

Social shaping implies that what the technology comes to be is the upshot of social processes of negotiation between different interest groups who view the advantages and disadvantages of the technology differently. The upshot of these processes involves the reaching of a closure around the definitions of the technology and the final version of the technology depends on which relevant social group's conceptualization wins out. The iconic example for this approach is the bicycle (Pinch and Bijker, 1987; Bijker, 1995). Although it might seem that the design of bicycle current today is simply the most efficient way for it to be, it can be shown that the self-evident design of the bicycle came about through processes of negotiation around the definitions of uses and problems of the relevant social groups. Technologies possess interpretive flexibility, such that not only do relevant social groups view the technology differently, but the technology could be said actually to be a different thing for each. Only in retrospect does the design that emerged come to seem self-evidently the best. Interpretive flexibility might seem to imply merely that perceptions of the artefact vary between different groups. Bijker (1987) acknowledges that 'artefactual flexibility' might have captured more explicitly the radical implications of different understandings for what the technology is.

The application of a social shaping approach to the Internet would imply that we conduct a detailed examination of the representations of the technology throughout its history, focusing on conflicting representations and the social groups that emerge from them. This approach might be able (if the model has general applicability) to unpack the processes that led to us being able to see the Internet in retrospect as either the product of military concerns or the triumph of a human will to communicate. Individual projects to set up community-based networks also could be analysed through the perspectives of the groups involved (Schmitz, 1997). The development of the Internet would be seen as the upshot of contingent social processes rather than the necessary outcome of either technical logic or human desire. The focus of this book is on the current state of the Internet rather than its history. Here the historical social shaping of the Internet is important in pointing to the problems of seeing the state at which the Internet has arrived as the result of a linear progress towards known goals, or as the embodiment of the concerns of any one group of people. Whatever the current uses of the Internet, it is useful to remember that they arise against a backdrop of negotiations about what the problem and the solutions might be. Considering the problems in this way makes it unhelpful to think of technical and social as two different things, as Bijker points out:

> A central adage for this research is that one should never take the meaning of a technical artefact or technological system as residing in the technology itself. Instead one must study how technologies are shaped and acquire their meanings

in the heterogeneity of social interactions. Another way of stating the same principle is to use the metaphor of the seamless web of science, technology and society, which is meant to remind the researcher not to accept at face value the distinctions between, for example, the technical and the social as these present themselves in a given situation. (1995: 6)

In analysing the Internet, what might seem technical features or inherent characteristics are therefore open to ethnographic investigation. Technical and social become constructs which are performed in different settings, rather than *a priori* explanatory distinctions (Rachel and Woolgar, 1995). The Internet can usefully be considered as thoroughly social (Grint and Woolgar, 1992).

Grint and Woolgar (1997), while acknowledging that the development of technologies is a contingent process, take issue with the utility of accepting that closure then occurs around what the technology is. For Grint and Woolgar the capacities of the technology are never fixed, and apprehending what the technology can do is always a site for interpretive work. While Pinch and Bijker (1987) focus on the interpretive flexibility of the technology in the past, Grint and Woolgar take pains to situate it in the present. They do so via the metaphor of technology as text. While the design process involves developers in embedding their notions of what users are like into the machine, consumption involves processes of negotiation and interpretation. The users 'read' the technology text in ways that are subject to configured relationships with the producers of the technology and with the technology itself. Aberrant readings are always possible from inadequately configured users. The technology as text metaphor suggests a focus on processes of development and consumption, viewing the relationship between producers and consumers as mediated but not determined by the technological text. Rather than possessing inherent qualities, the technology text 'makes available' readings which users/readers interpret in context. This is not to say that contexts possess inherent qualities either. The pertinent features of the context are produced in moments of interaction with the technology. Grint and Woolgar's notion of the effects of technology is also thoroughly social. The effects which are recognized are the result of contingent social processes depending upon by whom, to whom and in what contexts the effects are represented. For the explanations of the persuasiveness of particular accounts of the effects of a technology we are encouraged to look at social processes rather than attribute their success to a faithful representation of the technology's qualities.

The technology as text metaphor focuses attention on the contingency of practices through which the Internet is made meaningful in both production and use. For Grint and Woolgar, though, focusing on the material, bounded artefact of the computer gave them an obvious starting point for their analysis. In their aim to deconstruct the notion that the artefact had inherent qualities or effects, they were able to focus on the social relations around that material artefact. They also had a temporal focus, in that they could follow the progress of the new computer from inception through development to release on to the market. In applying the technology as text metaphor to the Internet some problems arise in deciding on appropriate field sites and sets of social relations to consider. While the computer hardware company in Grint and Woolgar's tale acts as a single point through which the technology finally delivered to the consumer must pass, with the Internet it is harder to identify any single track through which the technology is delivered to users.

Many groups of people, including hardware producers, Internet service providers, applications developers, developers of web pages and newsgroup contributors could be termed producers of the Internet. The Internet user might be found as a category in the work of Internet service providers, or of advertising agencies, or the marketers of new Internet-ready personal computers. We could design ethnographic studies to track the ways in which conceptions of the Internet user were embedded into particular access points, advertisements or pieces of hardware. We could investigate whom individual Internet users considered relevant producer communities, and then use that as a starting point to study the practices of those producers. Users of the Internet are often, however, producers too in terms of content. They (or at least, some of them) produce web pages, send email and post newsgroup messages. The concepts of producer and user are not routine ways in which social relations around the Internet are organized. The Internet is delivered at the point of buying a computer or signing up with an ISP, but it is also delivered up, and differently rendered, in every logging on, surfing session or newsgroup encounter. While Grint and Woolgar (1997) were relatively easily able to render the computer construction company as an adequate site for an ethnography of computers, the recognition of sites for the ethnography of the Internet is less straightforward.

The technology as text metaphor is therefore less straightforwardly applicable to the Internet than it is to bounded and located technological artefacts. It is however useful in focusing attention on the potential of a thoroughgoing constructivist approach to technologies that denies them an asocial core. It suggests that the making of the Internet can be explored through a detailed ethnographic attention to the ways in which the technology and its contexts are constructed. A first step is to disaggregate the Internet, and leave go of the idea that a study of the construction of *the* Internet is possible. An alternative to attempting to identify relevant groups in advance is to start with a particular use of the Internet and use that as a tool to explore the construction of sites of production and consumption without specifying them in advance. In this model, the ethnographer does not go to a single site or context and remain there, but focuses on travelling between sites as an analytic device. Chapter 3 describes an approach to ethnography of the Internet that embraces this ambivalence about the appropriate sites to study production and consumption of the Internet.

Research in the sociology of technology has shown that the properties we take to be self-evidently attached to technologies can more usefully be thought of as the upshot of a contingent set of social processes. In the sociology of the media the categories of analysis are slightly different, notably in that users become audiences, but the preoccupations are broadly similar. Here the concern has been with the relationships between media texts and their audiences. The question, crudely put, is whether media texts possess inherent qualities such as ideological messages made available to and/or unthinkingly absorbed by audiences, or whether audiences actively construct meanings undetermined by the content of the media texts they view. Latterly, a prominent view has been that the production of a media text constructs a relationship with the audience, which actual audiences may either orient to, reinterpret or reject. The upshot, as in the constructivist approach to technology, is to focus attention on the social processes through which media texts are produced and consumed:

> Scholars of television and popular culture have increasingly realized that the meaning of a text, including its progressive or reactionary ideology, cannot be ✓ ascertained by textual analysis, but only by a knowledge of situated audiences and readers – hence the turn to ethnography in cultural studies recently. (Goodwin and Wolff, 1997: 142)

Ethnographic studies of production and consumption contexts have displayed the active processes of meaning creation that surround the media text, and have questioned the idea of a straightforward process of communication of ideas from sender to receiver. In his social theory of the media, Thompson (1995) stresses that understanding the media involves ✓ looking both at their content and at the ways in which they are produced and used. Thompson's understanding of the social context is more concerned with the circumstances in which media messages are produced and consumed than with the ways in which the media technologies themselves are shaped. There has also, however, been a recognition of communications media as technologies. In a parallel move to the social shaping approaches described above, Williams (1990) argues that television can be seen as both a technology and a cultural form. Williams proposes that television arose through particular sets of concerns, and its uses have developed in response to social concerns in ways that have come to seem natural but are far from being so. Viewing television as both technology and cultural form allows Williams to investigate the interrelations between the institutions that surround and produce television, and the detail of the content including the forms of programme produced, the flow of programming and the way in which the content of television is organized into a sequence, and the detail of the forms of address that the programmes contain. The breadth of this reach leaves no aspect of television as innocent, neutral or self-evident.

Williams displays the paucity of explanations that posit the medium as a cause of social effects. The uses of television and radio were far from obvious from the outset, but were actively developed by producers based on their understandings of the potential of the medium and the characteristics of the audience (Scannell, 1996). For producers the audience is a category oriented to through various kinds of knowledge including ratings figures, surveys and focus groups, stereotyped portrayals of idealized knowledge and the use of personal experience and preferences. The audience is an imagined category that producers orient to in making their work meaningful (for example, Pekurny, 1982; Espinosa, 1982; Gill, 1993). The audience also acts as the 'money arrow' (Ettema and Whitney, 1994) which makes media production meaningful in an economic sense. The construction of the audience within production is a complex and situated practice.

'Audience' is therefore far from a straightforward category. If producers, whose livelihoods depend upon it, have trouble in knowing their audiences, the problems in knowing the audience for ethnographers are going to be even more acute (Hartley, 1987; Radway, 1988; Turner, 1996). Production is a relatively bounded pursuit. Groups of producers are often institutionally contained and separately located. They are therefore quite easy for an ethnographer to find (if not necessarily easy to access: Espinosa, 1982). Audiences, by contrast, are dispersed and fragmented in time and space (they do not group together within an institutional location and they only act as an audience for some of the time). It is, however, no less important to have a rich and detailed understanding of the ways in which they interpret media and media technologies. There is a commitment within media studies to focusing on television use as a part of everyday life (for example, Bausinger, 1984; Silverstone, 1992; Livingstone, 1998), and a similar approach has been taken to other information and communication technologies within domestic contexts (for example, Frissen, 1997; Silverstone and Hirsch, 1994). Bausinger suggests that 'technology in the everyday can only ever be grasped conjuncturally' (1984: 346), as a part of ongoing interactions within the home. It would therefore be artificial to separate out television as a topic for study. Such injunctions to study audiences *in situ* and as part of a multiplicity of ongoing interactions are theoretically pleasing, but hard to put into practice.

For ethnographers the problems of knowing the audience revolve around the difficulties of finding an appropriate site and conducting a study of practices that mainly occur in the private space of the home. Since living within a household for an extended period is largely impractical, applications of ethnographic approaches to the media audience have involved some creative adaptations. While retaining the ethos of fidelity to the processes of meaning construction *in situ*, ethnographic studies of the media audience have often dispensed with the concern of ethnography with holistic analysis. This is a strategic application of ethnography to a particular problem, and so is quite distinct from the anthropological conception of what it is to be ethnographic. Given the difficulties of extended participant observation in domestic settings, group discussions, television viewing sessions and extended interviews have been used to explore the ways in which audiences understand the medium and their audiencehood (for example, Morley, 1980; 1992; Lembo, 1997). Similar strategies could no doubt be used to study the interpretive practices of Internet lurkers, if one could locate them in sufficient numbers. Interviews with Internet users have certainly proved informative (Turkle, 1995; Shaw, 1997; Clark, 1998; Markham, 1998), and could be extended further to include accompanied online sessions, allowing the interviewer to discuss interactions with the informant as they happen.

In sum, work in sociology of technology and in media sociology sustains a view of technologies, including communications media, as thoroughly socially shaped. Both propose that the content of media/technology is open to ethnographic analysis in production and use. Categories such as producer, user and audience are constructed through the practices of production and consumption. It is only through these practices that an understanding of the capabilities of the technology arises, in situated contexts. Research on television is particularly pertinent in a consideration of the Internet. In television it has been argued that the content carried is created by producers in relation to their understandings of both the audience and the technology itself. Television in this sense parallels the Internet, in that Internet content can be seen as thoroughly shaped by ideas of what the technology does and who the audience are, as Chapter 5 will illustrate. The settings in which television content is consumed are diverse and spatially distinct. In the Internet, however, the sites of production of content are also markedly dispersed as compared with both television and the technologies considered by Grint and Woolgar (1997). In two senses the users of the Internet are involved in the construction of the technology: through the practices by which they understand it and through the content they produce. The dispersal of sites of production fragments the notion of producer while the technology makes situated interpretations of the technology at least partially available to other users. These processes complicate the identification of appropriate ethnographic field sites.

Tracing complex connections

The first section of this chapter explored challenges to the 'reduced social cues' model of CMC effects. Even within organizational groups, the attribution of social effects to technical characteristics has proved controversial. The recognition that 'effects' are different in different contexts goes some way to explain the often conflicting results that experimental studies produced. Schmitz and Fulk (1991) and Fulk (1993) propose that CMC be seen as socially constructed rather than a given technology with foreseeable effects. As Fulk et al. (1992) point out, organizational contexts vary widely, and so the apparent impacts of CMC might be expected to vary widely. By extrapolation, we might also expect that studies of CMC use in organizations might differ radically from studies of its use in other social settings. The Internet, and particularly the social context of group forums like newsgroups and MUDs, has complicated relationships with diverse organizational and domestic settings. The Internet can also, as argued in the second section of this chapter, be seen as a cultural artefact shaped by social processes in production and in use. The technology as text metaphor provides one way of exploring the producer/user relations enacted in the text and its interpretations. While the Internet might be seen as a culture in its own right, the meanings and perceptions which participants bring to that culture may be shaped by the settings from which they access the Internet and the expectations that they have of it. As Baym (1998) points out, the online and offline worlds are connected in complex ways. The space in which online interactions occur is simultaneously socially produced through a technology that is itself socially produced:

> CMC of course, is not just a tool; it is at once technology, medium, and engine of social relations. It not only structures social relations, it is the space within which the relations occur and the tool that individuals use to enter that space. It is more than the context in which social relations occur (although it is that too), for it is commented on and imaginatively constructed by symbolic processes initiated and maintained by individuals and groups. (Jones, 1995: 16)

The Internet can be seen as textual twice over: as a discursively performed culture and as a cultural artefact, the technology text. In neither sense are its uses and interpretations determined by the text. The distinction between Internet as culture and as cultural artefact is a heuristic device for thinking about the indeterminacy of the Internet. It is not, however, to be taken as a distinction that is real in the experience of users of the technology, or as a straightforward reflection of an online/offline boundary. The distinction between culture and cultural artefact replays the real/virtual distinction and if accepted unproblematically may obscure the processes through which this boundary is itself constructed. The heuristic distinction acts as an incentive to finding an ethnographic approach to the Internet which takes both aspects into account and explores the connections between them. Treating the Internet as a cultural artefact interrogates the assumptions which viewing the Internet as a site for culture entails, and highlights the status of the Internet as itself a cultural achievement based on particular understandings of the technology.

It could be argued that existing ethnographic approaches to the Internet as culture have neglected some important aspects of the construction of the Internet as cultural artefact, through their focus on the bounded social spaces of the Internet. This chapter has argued for the contribution of ethnography to the understanding of the Internet both as culture and as cultural artefact. It appears that emphasis can usefully be placed on the production of meaning in context, where context is understood as both the circumstances in which the Internet is used (offline) and the social spaces that emerge through its use (online). Stone (1991) describes the online and offline as both being 'consensual loci', each with their own locally defined version of 'reality'. We know very little about the ways in which these two contexts are connected. On one level this is a practical problem: the settings where we might observe Internet culture are different from the ones in which we would observe the Internet in use. One setting is virtual and the other a physical place. It is far from straightforward to design a study that encompasses both aspects of the Internet (Star and Kanfer, 1993). While it might be relatively straightforward to observe and participate in a newsgroup, it is more difficult to visit users of that newsgroup individually and form judgements of the context in which their use of the newsgroup arises. Similarly, while studying users of the Internet in their working or domestic environments is potentially straightforward, it is harder then to form a prolonged engagement with their online activities since this is generally construed as a solitary activity. The practical problem of designing an ethnographic study of the Internet is also a statement about methodological foundations. The 'problem' is a result of a narrow conception of ethnography, focused on prolonged engagement in a bounded social space, whether that be a village, a club, a computer company or a newsgroup. The next chapter explores some strands from current ethnographic thinking that suggest an ethnographic approach to the Internet beyond bounded social locations. This approach plays on the profound ambivalence about the appropriate sites for investigation that stems from seeing the Internet as textual twice over.

3   The Virtual Objects of Ethnography

The crisis in ethnography

Ethnography has changed a lot since its origins as the method anthropologists used to develop an understanding of cultures in distant places. It has been taken up within a wide range of substantive fields including urban life, the media, medicine, the classroom, science and technology. Ethnography has been used within sociology and cultural studies, although it retains a special status as the key anthropological approach. In new disciplinary settings, the emphasis on holistic description has given way to more focused and bounded studies of particular topics of interest. Rather than studying whole ways of life, ethnographers in sociology and cultural studies have interested themselves in more limited aspects: people as patients, as students, as television viewers or as professionals. The ethnography of familiar and nearby cultures has also augmented the ethnography of remote and apparently exotic ways of life. These settings have brought their own challenges as ethnographers struggle to suspend what they take for granted about their own cultures, and attempt to negotiate access to settings where they may be dealing with the culturally more powerful (Jackson, 1987). The upshot of these developments has been a wide diversity of approaches to ethnography, although these share a fundamental commitment to developing a deep understanding through participation and observation. Hammersley and Atkinson provide a basic definition, applicable to most studies, of what ethnography is:

> In its most characteristic form it involves the ethnographer participating, overtly ⌐
> or covertly in people's daily lives for an extended period of time, watching what
> happens, listening to what is said, asking questions – in fact, collecting whatever
> data are available to throw light on the issues that are the focus of the research.
> (1995: 1)

The practice of ethnography has continually faced challenges concerning objectivity and validity from the harder sciences. A methodology that offers little in the way of prescription to its practitioners and has no formula for judging the accuracy of its results is vulnerable to criticism from methodologies such as surveys, experiments and questionnaires that come equipped with a full armoury of evaluative techniques. In the face of these critiques the popularity of qualitative methodologies, including ethnography, is based on their strong appeal as ways of addressing the richness and complexity of social life. The emphasis on holism in ethnography gives it a persuasive attraction in dealing with complex and multi-faceted concepts like culture, as compared with the more reductive quantitative techniques. Ethnography is appealing for its depth of description and its lack of reliance on *a priori* hypotheses. It offers the promise of getting closer to understanding the ways in which people interpret the world and organize their lives. By contrast, quantitative studies are deemed thin representations of isolated concepts imposed on the study by the researcher.

One response to positivist-based, quantitative critiques of ethnography has centred on claims that ethnography produces an authentic under-standing of a culture based on concepts that emerge from the study instead of being imposed *a priori* by the researcher. Cultures are studied in their natural state, rather than as disturbed by survey techniques or experimental scenarios. This argument depends upon a realist ethnography which describes cultures as they really are (it also, of course, depends on accepting realism and objectivity as the aspiration of any methodology). More recently the realist and naturalistic project has come into question from within the qualitative field, as realist notions more generally have been challenged by constructivist approaches to knowledge (Berger and Luckman, 1971). The basis for claiming any kind of knowledge as asocial and independent of particular practices of knowing has come under attack, and ethnography has not been exempt. The naturalistic project of documenting a reality external to the researcher has been brought into question. Rather than being the records of objectively observed and pre-existing cultural objects, ethno-graphies have been reconceived as written and unavoidably constructed accounts of objects created through disciplinary practices and the ethno-grapher's embodied and reflexive engagement. These developments in epistemology have constituted what Denzin describes as a 'triple crisis of representation, legitimation, and praxis' (1997: 3) for qualitative research, including ethnography. The triple crisis that Denzin describes threatens ethnography on all fronts: its claims to represent culture; its claims to authentic knowledge; and the ability of its proponents to make principled interventions based on the knowledge they acquire through ethnography. Marcus relates the comprehensive nature of the challenge to ethnography:

> Under the label first of 'postmodernism' and then 'cultural studies', many scholars in the social sciences and humanities subjected themselves to a bracing critical self-examination of their habits of thought and work. This involved reconsiderations of the nature of representation, description, subjectivity, objec-tivity, even of the notions of 'society' and 'culture' themselves, as well as how scholars materialized objects of study and data about them to constitute the 'real' to which their work had been addressed. (1997: 399)

The 'crisis', rather than suggesting the abandonment of ethnography altogether, can be seen as opening possibilities for creative and strategic applications of the methodology. The 'ethnography of ethnography' (Van

Maanen, 1995) occasioned by the new epistemology entails a re-examination of features of the methodology that might have seemed self-evident. The whole methodology is thus opened up for re-examination and refashioning. This provides an opportunity for reshaping and reformulating projects in the light of current concerns. Recognizing that the objects we find and describe are of our own making entails owning up to the responsibility that recognition imposes. It offers up the opportunity of making the kind of research objects we need to enter and transform debates, and opens up the relationships between research subjects, ethnographers and readers to reconfiguration. This chapter takes the ethnographic 'crisis' as an opportunity for making a form of ethnographic enquiry suited to the Internet, involving a different kind of interaction and ethnographic object from those with which ethnography has traditionally been concerned. This approach involves embracing ethnography as a textual practice and as a lived craft, and destabilizes the ethnographic reliance on sustained presence in a found field site.

The aim of this examination of ethnography is to find a different way of dealing with some problems with an ethnographic approach to the Internet as described in Chapter 2. These problems include the authenticity of mediated interactions as material for an ethnographic understanding and the choice of appropriate sites to study the Internet as both a culture and a cultural object. The problems with an ethnographic approach to the Internet encompass both how it is to be constituted as an ethnographic object and how that object is to be authentically known. Within a naturalistic or realist version of the ethnographic project these issues seem to render the ethnography of the Internet highly problematic. The aim of this chapter is to examine some recent developments in ethnographic thinking that are particularly useful in developing an alternative approach to the study of the Internet. The account will focus on three crucial areas for looking at the Internet ethnographically. These areas are:

- the role of travel and face-to-face interaction in ethnography
- text, technology and reflexivity
- the making of ethnographic objects.

The examination of these areas is used to formulate the principles of a virtual ethnography that draws on current ethnographic thinking and applies it to the mediated and spatially dispersed interactions that the Internet facilitates.

Ethnography and the face-to-face

A major issue to be confronted in designing an ethnographic study of the Internet is the appropriate way of interacting with the subjects of the research. Ethnography has traditionally entailed physical travel to a place, which implies that face-to-face interaction is the most appropriate. Before the widespread availability of CMC, mediated forms of communication simply did not seem sufficiently interactive to allow the ethnographer to test ideas through immersion. If mediated interaction is to be incorporated into an ethnographic project, the basis for focusing ethnographic engagement or immersion on face-to-face interaction needs to be considered. The availability of mediated interaction provides the opportunity to question the role of face-to-face interaction in the construction of an ethnography. We can then examine what it is about their reliance on face-to-face interaction that makes ethnographers' accounts of their research convincing, and explore the possibilities for a reconceptualization of ethnographic authenticity that incorporates mediated interaction on its own terms.

The way of considering face-to-face interaction discussed here owes its basis to the 'representational crisis' (Denzin, 1997). The publication of *Writing Culture* (Clifford and Marcus, 1986) marked a growing recognition that ethnographic writing was not a transparent representation of a culture. The written products of ethnography were narratives or accounts that relied heavily on the experience of particular ethnographers and on the conventions used to make the telling of those accounts authoritative and engaging (Van Maanen, 1988). Ethnography was a 'story-telling institution' (Van Maanen, 1995), and the stories told could be more or less convincing, but were not necessarily to be evaluated on a basis of their truth to a pre-existing 'real' culture. Whatever the sincerity with which they were told, ethnographic stories were necessarily selective. Ethnographies were 'textual constructions of reality' (Atkinson, 1990). This perspective provides an opportunity to analyse the importance of face-to-face interaction by looking at the role that is played in accounts by the fact of the ethnographer having been to a field site for a sustained period. The primacy of the face-to-face in ethnography can be understood by reflecting upon the way in which ethnography's production as an authoritative textual account has traditionally relied upon travel, experience and interaction. This is particularly useful as a way of avoiding making *a priori* judgements of the richness (and ethnographic adequacy) or otherwise of communications media: an assumption that has proved problematic in relation to CMC (Chapter 2).

Travel has played an important part in the construction of an ethnographic authority. The days of reliance on second-hand accounts and the tales of travellers are cast as the 'bad old days', in which the ethnographer was insufficiently embroiled with what was going on to be able to provide an authoritative analysis, and, worse, could be misled by relying on the re-representations of others. Kuper (1983) equates the 'Malinowskian revolution' in ethnography as comprising the uniting of fieldworker and theorist in a single body, such that the one who went, saw and reported was also the one who analysed. The concept of travel still plays an important part in distinguishing ethnography from other analytic approaches. As Van Maanen states:

Whether or not the field worker ever really does 'get away' in a conceptual sense is becoming increasingly problematic, but physical displacement is a requirement. (1988: 3)

Van Maanen seems here to be casting the problem as ethnographers taking their own analytic frameworks with them, and therefore failing to address the field site they visit on its own terms, as they have claimed. While for him physical travel is not enough to ensure conceptual distance, travel to a field site is a prerequisite for the ethnographic analysis. It is still not clear, however, what it is that makes travel so fundamental. Some clues are provided by analyses of the ways in which ethnographers write about their experience of travelling and arriving. The role played by travel in constructing ethnographic authority is pointed to by Pratt in her analysis of the role of 'arrival stories' in ethnographers' accounts:

They [arrival stories] play the crucial role of anchoring that description in the intense and authority-giving personal experience of fieldwork . . . Always they are responsible for setting up the initial positionings of the subjects of the ethnographic text: the ethnographer, the native, and the reader. (1986: 32)

Travel in this analysis becomes a signifier of the relationship between the writer and readers of the ethnographic text and the subjects of the research. The details that the ethnographer gives of the way they got into the field encourage us as readers to accept the account that follows as authentically grounded in real experience. Along with travel comes the notion of translation (Turner, 1980). It is not sufficient merely to travel, but necessary also to come back, and to bring back an account. That account gains much of its authoritative effect with the contrast that it constructs between author and reader: the ethnographer has been where the reader cannot or did not go. It is instructive to note that the critique of Margaret Mead's *Coming of Age in Samoa* (1943) was based on another ethnographer having been there too, and having experienced a different cultural reality to the one Mead described (Freeman, 1996). The authority of the critique depends on Freeman's travel. A critic who had not been there might have found Mead's account implausible, but probably could not mount such a detailed and persuasive refutation.

The ethnography of the Internet does not necessarily involve physical travel. Visiting the Internet focuses on experiential rather than physical displacement. As Burnett suggests, 'you travel by looking, by reading, by imaging and imagining' (1996: 68). It is possible for an ethnographer sitting at a desk in an office (their own office, what's more) to explore the social spaces of the Internet. Far from getting the seats of their pants dirty, Internet ethnographers keep their seats firmly on the university's upholstery. The lack of physical travel does not mean, however, that the relationship between ethnographer and readers is collapsed. Baym (1995c) has her own version of an arrival story, as does Correll (1995). Both focus not on the ways in which they physically reached a field site, but on the ways in which they negotiated access, observed interactions and communicated with participants. These descriptions set up a relationship in which the ethnographer has an extensive and sustained experience of the field site that the reader is unlikely to share (besides an analytic distance which mere participants are unable to share). Methodological preambles are far from innocent in the construction of ethnographic authority. The ethnography described in this book is no different. Chapter 4 is there not just to tell you what I did, but to convince you that I did something that authorizes me to speak. Devices such as the technical glossary at the end of this book display the ethnographer's competence with the local language, just as do the glossaries included with ethnographies conducted in distant places and other languages. Whether physical travel is involved or not, the relationship between ethnographer, reader and research subjects is still inscribed in the ethnographic text. The ethnographer is still uniquely placed to give an account of the field site, based on their experience of it and their interaction with it.

The contrast between ethnographer and reader that forms a large part of the authority claim of the ethnographic text depends not just on travel, but also on experience. Again, we have a contrast with the bad old days when ethnographers remained on the verandah (conveniently close to informants but not too close) and failed to engage fully in the field. As Van Maanen says of the genre of realist tales, 'the convention is to allow the field-worker's unexplicated experience in the culture to stand as the basis for textual authority' (1988: 47). In some renditions, this experience of the culture informs the written ethnography by allowing the ethnographer to sense the culture, in ways that extend beyond sight:

> The experience of fieldwork does not produce a mysterious empowerment, but without it, the ethnographer would not encounter the context – the smells, sounds, sights, emotional tensions, feel – of the culture she will attempt to evoke in a written text. (Wolf, 1992: 128)

From these observations a sense of ethnographic presence begins to emerge in which 'being there' is unique to the ethnographer. The ethnographer who really went there is set up as the one with the authority to interpret, over and above the reader who might wish to interpret, but does not have access to a claim of having been there. Readers are thus always dependent on the second-hand account of the ethnographer. The ethnographic authority is not a transferable one: it resides always and only with the ethnographer who was there. The authority of the ethnographer is also not transferable, within this model, to the subjects of the study whom we might naively assume were also there. The research subject lacks the analytic vision of the ethnographer, and thus cannot coexist in the analytic space of the ethnography. Ethnography acts to construct an analytic space in which only the ethnographer is really there. Ethnographers exist alone in an analytic space which preserves their authority claim. According to Turner, "'the field" can be conceived of as a space – better an attitude – which far from being neutral or inert, is itself the product of "disciplinary technologies"' (1989: 13). Attempts may be made to cede this space, as in the exercise in coauthorship described by McBeth (1993), but it is the ethnographer's right to grant or withhold access.

Rosaldo (1989) evokes another sense in which experience is vital to the ethnographer. He describes his inability to comprehend the headhunter's conflation of grief with rage, until he himself suffers intense grief and finds himself angry. This foregrounds the necessity of lived experience and participation for full understanding. The ethnographer is not simply a voyeur or a disengaged observer, but is also to some extent a participant, sharing some of the concerns, emotions and commitments of the research subjects. This extended form of experience depends also on interaction, on a constant questioning of what it is to have an ethnographic understanding of a phenomenon. The authority of interaction, of juxtaposing ethnographic interpretations with those of the native, and opening them up to being altered, is another aspect of the authority that ethnography gains from the face-to-face.

The definition of ethnography as participation given by Hammersley and Atkinson (1995: 2) highlights the interactive aspect of ethnographic research. The researcher does not just observe at close quarters, but interacts with the researched to ask questions and gain the insights into life that come from doing as well as seeing. As Pratt points out, ethnography distinguishes itself from other kinds of travel, and from the accounts offered by other kinds of travellers:

> In almost any ethnography dull-looking figures called 'mere travellers' or 'casual observers' show up from time to time, only to have their superficial perceptions either corrected or corroborated by the serious scientist. (1986: 27)

At least part of this distinction stems from an assumption that ethnography is an active attempt at analysis, involving more than just soaking up the local atmosphere. As Wolf says:

> We do research. It is more than something that simply happens to us as a result of being in an exotic place. (1992: 127)

This interaction also involves the ethnographer in leaving herself open to being taken by surprise by what occurs in the fieldwork setting. By being there, participating and experiencing, the ethnographer opens herself up to learning:

> Fieldwork of the ethnographic kind is authentic to the degree that it approximates the stranger stepping into a culturally alien community to become, for a

time and in an unpredictable way, an active part of the face-to-face relationships in that community. (Van Maanen, 1988: 9)

Again we are back to face-to-face interaction as an intrinsic part of ethnography. The importance of the face-to-face in Van Maanen's account is that being physically present forces the ethnographer to be a participant in events and interactions. An ethnographer who managed to be an invisible observer (a cultural lurker?) would leave the setting undisturbed, but would also leave their interpretations of it undisturbed by trial in practice. The suggestion is that the ethnographer, by opening herself up to the unpredictability of the field, allows at least part of the agenda to be set by the setting. This claim to act as a neutral voice for the field has been used to enhance the ethnographer's authority. As Pratt points out, this does create a paradox for the ethnographic account:

> Personal narrative mediates this contradiction between the involvement called for in fieldwork and the self-effacement called for in formal ethnographic description, or at least mitigates some of its anguish, by inserting into the ethnographic text the authority of the personal experience out of which the ethnography is made. It thus recuperates at least a few shreds of what was exorcised in the conversion from the face-to-face field encounter to objectified science. (1986: 33)

Ethnographers in cyberspace can, of course, lurk in a way that face-to-face ethnographers cannot readily achieve. An observer who might be physically visible and marked as different in a face-to-face setting even when silent, can simply merge invisibly with all the other lurkers in an online setting. To do this, however, is to relinquish claims to the kind of ethnographic authority that comes from exposing the emergent analysis to challenge through interaction. Both Baym (1995c) and Correll (1995) make clear that their findings are the result of observation and interaction.

Correll (1995) stresses that besides her online work she also met some of her informants face-to-face, and thus could verify some things that they said online about their offline lives. While this is presented as a way of triangulating findings and adding authenticity to them, it could also be seen as a result of the pursuit of ethnographic holism. In this case, the group did hold periodic meetings, and Correll took advantage of this convention. Many inhabitants of cyberspace, however, have never met face-to-face and have no intention of doing so. To instigate face-to-face meetings in this situation would place the ethnographer in an asymmetric position, using more varied and different means of communication to understand inform-ants than are used by informants themselves. In a conventional ethno-graphy involving travel, the ethnographer is in a symmetrical position to that of informants. Informants too can look around them, ask questions, and try out their interpretations, although of course they are unlikely to analyse the results in the same way or publish them as a book! The ethnographer simply exploits the role of the stranger, new to the culture, who has deliberately to learn what others take for granted. The symmetry here is that of the ethnographer using the same resources and the same means of communication as available to the subjects of the research. This leaves us with a paradox: while pursuing face-to-face meetings with online informants might be intended to enhance authenticity via triangulation (Silverman, 1993; Hammersley and Atkinson, 1995), it might also threaten the experiential authenticity that comes from aiming to understand the world the way it is for informants. Rather than accepting face-to-face communication as inherently better in ethnography, a more sceptical and symmetrical approach suggests that it should be used with caution, and with a sensitivity to the ways in which informants use it.

The question remains then whether interactions in electronic space should be viewed as authentic, since the ethnographer cannot readily confirm details that informants tell them about their offline selves. Posing the problem in this way, however, assumes a particular idea of what a person is (and what authenticity is). Authenticity, in this formulation, means correspondence between the identity performed in interactions with the ethnographer and that performed elsewhere both online and offline. This presupposes a singular notion of an identity, linked to a similarly singular physical body. As Wynn and Katz (1997) point out, critiques of this singular notion of identity are well established and in no way rely upon the new technologies. The person might be better thought of as a convenient shorthand for a more or less coherent set of identity performances with reference to a singular body and biography. We might usefully turn our attention, rather than seeking correspondence and coherence ourselves, to looking at the ways in which new media might alter the conditions of identity performance (Meyrowitz, 1985). Standards of authenticity should not be seen as absolute, but are situationally negotiated and sustained. Authenticity, then, is another manifestation of the 'phenomenon always escapes' rule (Silverman, 1993: 201). A search for truly authentic knowledge about people or phenomena is doomed to be ultimately irresolvable. The point for the ethnographer is not to bring some external criterion for judging whether it is safe to believe what informants say, but rather to come to understand how it is that informants judge authenticity. This also entails accepting that 'the informant' is a partial performance rather than a whole identity.

Rather than treating authenticity as a particular problem posed by cyberspace that the ethnographer has to solve before moving on to the analysis, it would be more fruitful to place authenticity in cyberspace as a topic at the heart of the analysis. Assuming *a priori* that authenticity is a problem for inhabitants of cyberspace is the same kind of ethnographic mistake as assuming that the Azande have a problem in dealing with the contradictions inherent in their beliefs about witchcraft. It should be addressed as an issue for the ethnography as and when it arises during interaction. The issues of authenticity and identity are addressed again in Chapter 6 in the light of an ethnographic exploration of an Internet event.

Despite this transformation of the authenticity issue from a problem for the ethnographer to a topic for the ethnography, it is fair to say that the ethnography will always have to meet a different standard of authenticity to that prevailing in interactions in the field: the ethnography is ultimately produced and evaluated in an academic setting (Stanley, 1990). What faces the ethnographer is a translation task between the authenticity standards of two different discourses.

Text, technology and reflexivity

In the previous section, the Internet was described as a site for interaction, which, although it might not entail face-to-face communication, was still in some sense ethnographically available. This argument is based on the assumption that what goes on within the Internet is social interaction. Another way of looking, however, would see cyberspace as composed of texts, rather than being interactive. There is no definite fixed line between the two concepts. The distinction is useful in so far as it plays out different ideas about what constitutes and characterizes the two phenomena. Interaction tends to be thought of as entailing a copresence of the parties involved, and a rapid exchange of perspectives which leads to a shared achievement of understanding between those involved (although not, of course, a completely transparent understanding). What we call a text could be thought of as a temporally shifted and packaged form of interaction. While spoken interaction is ephemeral (unless transcribed by social scientists) and local, texts are mobile, and so available outside the immediate circumstances in which they are produced. Texts possess the potential for availability outside their site of production, and hence make possible the separation of production and consumption. Newspapers, television programmes, memoranda, correspondence, audio and video tapes, and compact discs all have a taken-for-granted mobility: they are packaged in a form which means they can be transferred from one person to another. Where clarification is needed, the readers of a text cannot readily ask the authors what they meant. The focus in consuming texts is therefore placed far more on the interpretive work done by readers and less on a shared understanding between authors and readers. We tend (now) not to see texts as transparent carriers of the meanings intended by their authors. It could be said, then, that what we see on the Internet is a collection of texts. Using the Internet then becomes a process of reading and writing texts, and the ethnographer's job is to develop an understanding of the meanings which underlie and are enacted through these textual practices.

There is probably little to be gained from itemizing which aspects of the Internet should be seen as interactive sites or texts. Rather, it is important to keep in mind that they can be both. There is no doubt, however, that some parts seem more interactive than others. IRC, MUDs and newsgroups can seem quite interactive, even approaching the informality of spoken conversation. Although not all contributions are visibly acknowledged, enough receive responses for the impression of an ongoing conversation to develop. The early ethnographers of the Internet have had no problems in rendering these settings as appropriate sites for ethnographic interaction. The WWW, as discussed in Chapter 2, seems to pose more of a challenge to those looking for interactive sites. In contrast to newsgroups, the WWW seems to be a collection of largely static texts (although some of these contain interactive settings or discussion lists). The texts of static web pages might be interlinked, and might change over time, but viewed individually they make available no obvious way in which the ethnographer might interact. The ethnographer could visit other web pages and then develop their own web page as a response, but this hardly meets the standards for knowledge exposed to test through interaction and experience described above. This might seem to mean that the WWW is not available for ethnographic enquiry. The ethnographic approach seems to come to a full stop at the point at which the technology no longer promotes interactions in which the ethnographer can play a part. It is worth looking at the ways in which texts have been used by other ethnographers, in order to find some ways forward.

Traditionally, oral interactions have been foremost for ethnographers, and texts have taken a somewhat secondary role as cultural products, worthy of study only as far as they reveal something about the oral settings in which culture resides. Hammersley and Atkinson (1995) interpret this reliance on oral interaction as part of the 'romantic legacy' of ethnography, which tends to treat speech as more authentic than writing. They suggest that texts deserve a more detailed appraisal, and that judgement about the authenticity of written accounts should be suspended. Rather than being seen as more or less accurate portrayals of reality, texts should be seen as ethnographic material which tells us about the understanding which authors have of the reality which they inhabit. Texts are an important part of life in many of the settings which ethnographers now address, and to ignore them would be to produce a highly partial account of cultural practices. Rule books, manuals, biographies, scientific papers, official statistics and codes of practice can all be seen as ethnographic material in the ways in which they present and shape reality and are embedded in practice. Ethnographers should neither dismiss texts as distorted accounts nor accept them as straightforward truths, but should draw on their own 'socialized competence' in reading and writing to interpret them as culturally situated cultural artefacts (1995: 174).

Thompson (1995) also stresses the importance of combining a view of texts (here, media texts) with understandings of the situationality of those texts. What Thompson calls 'mediated quasi-interaction' (1995: 84) is facilitated by the texts of the mass media. The mobility of texts enabled by mediated quasi-interaction, resulting in a separation in space and time of producers and consumers, is one of the key features in analysing the social effects of the mass media. Thompson stresses that while symbolic or semiotic interpretations of the content of texts may be useful, it is important also to address the situated writing and reading practices which make those texts meaningful. Hammersley and Atkinson (1995) and Thompson (1995) therefore converge on a view that the analysis of texts needs to take into account their context. Only then can we make sensible, culturally informed judgements of their significance, and indeed only then can we determine their status as accounts of reality. This does not necessarily entail judging them as true or false accounts, but it does enable a view of the text as an account which has a situated author producing text within a cultural context and a situated audience interpreting text within other cultural contexts. Viewing texts ethnographically, then, entails tying those texts to particular circumstances of production and consumption. The text becomes ethnographically (and socially) meaningful once we have cultural context(s) in which to situate it.

Swales (1998) develops a model he calls textography for his attempt to combine an analysis of texts with an understanding of their relationship to other texts and the working lives of their authors. He explicitly states that this work is a partial one and he is unable to do justice to the 'complex situationalities' of 'personal, curatorial, institutional and disciplinary' influences (1998: 142). The strategic focus on textual production leaves many other aspects unexamined. For this partial approach Swales chooses a spatially defined sample: a university building occupied by three very different departments. The spatial proximity highlights the distinctive disciplinary practices of textual production that are uncovered. Through interviews with the authors of texts and observations of them in their working context, accounts of textual practices which the authors recognize but would not have given themselves are built up. Distinct disciplinary practices are sustained by the textual links between distant sites. These textual links are made manifest in the documents which are found in the offices of those studied and which are used in their work as reference and as models for their own writing. In addition to the working context of the authors, Swales therefore implies a second context, the intertextual context provided by the texts themselves. The discipline to which Swales's authors orient exists for him in and through the texts which constitute it: a feature which is emphasized by his reliance on study within the bounded space of the departmental building. In the same way, we might think of the intertextual context of the Internet as being the space into which the work of web authors is inserted and a context to which authors orient themselves.

In the case of the Internet, tying texts to social contexts of writing is relatively straightforward. Individual web authors can be approached for their interpretations of their practices. Given an accessible field site, an ethnographer could follow the progress of development of a web site and explore the interpretations of those involved as to the capacities of the technology and the identity of the audience being addressed. This analysis could be combined with an analysis of the content of the resulting web site. In this portrayal, the ethnography is a physically located one which renders the Internet as a repository of texts rather than a site for social interaction. A webography could become a strategically oriented and partial form of ethnography, like a textography. To take this kind of detailed approach to the influences and assumptions antecedent to the appearance of a page on the WWW would be a step forwards from analysing the web pages themselves as isolated phenomena, but would still be a relatively conservative approach. We would still be tied to a bounded physical location, and the influences which we were able to take into account would be largely those which occurred in that setting. This approach would not, therefore, be taking on board the spatial implications of mediated interaction. The more complex issue is how to incorporate the availability of texts (or interactions) across physical locations which the Internet enables. This issue is considered in the next section of this chapter, on the making of ethnographic objects.

While saying that contexts like newsgroups are interactive makes them ethnographically available, viewing newsgroup contributions as textual can also provide some valuable insights. A textual focus places emphasis on the ways in which contributions are justified and rendered authoritative, and on the identities which authors construct and perform through their postings. This approach to ethnography suggests a discourse analytic stance, which remains ambivalent about the nature of the discourse which is under analysis. The reality which texts construct can be evaluated on its own terms, without recourse to an external, pretextual reality (Potter and Wetherell, 1987; Potter, 1996). Here, again, the distinction between text and interaction blurs, since the material of discourse analysis encompasses textualized records of interaction as well as solely written texts. Discourse analysis is primarily concerned with the reality which texts construct. It has been criticized for the lack of ways of verifying the interpretations which it produces, although Potter counters this with a claim that at least if the analysis is at fault, the original text is made available for readers to develop their own interpretations:

> Nevertheless there is an important sense in which this approach democratizes academic interaction. For example, the reader does not have to take on trust the sensitivity or acuity of the ethnographer. (1996: 106)

For individual textual fragments this may be appropriate, but for more complex corpora of material the democratic approach may be rather taxing to readers asked to duplicate the analytic effort of the original analyst. We do not always read academic texts in order to discover the author wrong and substitute our own analysis, however much this might sometimes seem to be the case. Availability of data does not imply democracy either, since texts are generally constructed to produce an authoritative position for their authors and discourse analysts are rarely exempt. Rather than replacing ethnography, discourse analytic approaches to Internet texts could usefully coexist with ethnographic approaches to Internet interaction. This combination could help to maintain analytic ambivalence about what the phenomena being studied *really* are. Both approaches, however, share a problem of observability: potential interactants who choose to remain silent, and potential authors who fail to write, are lost to the analysis.

Hammersley and Atkinson (1995) pay considerably more attention to the authors of texts than to the readers. This is no doubt in part due to the problems in making the interpretation of texts ethnographically visible. It is far easier to study the work of producers than consumers: producers embody their concerns in the technologies they produce, and the work of constructing a technology is highly visible and observable. By contrast, users leave no visible marks on technologies, and interpreting the technology is often something they simply get on and do. Ethnographers can, of course, as they routinely do, attempt to make the invisible visible by asking questions or exploring scenarios with willing informants. To make these practices visible the ethnographer has to work harder at producing interpretations from informants, and is opened up to criticisms of having produced a partial or biased account. Another response to this kind of ethnographic invisibility of interpretive and embodied work is to incorporate a reflexive understanding (Cooper et al., 1995). The ethnographer can use an active engagement with the Internet as a reflexive tool to a deeper understanding of the medium. Reflexivity can therefore be a strategic response to the silence of web surfers and newsgroup lurkers. It can also be a way of acquiring and examining the 'socialized competences' which Hammersley and Atkinson (1995: 174) suggest that ethnographers aim for. In learning how to use the Internet and in using it to reach their field site and collect their data, ethnographers of the Internet can use their own data collection practices as data in their own right. As discussed in Chapter 2, an ethnographer of the Internet cannot hope to understand the practices of *all* users, but through their own practices can develop an understanding of what it is to be *a* user.

Ethnographers are traditionally warned about the dangers of 'going native' or losing their sceptical approach to things which their informants take for granted. If the ethnographer too comes to take these things for granted, their ethnographic edge as a cultural commentator will have been lost. These kinds of insecurities, still firmly grounded in a realist notion of ethnography, may help to explain some of the reluctance of ethnographers to engage fully in the work which their informants do, and move further along the spectrum from observer to participant. This may explain why ethnographers often develop only limited competences in the technical work which their informants do, as if incompetence was in some way strategic in maintaining strangeness. Often, admittedly, periods of training and required background knowledge simply pose too great a hurdle for the ethnographer to achieve any kind of competence without thoroughly disrupting (and entertaining) the informants they set out to study. In the case of the Internet, however, the obstacles to competence are not so great:

the sheer mass of web pages and newsgroup contributions out there testify that it cannot be so hard, surely, if all these people can do it. The process of becoming competent in use of the Internet is a way for the ethnographer to find out just how hard it is, and in what specific ways it is made either hard or easy. Rather than forming a barrier to ethnographic strangeness to be guarded against, competence in using the Internet acquires a multiple significance: as a ground for reflexive exploration of what it is to use the Internet; as a means to deeper engagement and conversations with other users of the Internet; as a way to developing an enriched reading of the practices which lead to the production and consumption of Internet artefacts. With due (sceptical) caution, it appears that there are good grounds for an ethnographer of the Internet to become competent in its use. The processes through which field sites are found and materials collected become ethnographic materials in themselves.

The reflexivity discussed above is a strategic use of reflexivity as a method for interrogating the field. This kind of reflexivity could be incorporated relatively comfortably into a realist account, as a way of giving more authentic and deeper portrayals of what it is to be a cultural member. Reflexivity, however, is a much-contested term, which has precise but quite different meanings in different disciplinary settings (Woolgar, 1991b). In some incarnations reflexivity has a less comfortable relationship with realism. When juxtaposed with ideas about the social construction of knowledge, the claims of ethnography to provide an objective, factual portrayal of culture become suspect. Here reflexivity is applied not just to the work of individual ethnographers, but to the methodology as a whole. Folding back ideas about the constructed nature of knowledge on to ethnography itself poses an interesting paradox: ethnographic knowledge too might be a cultural construct. This paradox becomes particularly apparent for ethnographers of knowledge production, who might claim to be producing objective descriptions of the ways in which what scientists think of as objective fact turns out to be the upshot of social processes. If knowledge is seen to be a social construct, then ethnography has very weak claims to be held exempt, and the case for validating ethnographies on the basis of their truthful representation of underlying reality becomes suspect. Three distinct strategies for dealing with this paradox have become notable.

One approach is to rehabilitate member understandings of culture alongside the ethnographer's account, thus addressing and to some extent redressing the previous imbalance which claimed a privilege for ethnography. This can imply the ethnographer's sensitivity to the ways in which the subjects of the research understand their own culture:

By including and focusing upon the ways people perceive and define the cultural space within which they exist and their own place in it, these studies therefore view distinctions between external and internal points of view as processes of life that are contingent upon the particular contexts in which they are made. (Hastrup and Olwig, 1997: 11)

This approach to reflexivity denies the privileging of the ethnographic account and blurs the boundaries between ethnographic and member understandings. The two are different, but neither is necessarily privileged. The second distinct approach is to place the focus on the ethnographer, reflecting on the particular perspective, history and standpoint which led this ethnographer to be giving their particular account of this setting. This can imply a focus on the ways in which the presuppositions and cultural positioning of the ethnographer shape the study. In this sense, reflexivity is a sensitizing device to counteract the tendency to present ethnographic reports as portrayals of an objective reality. Some view this kind of reflexivity as indulgence, a 'self-reflexive cul-de-sac' (Moores, 1993: 4) in which the ethnographer ends up telling readers more about herself than about the culture purportedly being described. It can also be a strategic device when used sensitively to explore differences of interpretation and understanding between ethnographers and subjects. Moores recognizes the strategic significance of Walkerdine's (1986; 1990) references to her own biography in shaping her reaction and those of the family she observed to a film both parties watched together. Ethnography can be a process of self-discovery and reflexivity can be a strategic element in developing insight.

A final approach attempts to incorporate a destabilization of ethnographic authority within the text itself. In contrast to 'politically correct' acceptances of the significance of member reflexivity and ethnographer standpoint, some ethnographers have taken a more 'epistemologically correct' approach to their ethnography. In the context of claims about the socially constructed nature of knowledge, which owe large parts of their force to ethnographies in scientific laboratories (Potter, 1996), some ethnographers have embraced the challenge this poses for their own knowledge-making practices. Epistemological correctness entails making clear the constructed nature of accounts, and has given rise to a range of approaches to presentation of ethnographic accounts which aim to make clear to readers their constructed and contingent nature (Woolgar, 1991b). Denzin (1997) reports on a variety of new ways of writing ethnography, based on recognition that writing is a constructive act rather than a straightforward reflection of reality.

The three approaches described above are not mutually exclusive, and are associated with differing political commitments and disciplinary histories. No doubt these approaches do not exhaust the possibilities for creative transformation of the ethnographic project in the light of the abandonment of a commitment to realism. Recently ethnographers have begun to explore the possibilities of hypertext and multimedia for expanding access to ethnographic materials and providing opportunities for readers to form their own narratives based on the material (Dicks and Mason, 1998; Slack, 1998). The ethnography which is presented in this book is told in a largely conventional style. I simply say the things which my experiences lead me to want to say, without claiming that these represent a single true reality, but also without strictly censoring those parts which might come across in a realist way. In part, this is because I am sceptical that there is an adequately configured readership for the new representational forms in ethnography (Traweek, 1992), and it is not clear that those who do exist overlap with the readership intended for this book. Marcus and Cushman (1982) identify six readerships of ethnography: the area specialist, the general anthropologist, social scientists other than anthropologists, students, action-oriented readers and popular readership. My readership could be any one of these, if we replace the anthropological area specialist with the new category of the cyberspace specialist. Modes of representation can be strategic choices which depend on the assumed readership (not forgetting that the ethnographic text is constructed by its readers). In this I adopt Hammersley's perspective, that:

> How we describe an object depends not just on decisions about what we believe to be true but also on judgements about relevance. The latter rely, in turn, on the purposes which the description is to serve. (1990: 609)

Ways of writing and strategies of familiarization and making strange depend on assumptions about what the audience will find familiar or strange already, and hence are inherently selective (Rosaldo, 1989). This suggests an approach which explicitly embraces the necessary selectivity and constructedness of accounts and which makes clear that this is the account I chose to give in the context of the questions which seem to me to be important. The ethnography which is presented in the next three chapters is neither a truth nor a fiction, but an account of an ethnographically constructed field of social interactions. Just because an ethnography is not a straightforward representation of the real does not mean that it cannot be sincere, unfashionable though sincerity is in playful postmodern times. What seems to be important is that we examine the circumstances which lead us to be telling this story about this object at this time and in this way. As Woolgar says:

> In short, we need continually to interrogate and find strange the process of representation as we engage in it. This kind of reflexivity is the ethnographer of the text. (1991b: 28)

One way in which I have addressed this issue is to compare my own interpretive and representational practices with those of my informants. Another part of examining how we come to be telling a particular ethnographic story is looking at the ways in which the object of the ethnography is constituted. While ethnographers in the past or in other settings may have been able to look at bounded physical settings, when studying the Internet the concept of the field site is no longer so straightforward. In the next section I consider the opportunities which this disruption offers.

The making of ethnographic objects

The traditional emphasis in ethnography on field sites which map on to physically bounded places has some important implications for the constitution of ethnographic objects. The objects produced and studied through ethnography, its communities and societies, have been largely understood in spatial terms (Clifford, 1992). While ethnographers have often been sensitive to the influences of external contacts and influences, fieldwork places an emphasis on culture as something which is local. A 'manageable unit', carved out on grounds of self-evident boundaries, often came to stand in for what culture was (1992: 98). A similar observation could be made about the more substantively based ethnographic projects with which sociology has often been concerned. Silverman (1993) uses Gubrium and Holstein's (1987) work to show that while we might think of the household as the place to go in order to study the family, there are multiple other sites in which the 'family' is performed, such as television programmes, courtrooms and policy forums. The sites which we choose to study are often based on common sense understandings of what the phenomenon being explored is, intrinsically linked with an idea about where that activity goes on, whether the activity be the technical work of software engineering or the experimental work of science (Low and Woolgar, 1993; Knorr-Cetina, 1992).

The tendency to treat the field site as a place which one goes to and dwells within reinforces an idea of culture as something which exists in and is bounded by physical space. This tendency is exacerbated by the historical roots of anthropology in the study of relatively isolated communities, and by the continuing practice of concentrating on a particular region. The very idea of the field as a place which the ethnographer goes to, and comes back from, implies that the ethnographer is the only link between the two and bolsters the impression of separate cultural sites, 'ours' and 'theirs' (Ferguson, 1997). In this way, the world as seen through ethnographic eyes becomes a 'mosaic of unique and distinct cultures' (Hastrup and Olwig, 1997: 12). In sociological approaches the ethnographic object may be carved out through a substantive focus: the school, the street corner, the doctor's surgery, the laboratory. This object, however, is still a bounded physical location, and the aim becomes to describe the life which occurs within that space. The strategic applications of ethnography within sociology carve out particular facets of life for substantive investigation and tend to treat a physical or institutional boundary as the limit for their ethnographic interest (Hammersley, 1990).

In the face of increasing media saturation in all parts of the world and the prevalence of migration, a concern has been growing within anthropology that the implied notion of bounded cultures requires re-examination (Clifford, 1992). More and more, cultures appear to be interlinked, aware of one another, and connected through physical mobility of people and things (Appadurai, 1996; Gupta and Ferguson, 1992; Marcus, 1995). Whole areas of anthropology, cultural studies, sociology and geography have become 'saturated with the vocabulary of mobility' (Thrift, 1996a: 297). This new emphasis provides opportunities for ethnographers to study the reflexive awareness which comes from the inter-visibility of different cultural locations. The balance of authority in ethnographic accounts subtly shifts, as it becomes harder to render the ethnographer/traveller as uniquely privileged in their ability to see across cultures:

> In the present postcolonial world, the notion of an authentic culture as an autonomous internally coherent universe no longer seems tenable, except perhaps as a 'useful fiction' or a revealing distortion. In retrospect, it appears that only a concerted disciplinary effort could maintain the tenuous fiction of a self-contained cultural whole. Rapidly increasing global interdependence has made it more and more clear that neither 'we' nor 'they' are as neatly bounded and homogeneous as once seemed to be the case. (Rosaldo, 1989: 217)

Theoretical developments have not necessarily been mirrored by changes in methodological orientation (Hastrup and Olwig, 1997). Recently, however, there has been a considerable effort to struggle with the implications of connectivity and interrelations for the conduct of ethnography. The concern with translocal phenomena in ethnography has been particularly apparent in science and technology studies (Franklin, 1995) and media and cultural studies (Radway, 1988). Two distinct but related responses to the issue of cultural interconnectedness have arisen. One way to deal with this is to aim for a richer, deeper and more holistic notion of the articulation of diverse cultural fragments within particular locations (Radway, 1988; Abu-Lughod, 1997; Hirsch, 1998). Situating their argument within media reception and consumption studies, these authors question the particular notions of audiences which emerge from studies based on the reception of a specific media text or technology. They argue that these studies fail to consider the multiple discourses, identities and locations in which the 'audience' or 'consumers' are implicated. Aiming for holism does bring some problems, and is somewhat at odds with Ang's (1996) suggestion that the way forwards for reception studies is to embrace partiality (in its several senses). The idea of a holistic study of a given context is a disciplinary fiction which fails to acknowledge the partiality and selectivity of any ethnographic description (Hammersley, 1990; Stanley, 1990). It also fails to take on board the full implications of interconnectedness: how can there be a holistic study of a site if its boundaries are unstable and only occasionally enacted? Where does the local stop and the global begin?

As a strategy, and leaving aside aspirations to holistic description, a multi-dimensional approach does have an appeal. This strategy would no doubt be a useful one for a study of the Internet. A useful complement to online studies which treat the Internet as a separate cultural sphere would be to conduct sustained contextual studies of the ways in which the Internet is articulated into and transforms offline relationships. This would enable a much richer sense of the uses of the Internet and the ways in which local relationships shape its use as a technology and as a cultural context. We could consider the ways in which domestic or working settings were transformed by the interpolation of the new context provided by the Internet, and the ways in which that context was transformed by local concerns. We could, to some extent, study the interplay between the different notions of context which local settings and Internet provide. Moving the study of the Internet to offline settings rather than online ones would be a strategic choice with some obvious benefits. It is difficult to see, however, how this approach would give more than a fleeting impression of the spatiality of the Internet itself and the ways in which the relations within it are organized by the interaction with and construction of separated sites. Concentration on a single geographic location could end up focusing on Internet as technology at the expense of Internet as cultural context. For my purposes, I am drawn away from holism and towards connectivity as an organizing principle. This focus is an attempt to remain agnostic about the most suitable site for exploring the Internet.

Efforts to struggle with ethnography's reliance on bounded locations by focusing on connectivity rather than holism have been made notably in the collection edited by Olwig and Hastrup (1997) and in Marcus (1995). Hastrup and Olwig suggest that a new sensitivity to the ways in which place is performed and practised is required. This might involve viewing the field, rather than a site, as being a 'field of relations' (1997: 8). Ethnographers might still start from a particular place, but would be encouraged to follow connections which were made meaningful from that setting. The ethnographic sensitivity would focus on the ways in which particular places were made meaningful and visible. Ethnography in this strategy becomes as much a process of following connections as it is a period of inhabitance. In similar vein, Marcus suggests that ethnography could (should?) be adapted to 'examine the circulation of cultural meanings, objects and identities in diffuse time–space' (1995: 96). He suggests a range of strategies for ethnographers to construct fields in the absence of bounded sites, including the following of people, things, metaphors, narratives, biographies and conflicts. The heterogeneity of this collection of organizing concepts suggests that this will not be easy, and that ethnographers who follow Marcus's advice will need to embrace the insecurity of never quite knowing when one is in the field. Among the problems which Marcus acknowledges that multi-sited ethnography will bring is an anxiety about diluting the fieldwork engagement that ethnography depends upon. The engagement from sustained immersion in a particular place is replaced, in part, by the sensitivity of the ethnographer to mobility across a heterogeneous landscape and the differential engagements which this enables and requires. This sensitivity is exemplified in the work of Martin (1994) on the concept of the immune system, and Heath (1998) in her ethnographic tracing of the transformations of Marfan syndrome between multiple locations and articulations. Both studies are explicitly multi-sited, in a straightforward 'more than one place' sense, but are also thoroughly concerned with connection and transformation. Both are able to show how knowledges and places have complex and often unpredictable relationships, and how knowledges are transformed in the processes of recombination and rearticulation which mobility entails.

Sites have a tendency to focus our attention on the ways in which things are kept together as part of a cultural unit. We are focused on the local, the contextual, the interrelated and the coherent. The ethnographic description itself has a tendency to make the field seem homogeneous (Friedman, 1997). By focusing on sites, locales and places, we may be missing out on other ways of understanding culture, based on connection, difference, heterogeneity and incoherence. We miss out on the opportunity to consider the role of space in structuring social relations (Thrift, 1996a). Castells (1996a; 1996b; 1997) introduces the idea that a new form of space is increasingly important in structuring social relations. This space is the space of flows, which, in contrast to the space of place, is organized around connection rather than location. Flows of people, information, money, circulate between nodes which form a network of associations increasingly independent of specific local contexts. The concept of the space of flows will be examined in greater depth in Chapter 5. Here, it serves as a reminder that the organization of social relations is not necessarily linked to local context in a straightforward way. By analogy, the field site of ethnography could become a field flow, which is organized around tracing connections rather than about location in a singular bounded site.

The emergence of multi-sited ethnography, conceived of as an experiential, interactive and engaged exploration of connectivity, is encouraging news for ethnography of the Internet. It offers up possibilities for designing a study which is based on the connections within and around the Internet and enabled by it but not reliant on any one understanding of it. Chapter 2 discussed the reliance of accounts of Internet culture on bounded social settings such as newsgroups and MUDs. In focusing thus narrowly on boundaries which seemed self-evident, it was suggested that these ethnographies missed out on some of the potential offered by ethnography as a way of investigating the making of bounded social space and the importance of interaction between differently connected spaces. Online ethnographies despatialize notions of community, and focus on cultural process rather than physical place. This can, however, be at the expense of minimizing connections with offline life. Despatializing notions of community, in itself, does not guarantee that justice will be done to the complexity of connections which the new technology makes possible. To do this, we need to turn from (static, located) boundaries to networks and connections (Strathern, 1996). Following Strathern's advice, the ethnographer could usefully follow connections and also pay attention to the ways in which connections available in principle are cut in practice to limit the infinite extension of networks. Whether the online is separate from the offline, and in what ways, becomes an intrinsic part of the ethnography rather than a prior assumption. Connective ethnography turns the attention from 'being there' to 'getting there' (Clifford, 1992). We can ask what people are doing in their web pages and newsgroup postings: what does their traversal of space mean to them, and what does it achieve? Abandoning the offline/online boundary as a principled barrier to the analysis allows for it to be traversed (or created and sustained) through the ways in which connections are assembled.

To take a connective approach is not to suggest that no bounded locations exist on the Internet, or that the 'being there' is never important on the Internet. As Clifford (1992) and Featherstone (1995) suggest, diverting attention to travel does not mean assuming that everyone is a traveller and nobody dwells any more. This kind of connective ethnography remains agnostic about the 'real' existence of places and categories. Rather than cataloguing the characteristics of Internet communication, the virtual ethnographer asks, not what is the Internet, but when, where and how is the Internet (Moerman, 1974)? A connective ethnography could be a useful adjunct to space-based approaches. The World Wide Web, as a mixture of varyingly interlinked cultural sites and cultural connections, could form a model for a new way of orienting an ethnography to the field. This is not to say that web surfing is going to be used to stand in for ethnographic engagement. Following hypertextual links may be part of the strategy, but connectivity is also performed in the borrowing of material and images from other sites and other media, by the authorship and readership of sites, by the portrayals of the Internet in other media, and in myriad other ways. Connection could as well be the juxtaposition of elements in a narrative, the array of pages thrown up by a search engine, or a set of hyperlinks on a web page as an instance of communication between two people. The goal of the ethnography becomes to explore what those links are, how they are performed and what transformations occur *en route* in a snowballing approach (Bijker, 1995) that is sensitive to heterogeneity. Each performance of a connection becomes an invitation to the ethnographer to move on. This suggests an active engagement through exploration and interaction rather than a disengaged textual analysis.

Accepting a multi-sited or connective notion of ethnography opens up many different ways of designing and conducting an ethnographic project. Choices and movements are made on the basis of strategic and often arbitrary decisions, which dictate the shape and boundaries of the resulting ethnographic object. We end up with a multitude of different sites and sources for studying the Internet, even if we rely only on those most obviously and intuitively relevant. A first attempt at cataloguing sites in which the Internet is enacted and interpreted produces the following non-exhaustive list:

- web pages
- accounts of making web pages
- instructions on how to make web pages

- programs to help in making web pages
- reviews of web pages
- media reports on Internet events
- magazines and newspaper supplements devoted to the Internet
- fictionalized accounts of Internet-like technologies
- computer equipment retailers
- software developers
- stock markets
- newsgroups
- MUDs
- IRC
- video conferences
- accounts of the purpose of newsgroups
- Internet service providers' advertising and introductory materials
- Internet gateways and search engines
- homes and workplaces where the Internet is used, and the practices we find there
- training courses
- conversations between friends, families and work colleagues
- academic Internet studies like this one.

A holistic understanding of the Internet seems a futile undertaking in the face of this list. However hard the ethnographer works, she or he will only ever partially experience the Internet (Thornton, 1988). The challenge addressed in Chapter 4 is to incorporate as many of these sites and sources as practicable while retaining a coherent but explicitly partial ethnographic project. What follows is the story of one journey through which an Internet was made, by following connections motivated by the foreshadowed problems in Chapter 1.

The principles of virtual ethnography

This chapter and the preceding one have reviewed literature on ethnographic methodology to develop an approach to the Internet which embraces the complexity offered by this form of mediated interaction. In the next three chapters I attempt to flesh out the conclusions reached in this literature review by discussing a project designed to put this approach into action. First, however, it is worth reiterating the principles for virtual ethnography which form the foundations for the experiment in ethnography described here.

1 The sustained presence of an ethnographer in the field setting, combined with intensive engagement with the everyday life of the inhabitants of the field site, make for the special kind of knowledge we call

ethnographic. The ethnographer is able to use this sustained interaction to 'reduce the puzzlement' (Geertz, 1993: 16) which other people's ways of life can evoke. At the same time, ethnography can be a device for inducing that same puzzlement by 'displacing the dulling sense of familiarity with which the mysteriousness of our own ability to relate perceptively to one another is concealed from us' (1993: 14). Virtual ethnography is used as a device to render the use of the Internet as problematic: rather than being inherently sensible, the Internet acquires its sensibility in use. The status of the Internet as a way of communicating, as an object within people's lives and as a site for community-like formations is achieved and sustained in the ways in which it is used, interpreted and reinterpreted.

2 Interactive media provide a challenge and an opportunity for ethnography, by bringing into question the notion of a site of interaction. Cyberspace is not to be thought of as a space detached from any connections to 'real life' and face-to-face interaction. It has rich and complex connections with the contexts in which it is used. It also depends on technologies which are used and understood differently in different contexts, and which have to be acquired, learnt, interpreted and incorporated into context. These technologies show a high degree of interpretive flexibility. Interactive media such as the Internet can be understood as both culture and cultural artefact. To concentrate on either aspect to the exclusion of the other leads to an impoverished view.

3 The growth of mediated interaction renders it unnecessary for ethnography to be thought of as located in particular places, or even as multi-sited. The investigation of the making and remaking of space through mediated interactions is a major opportunity for the ethnographic approach. We can usefully think of the ethnography of mediated interaction as mobile rather than multi-sited.

4 As a consequence, the concept of the field site is brought into question. If culture and community are not self-evidently located in place, then neither is ethnography. The object of ethnographic enquiry can usefully be reshaped by concentrating on flow and connectivity rather than location and boundary as the organizing principle.

5 Boundaries are not assumed *a priori* but explored through the course of the ethnography. The challenge of virtual ethnography is to explore the making of boundaries and the making of connections, especially between the 'virtual' and the 'real'. Along with this goes the problem of knowing when to stop. If the concept of ethnography (and/or culture) as having natural boundaries is abandoned for analytic purposes, we can also abandon the idea of a whole ethnography of a given object. Stopping the ethnography becomes a pragmatic decision. The ethnographic object itself can be reformulated with each decision to either follow yet another connection or retrace steps to a previous point. Practically it is limited by the embodied ethnographer's constraints in time, space and ingenuity.

6 Along with spatial dislocation comes temporal dislocation. Engagement with mediated contexts is interspersed with interactions in other
   spheres and with other media. Virtual ethnography is interstitial, in
   that it fits into the other activities of both ethnographer and subjects.
   Immersion in the setting is only intermittently achieved.

7 Virtual ethnography is necessarily partial. A holistic description of any
   informant, location or culture is impossible to achieve. The notion of
   pre-existing, isolable and describable informants, locales and cultures
   is set aside. Our accounts can be based on ideas of strategic relevance
   rather than faithful representations of objective realities.

8 Virtual ethnography involves intensive engagement with mediated
   interaction. This kind of engagement adds a new dimension to the
   exploration of the use of the medium in context. The ethnographer's
   engagement with the medium is a valuable source of insight. Virtual
   ethnography can usefully draw on ethnographer as informant and
   embrace the reflexive dimension. The shaping of interactions with
   informants by the technology is part of the ethnography, as are the
   ethnographer's interactions with the technology.

9 New technologies of interaction make it possible both for informants
   to be absent and to render them present within the ethnography. In the
   same way, the ethnographer is both absent from and present with
   informants. The technology enables these relationships to be fleeting or
   sustained and to be carried out across temporal and spatial divides. All
   forms of interaction are ethnographically valid, not just the face-to-
   face. The shaping of the ethnographic object as it is made possible by
   the available technologies *is* the ethnography. This is ethnography *in*,
   of and *through* the virtual.

10 Virtual ethnography is not only virtual in the sense of being disembodied. Virtuality also carries a connotation of 'not quite', adequate
   for practical purposes even if not strictly the real thing (although this
   definition of virtuality is often suppressed in favour of its trendier
   alternative). Virtual ethnography is adequate for the practical purpose
   of exploring the relations of mediated interaction, even if not quite the
   real thing in methodologically purist terms. It is an adaptive ethnography which sets out to suit itself to the conditions in which it finds
   itself.

Principles 1 to 9 should follow fairly self-evidently from the discussions of
this chapter and the previous one, and follow on from some of the main
currents in ethnographic thinking discussed in those chapters. Principle 10,
however, probably needs further explanation. Ethnography always has
been adaptive to the conditions in which it finds itself. This may help to
explain the traditional reluctance of ethnographers to give advice to those
about to start fieldwork. There are no sets of rules to follow in order to
conduct the perfect ethnography, and defining the fundamental compo-
nents of the ethnographic approach is unhelpful. The focus of ethnography

on dwelling within a culture demands adaptation and the possibility of overturning prior assumptions. In virtual ethnography the adaptation of methodology to circumstance raises the issues which principles 1 to 9 address.

There seems to be a contradiction here. If we adhere to principle 10 then it would seem that we undermine the other nine principles, since to be adaptive and adequate to the purpose would seem to make adherence to principles in itself problematic. There is a temporal shift here. Most readers of ethnography will recognize the written product of an ethnography as being an after-the-event construction, the product of an overlapping but largely linear process of planning, data collection, analysis and writing. The written product rarely reflects this sequence of events, and methodological considerations which arose during the data collection phase may be presented as preceding and even justifying the decisions which gave rise to them. This text is no different in the liberties it takes with the temporal sequence. The methodological principles detailed here arose through the conduct of the ethnography itself, as it became clear what an adaptive ethnography might look like in the context of the Internet. In this sense principle 10, although it is presented last, is the fundamental principle which underlies the rest and makes them possible. Adapting and inter-rogating ethnography keeps it alive, contextual and relevant. After all, if we are happy enough that technologies are appropriated and interpreted differently in different contexts, why should we not be happy for ethno-graphy to be similarly sensitive to its contexts of use? It is no more a sacred and unchanging text than the technologies which it is used to study. In the following chapter I describe the ethnographic project which forms the basis for this book. In describing the case, I will also attempt to retrieve some of the decisions which gave rise to the methodological principles listed above.

4   The Making of a Virtual Ethnography

The Louise Woodward case

In line with the principles of virtual ethnography established in Chapter 3, the object of this virtual ethnography is a topic and not a location. The topic concerns a media event which gained high levels of attention in both the US and the UK and some coverage in other parts of the world, and was accompanied by large amounts of activity on the Internet. The Internet was used in some innovative ways in the case and it received prominent media coverage. These phenomena were both reflective of and constitutive of the status of the Internet as culture and cultural object at the time, making this a rich setting in which to explore what the Internet has come to mean. The case which I chose to explore was that of Louise Woodward, a teenage British nanny tried in Boston for the murder of the child who had been in her care. It is not the aim of this book to give a definitive account of the Louise Woodward case. The book is not intended to be about Louise, and I am not setting out to discuss the case, the evidence or the outcomes in any depth. Rather, the aim is to use the Internet events surrounding the case as a site for exploring some of the meanings of the Internet at the time. First, however, I need to map the basic facts of the case. The progress of the case provides the context within which the various media and Internet representations came about (and which they helped to create).

Matthew Eappen, the 8-month-old child of Deborah and Sunil Eappen, died on 9 February 1997. Matthew had suffered a brain haemorrhage and 'shaken baby syndrome' was diagnosed, suggesting that someone had treated him roughly enough to cause damage inside his skull. The Eappens had been employing 18-year-old Louise Woodward as an au pair and she had been responsible for minding their two children for long periods. The Eappens were American and were living in the Boston area. Louise was British and came from a small town called Elton in Cheshire. Louise was interviewed by police and arrested shortly after Matthew's admission to hospital, and when he died was charged with his murder.

The trial opened on 7 October 1997, amid intense media interest in both the US and the UK. Courtroom proceedings were televised on cable and satellite channels and there was heavy coverage on television news bulletins and in newspapers throughout the trial. What had seemed a watertight case for the prosecution was brought into question by the defence and by the production of new medical interpretations of Matthew's injuries. Deborah Eappen appeared on television arguing that Louise was guilty and that she should receive a life sentence. After deliberation, on 30 October 1997 the jury returned a murder verdict. There then followed an unusual twist: at the defence's request the judge prepared to consider whether to accept the jury's verdict or to overturn it and impose his own ruling, an option available to him under Boston law. The judge announced that it was his intention to release his ruling on the Internet, rather than using the traditional method of handing out paper copies from the courthouse. This decision was discussed at length on television and radio, in newspapers, and on the Internet itself. Initially one site, www.lawyersweekly.com, was nominated to release the ruling, then other mirror sites were set up when it became clear that the site would not be able to support the high levels of traffic that ensued. News media organizations competed to be granted the right to carry the ruling, anxious not to be excluded or left to discover the ruling along with the rest of the Internet world. Security systems were debated for ensuring that the news organizations would be able to verify that the electronic version of the ruling they received was indeed from the judge and was not a hoax. After several false alarms, the judge released his ruling on 10 November 1997. In the event, problems with the Internet release of the ruling meant that most people learnt of the ruling first through television or radio. The judge, Hiller Zobel, overturned the original murder verdict and substituted one of involuntary manslaughter. He passed a sentence of 279 days in state prison: the length of time which Louise had already served. At the end of the hearing Louise was free to leave jail, although required to remain in Massachusetts pending appeal. The appeal upheld the sentence of time being served and Louise returned home on 18 June 1998, first to Elton in Cheshire and later to begin a law degree at a British university.

Internet as culture

During the trial and the publicity build-up which surrounded it, the number of WWW sites related to the case grew. When the judge announced his intention to release his ruling on to a WWW site, interest in the WWW as a site for Louise-related information and opinion increased. Searches through www.infoseek.com for the phrase 'Louise Woodward' in web pages showed steadily increasing totals, from 165 on 5 November 1997 to 707 on 11 November 1997. Various different kinds of site could be distinguished, in addition to the sites of the news organizations which reproduced their offerings in other media. Support sites were particularly prominent. Apparently produced by individuals, these sites expressed concern for Louise, pointed out flaws in the prosecution case, and solicited support in lobbying for Louise both online and offline. As time went on, more and more of these support sites included cross-links to other support sites, particularly the Official Louise Woodward Campaign for Justice site. Visitors would be advised that they must visit the official site as well. In addition to the support sites, others emerged which presented themselves as more impartial and informative. These offered access to evidence and testimonies, enhanced by sound and video clips of courtroom proceedings. Other sites presented themselves as testing the mood of public opinion and offered visitors the opportunity to participate in an online poll on Louise's guilt or innocence. Some sites offered discussion forums or guest books for visitors to have their own say. Finally, it was apparent that some opportunists had realized that Louise Woodward was news and that having her name prominently displayed on your web page, whatever its main content or purpose, was a good way to ensure that your site came high up on search engine lists.

Newsgroups and other kinds of discussion list also showed a high level of interest in the case. Some discussion lists were set up with the prime purpose of providing a place for talking about the case. These discussions acquired regular contributors who entered into lengthy and heated debates about the minutiae of the evidence, the legal and cultural background, and the demeanour of Louise and the Eappens. The discussions in some newsgroups apparently quite unrelated to the case included passing comments which sometimes extended into long threads on aspects of the case. Within both web sites and newsgroups, therefore, the case of Louise Woodward provides a rich site for exploring the emerging culture of the Internet, including the temporal and spatial relationships, the interplay of authority and identity in the exchange of information and opinion, and the appropriation of the technologies of Internet communication for a multitude of purposes. It would be too narrow, however, to take these emerging Internet phenomena as arising completely anew within the Internet itself. It is a premise of this book that it is also worth exploring the ways in which use of the Internet is shaped by perceptions of it as a communications medium and as a technology with specific meanings for those who use it. For this it is useful to turn to the meaning of the Internet as a cultural artefact.

Internet as cultural artefact

The status of the Internet as a communications medium received much media attention at a particular point in the Woodward case, when Judge Hiller Zobel announced his intention to release his final ruling to a World Wide Web site. The following day (5 November 1997) the story was on the front pages of the UK national newspapers. The newspapers and the national television news found themselves in the position of explaining to their readers what the Internet was for and what it was sensible to do with it. The newspaper coverage presented various interpretations of the Internet. *The Sun* was unequivocal with its headline: 'Internut!' Some newspapers chose to tell their readers how they could get online themselves. Others chose to question the claim that releasing the verdict on the Internet was the fairest way to distribute the ruling, by stressing the numbers without access to the Internet. The judge's decision was interpreted and explained: some found it eminently sensible, while others put it down to the judge's 'computer crazy' son or found it bizarre given that the judge did not own a television.

Throughout the case, television reporters were posted to the steps of the courtroom, to the streets of Boston to test the mood of the American public, and to a pub in the village in Cheshire which formed the headquarters of the official campaign. Television reports flitted from one site to another, incorporating interviews in the various locations and footage from the courtroom proceedings. To cover events on the Internet, the location footage showed people sitting in front of computers, before zooming in on a World Wide Web page. The ITV programme showed a Boston cybercafé. The BBC news showed their own newsroom. Both attempted to find a suitable location to take viewers to the Internet. If television news is about taking viewers to the significant locations for authoritative statements on what was going on there, the Internet was a location which now had to be incorporated into the coverage. It became a significant location for events in the Louise Woodward case. For a brief period of time the Internet became the place to be to receive the latest and most authoritative news: a privileged location. This status did not last. By the following week the newspapers and television were reasserting their reliability and immediacy over the Internet, which failed the test.

Newspaper, television and radio coverage provides a perspective on the public constitution of the Internet as a cultural artefact. Both in their explicit commentaries on the judge's decision to release his ruling on the Internet and in their efforts to portray the Internet as a significant location for events, the media coverage constituted the Internet as an object with particular capacities. In so doing, the media struggled to make the Internet a meaningful object for their readers and viewers. It would be a mistake, however, to take these public statements as defining or determining the reactions of viewers and readers. They coexist with a mass of other references to the Internet in advertisements, newspaper supplements, dedicated magazines, government policies, training courses, workplaces, schools and homes. The way in which these influences are combined to produce an image of communication through web site or newsgroup as a form of social action is the key puzzle for the ethnography.

In the Louise Woodward case, the Internet as culture and the Internet as cultural artefact were intertwined. The first task of the ethnographer is to work out what is going on: in the courtroom, in the press, on television, and by sustained presence in online environments as new World Wide Web pages are produced and as people contribute their views to online discussions. Tracing the complex connections between the different sites as they are formed and reformed requires mobility and a sensitivity to the ways in which places and events are rendered. If events are no longer bounded in particular places, then ethnography can usefully attempt to follow. At the same time it is important to be a part of the settings in which people are discussing the case, making sense of the coverage available to them, and locating themselves in particular places in relation to it.

The course of the ethnography

As described in Chapter 3, the principles of virtual ethnography did not exist fully formed at the outset. The development of the ethnography was an exploratory process, with each activity and each new form of data leading to another and further adding to the understanding of what ethnography could mean in this kind of context. I had not planned at the beginning what data I would collect or even what forms data would take. At every stage it was a question of using an ethnographic sensitivity to ✓ follow up leads which looked interesting. The identification of the Louise Woodward case as a suitable site for a virtual ethnography was a key defining moment for the ethnography which later resulted, but there were many other decisions along the way which shaped what the ethnography later came to be. In this section I attempt to retrieve some of those decisive moments in discussing the main forms of data which came to be available.

I, along with most of the informants whom I later found, first heard about Louise Woodward when her trial began. I had not noticed or taken any interest in reports of her arrest in the press, but when her case came to trial it became hard to ignore. Television news reported daily on the developments in court and reactions to them, building up to the verdict of murder passed by the jury. The Internet then came to the fore in a major way, with the judge's intention to report his verdict on the Internet. This awoke my interest and, quite casually at first, I started to look at some of the web sites which had already appeared. Assisted by Allegra, my research assistant, I started to carry out Internet searches to explore the range of Louise-related web sites that had been developed. Through Internet searches I later found a large amount of web pages and newsgroup discussions that had developed previously, but I had not had any reason to look for them until this point.

The process which led up to the release of the judge's verdict was followed in 'real time'. Visiting the sites where the verdict was to be released at the ✓ same time as following reports on television and in the newspapers gave us a sense of involvement in the case. The media reports set up an expectation that the verdict would be released on the Internet first, and that the result would be out soon. Instead of visiting static web sites we were expecting and hoping for developments and new information. Knowing that we were monitoring the case on the Internet, colleagues started to use us as a source of information, popping in to check whether anything had happened yet. We were disappointed and frustrated when sites were unavailable due to excess traffic and when the verdict was not released when predicted. It was at this point that the project first came to seem ethnographic: there was a ✓ sense of engagement with an ongoing and living event.

The sixth of the ten principles outlined in Chapter 3 proposes that virtual ethnography is an interstitial activity, which is slotted in amongst other activities. The importance of this feature became apparent during this phase of the ethnography. We were trying to keep track of events occurring to a schedule dictated by the Boston time zone and daily schedules and mediated through television, newspapers and the Internet, whilst attending to the regularities and demands of our own lives, jobs and need for sleep. Whilst media and the Internet are in principle available to us all the time in some form, in practice our engagement with them is interstitial: some spaces and some times lend themselves more easily to mediated interaction than others. The combination of Internet use with other simultaneous activities is certainly possible. It was thus, when the first news of the judge's ruling appeared on the Internet, that I found myself in my office, feet up on the desk and leaning back in my chair, engaged in a prearranged telephone meeting via the receiver I held in my left hand, following discussions on a topic totally unrelated to Louise, while clicking my mouse with the right hand visiting Louise Woodward web sites, and listening to conversations through the door of my office and trying to work out whether Allegra had realized that the ruling was out. The excitement of this multiple engagement is hard to recapture now – indeed with a bit of ethnographic distance it seems a little sad to have found it so exciting – but it was real enough at the time. The feeling was one of being multi-present and thoroughly engaged.

This phase of the ethnography was a breathless race to capture as much as possible of the ephemeral activities on the web related to Louise Woodward. We were dealing in large part with fast changing web sites, often belonging to news organizations, where newness and reflection of the latest events were paramount. If one did not see a particular story or update when it appeared, one would have missed it altogether. By tracking changes across web sites and following links between them, a picture of the web as dynamic and developing complex patterns of association and spatio-temporal relationships emerged. Chapter 5 discusses the emergence of spatio-temporal patterns in Internet activities related to Louise Woodward and could only be written because of these phases of intense engagement with developments in 'real time'.

The period after the release of the judge's verdict and before the appeal was settled were by contrast much calmer. Web sites still existed and newsgroup discussions went on, but the pace was much slower. This felt like a good time to try to get beyond the activities observed on the web and make contact with the developers of some of the web sites and some of the contributors to the newsgroups. Rich though the observational data were, they still left unanswered many questions concerning the understandings, motivations and experiences of those who contributed. The observation-only phase of the ethnography, combined with my experience in use of email, newsgroups and web sites, gave me the confidence to risk a more active entry into the field (Lindlof and Shatzer, 1998).

With regard to the developers of web sites, a strategic decision was made to focus on the developers of the support sites which solicited support either for Louise or for the Eappen family. These sites were chosen rather than the sites created by news media organizations. This decision was made on the pragmatic grounds that accessing individual informants might be easier with amateurs than with large professional organizations. The organizational context in which web sites are developed and maintained would undoubtedly form a rich and fascinating research site, but one simply outside the possibilities for this particular study. The decision to focus on amateur support sites was also made on the grounds that they might provide an interesting field to research. The World Wide Web opens up the possibility for individuals to communicate on a world wide basis and at least to some extent to compete with the media organizations. The experience and understanding of the individuals involved in this innovation seemed a useful phenomenon to investigate.

Web sites which mentioned Louise were found using a search engine (www.infoseek.com) and sites were visited to determine whether they were still available and whether they seemed to be the product of a major news organization or an individual. A list of web sites which appeared to be the product of an individual was drawn up. This list was certainly incomplete: no search engine can index all available sites; some sites may have come and gone before the search was carried out; some may not yet have been indexed; and the search was limited by the ethnographer's patience in visiting all of the hundreds of sites listed by the search engine. The list resulting from the search engine was augmented by the lists of links presented on some of the Louise Woodward sites visited: a list on the Official Louise Woodward Campaign for Justice site (www.louise.force9. co.uk) was particularly helpful. A list of 35 particularly promising looking sites resulted, all of which contained some contact details for the author of the site. Each of these web authors was contacted via email and asked whether they would be willing to answer some questions about their site. The initial email which was sent is as follows:

I am a researcher in communications and I have been looking at the role played by the Internet in the Louise Woodward case. I'm particularly interested in sites like yours, which provided an alternative route way of communicating for people interested in exchanging information about Louise or expressing support. I'm researching this case because I feel that it's important to look at specific cases in order to understand the potential of the Internet, rather than relying on the generalised hype and scaremongering that you sometimes see in the newspapers.

I'd be really grateful if you would spare a little of your time to tell me about your site. If you agree to help, I'll mail you a few questions. Your answers can be as long or short as you like. You could really help me by spending as little as 10 minutes telling me about your experiences. In anything I use from what you say, I will make sure that no clues are given to your identity.

If you want to check out my credentials I have a (very boring) web site at http://www.brunel.ac.uk/~xxctcmh/cmh.htm. This has a link to information on CRICT, the research centre that I'm a part of, which will show you the kind of research I do.

I hope you will help. Sorry to have wasted your time if you're not interested.

Christine Hine

Composing this message took some thought. This was the first way in which my potential informants would be able to judge me, and as Lindlof and Shatzer (1998) point out, self-presentation is crucial in forming relationships with potential informants in online settings. While ordinarily I might expect to set up an extended meeting, or at least have the luxury of a telephone call to explain myself and correct any misconceptions, here I felt I had to try to make a good impression straight away, at least to prompt people to respond and to ask for clarification if they wanted it. When thinking about the medium of email much attention has been paid to the messages themselves, how people express themselves, how they represent emotions and so on (for example, Rice and Love, 1987; Argyle and Shields, 1996), but little has been made of the silences in between and how people make sense of them. The ability to interpret silence in a meaningful way is however crucial to the use of asynchronous communications like email, where a response could be (but rarely is) instantaneous. In ordinary circumstances, when sending email to a colleague or to a friend, I can tell myself stories to make sense out of non-response: they may not be in the office today; they may be busy teaching; they might not think my message called for a response. I call on my background knowledge of their lives and fill in details drawn from my own use of email. In the case of these potential informants the stories that I have to tell myself revolve around my inadequacies: maybe my approach put them off; maybe they thought I was being pushy; maybe I looked too amateurish; maybe they have been bothered by researchers before. At this stage I had no background to suggest how soon, or whether, there might be responses to my message.

My initial email acquired a major significance, as my first and possibly only opportunity to perform my identity as a researcher. I thought about which name to use, and settled on Christine, rather than Chris, which I tend to use more often in my work communications. I was aware, in making this decision, that gender persists as an important feature in people's computer-mediated interactions and their ethnographic interactions (Bell, 1993), and I did not want to disconcert potential informants by leaving my gender ambiguous. In my initial message I decided to stress the general aspects of my research first and foremost, to try to diffuse any suspicion that I might be taking a ghoulish interest in Louise's case or be biased for or against her in any way. I felt that it was necessary to explain some of the research methods and give what assurance I could. I also felt that it was important to give these potential informants some information about myself, and revealing a web address of my own seemed both a practical and a culturally acceptable way to do this. I drew on a practice now common among users of email, which directs those wanting further information to a web site address. Comments from those who chose to reply showed that many did indeed visit the web site to check my credentials and offered their own assessments of previous work that I had done.

Of the 35 email messages originally sent, 5 failed to be delivered, due to faulty or untraceable addresses; 30 were apparently delivered, although without any reply or confirmation of receipt it is not possible to know whether their recipients ever read them, or simply deleted them unread, or decided not to participate. Of the recipients of the original message, 11 replied, 10 of them expressing willingness to answer questions. One, the author of a distinctly humorous site referring to Louise, made the simple answer 'Huh?'; my explanatory reply to this message received no response. I sent a list of initial questions to the willing informants:

> Thanks very much for agreeing to look at the questions. These are general questions, so just skip any that aren't appropriate (or of course all of them, if you don't like them at all!). Once again, just write as much as you want to. This isn't a survey where I'm trying to fit you into neat categories – I'm interested in your opinions. Your identity will be kept confidential.
>
> Developing the page
> When did you first develop the page?
> Where did you get the images from?
> Where did you get the contents from?
> Where did you get the links from?
> Did you include a link to the Official Campaign site? If so, when and why?
> Why does your page look and feel the way it does?
>
> Updating the page
> Have you updated the page at all as the case progresses?
> If so, when and why do you update the page?
>
> Who visits the page?
> Do you check counter, visitor logs or guestbook to see who visited the page?
> Have you been surprised (or disappointed) by the number of visitors?
> Have you met (IRL or electronically) any new people through your page?
> Do you know (in either sense) any developers of other Louise Woodward sites?
> Have you made any attempts to promote your page, e.g. web rings, telling friends, submitting to indexes, notifying owners of other sites?
>
> General
> How much experience do you have of the web as a user? And as a developer of pages?
> What made you decide to develop your own Louise Woodward page?
> Have you done any other campaigning (letter writing, emails etc.) in the Louise Woodward case?
> Did you ever take part in campaigns like this pre-web?
> Has the experience of having a Louise Woodward page turned out the way you expected it to?
> How useful do you think the web is for campaigns like this?
>
> Sorry to bombard you with questions. Thanks again for agreeing to take a look.

Each of the messages I sent was tailored individually to things that were said in the emails sent in response to my initial request: mentions of web addiction, questions on how I found their site, comments on my research or my identity. Even at this stage I felt it important to develop a personalized approach rather than relying on a standardized questionnaire. I was dissatisfied with the list of questions which I sent out, as being rather stark and predetermining the issues, but it seemed to be the best way of beginning to get some insight into the background of the pages. Answers to the questions varied in length from a few words to paragraphs on each question. I acknowledged receipt of answers, asked clarification questions and thanked respondents with virtual bunches of flowers (www.virtualflorist.com). Along with the answers to questions I explored the web pages produced by informants, including and beyond their Louise Woodward sites, and I kept printouts and field notes on visits to those sites. In the case of several informants this led to a sustained interaction over several weeks and a rich insight into their involvement with web pages and the Louise Woodward case. I sent messages when sites were updated, and when developments in the case occurred I sent some messages asking informants if they were planning to update their sites. I was offered video tapes of broadcasts I had missed. I developed a range of serious, flirtatious, jokey and professional-style relationships with informants who were all male but of a range of ages from 16 years old into apparent middle age. The majority were convincingly sincere and interested in the research itself. Several informants were 'folk theorists' of the Internet, with their own theories of its revolutionary potential, and in this sense it was sometimes hard to maintain a distinction between the researcher and the researched (Cooper, 1998). They often asked to read the results of the research, and I promised to put a shortened version on my own web site.

In this ethnography I make a claim to be studying the relationship between offline and online, and yet I have restricted myself for practical reasons to online interactions. It was possible that any one of the answers I was given might have been made up, or indeed an entire electronic identity might be a fabrication. As Paccagnella (1997) points out, interpreting what people say online about their offline lives is 'always a hazardous, uncertain procedure'. The hazard arises not just because people can deliberately misrepresent themselves, but also because the ethnographer is lacking ethnographic immersion in the context about which statements are being made. The many and diverse contexts in which the Internet is used may leave the ethnographer thinking that they have understood when they only have a very vague or misleading idea of what that context is. By implication, Paccagnella treats as authentic that which has been verified through an ethnographic process of engagement and immersion, suggesting that the standards of authenticity for the ethnographer should be different to those of informants. While caution in interpreting the words of informants is always advisable, to take this stance seems to assume *a priori* that there is a boundary between offline and online interaction which is a barrier to the ethnographer. Asking people about their offline contexts is far from useless. The accumulation of interactions with informants and the other traces of their presence on the Internet enabled me to make some assessments: the identities which I experienced were plausible for purposes of the ethnography. At any time I could explore other traces left in web pages and newsgroup discussions by the person with whom I was in email contact. I experienced sustained and plausible identities: true for practical purposes, or virtual like the ethnography. The aim was not to judge whether the identities were authentic or not. Using electronic communications to conduct the ethnography allows for a reflexive examination of the ways in which we make that kind of distinction.

The activities of newsgroups became the focus of the next phase of the research, around the time when the appeal upheld the judge's original ruling and Louise flew home. The first task was to locate the newsgroups where the case was being discussed. To do this I used www.dejanews.com, a newsgroup indexing service which allows the entry of keywords to search the full text of newsgroup postings. Rather than trawling through postings from the very beginning of the case I decided to concentrate on more recent events, and initially I concentrated on one month, from 14 June to 14 July 1998. Through a combination of the use of the search engine and manual counting and indexing, I drew up a list of the newsgroups which had mentioned Louise that month. A very long tail of newsgroups were found to have made fewer than 10 mentions of Louise. Those which made 10 or more mentions of Louise Woodward are listed in Table 4.1.

There are several reasons to be sceptical of the value of this list for assessing the level of interest in the Louise Woodward case in the newsgroups concerned. Firstly, to accept it would be to express a high level of trust in the results with very little information on the mechanism of searching and collating results. Dejanews appears to be a highly reputable and efficient service, but we have no independent way of assessing its validity beyond the impression it gives of itself. All of the links followed do indeed appear to relate to postings which mention Louise Woodward, but there is no way of validating whether this is the complete set. In one particular way this is not a complete set of mentions of Louise Woodward in each newsgroup, since many messages are cross-posted to more than one newsgroup, but they are indexed under the newsgroup which appears first on the list. Finally, levels of traffic vary greatly between newsgroups, and the percentage of total traffic on the newsgroup which mentions Louise Woodward might be a better way of assessing interest in the case, but there appears to be no easy way of using dejanews to assess the total number of postings to a given newsgroup in a given period, including cross-postings.

The figures presented in the table are therefore not intended to be an absolute assessment of levels of discussion of the case in newsgroups. Rather they are intended, and were used within the ethnography, as a sensitizing device to focus the attention on some specific sites which showed concern with the case. I joined the newsgroups which appeared on the list above, reading postings which concerned the case and other postings to gain a sense of the topics which were discussed and the ways in which they were addressed. The aim was not to produce the kind of rich ethnography of a single setting which has been achieved by Correll (1995) and Baym

TABLE 4.1 *Newsgroups containing 10 or more mentions of Louise Woodward in messages posted between 14 June and 14 July 1998, retrieved via www.dejanews.com*

Newsgroup	Messages mentioning Louise Woodward
alt.politics.british	599
alt.true-crime	254
soc.culture.british	123
soc.culture.indian	96
alt.teens	95
alt.star-chamber.louise.woodward	71
rec.travel.air	66
alt.digitiser	60
alt.games.final-fantasy	58
uk.local.southwest	44
alt.astrology	39
alt.fan.oj-simpson	34
soc.culture.usa	31
alt.gossip.celebrities	28
alt.activism.death-penalty	27
uk.politics.misc	23
uk.people.teens	18
uk.media.tv.misc	17
alt.fan.rush-limbaugh	14
ne.general	13
alt.fan.howard-stern	12
ne.general.selected	12
uk.local.yorkshire	11
rec.arts.tv.soaps.cbs	10
uk.misc	10

(1995a; 1995b; 1995c; 1998). Rather, the aim was to track the different manifestations of the Louise Woodward case on the newsgroups and to investigate the ways in which the case was rendered differently within the spaces of different newsgroups, sacrificing depth for breadth. To provide some background on the understandings of contributors to newsgroups I posted a message to several newsgroups chosen from the list above.

As with the web site developers I introduced myself as a researcher in communications who was looking at the specific case of Louise Woodward on the Internet. I explained that I was concerned with how people got interested in the case, where they got their information from, and what they thought of the quality of information on newsgroups and web pages. As before, I offered people a promise of confidentiality and the chance to check my credentials through my web site. In contrast to the web site developers, very few newsgroup contributors replied. Hundreds, possibly thousands of people may have read the messages, but the responses were in single figures. This lack of response is fairly typical in my experience and that of others for generalized requests for research assistance from news-groups. Baym (1995c) suggests that 'response rates to surveys posted to online newsgroups is generally low, as people feel no obligation and have no incentive to respond'. With those who did reply I proceeded as with the web site developers, asking questions and developing a relationship. Some contacts did not proceed beyond an initial message with no response to my follow-up, while others endured for a longer period of time.

A final contact valuable to the research was the developer of the Official Louise Woodward Campaign for Justice site (www.louise.force9.co.uk). I was reluctant to make contact during the campaign, since I felt that the sensitivity of developments in the case might make members of the campaign reluctant to talk, and it would be unfair to try to persuade them. As the case progressed, and increasing numbers of the amateur supporter sites referred to the official site, I felt it was also increasingly important to contact the developer of the site. I became correspondingly more nervous about making sure that my first contact gave the right impression. When I finally found the courage to write, I began, as with my previous attempts to recruit informants, by explaining my credentials and setting out a broad context for the research I was hoping to carry out. I also explained that I had waited until the case was resolved before making contact. I hoped to portray myself as a genuine researcher with some sympathies for the complexities of working on such a high-profile campaign. At this stage I was sending my message to an anonymous 'webmaster', and I had no idea whether I was addressing an individual or a group of people, nor did I know how close the author of the site was to the campaign itself.

I was delighted when I received a reply to my message, and somewhat relieved to find that I was in touch with one individual, Peter, who had been the key figure behind the development of the official site. Peter was quite clear that he saw the case as a significant moment in the development of the Internet. He undertook to give me a history of the events surrounding the setting up and maintenance of the site. His story talked about the ways in which he came to know about the case both through living in the Elton area and, crucially for him, being involved in bulletin board discussions based in Boston. He told me how he became convinced of Louise's innocence, such that when the news broke that the jury had found Louise guilty, he drove to Elton to volunteer to produce a web site for the campaign. For him, producing a web site was an obvious means which he had at his disposal to help the campaign. The site developed over time, including increasing amounts of information on the case beyond the initial contact details for ways to register an opinion on the case which it contained. More people volunteered to assist with the site, and eventually a network of people, communicating via email, collaborated on producing the site. Peter felt that while this was an efficient way to work initially, ultimately it led to distrust and the breakdown of the group. Peter's final reflection on the case was as follows:

Why am I telling you this? Well, it's an important event which I feel should be noted. There are huge benefits of the internet as a communications medium, but I am also convinced that human nature does not work well on it.

How did I feel about doing the website? Well, I'm proud to have helped, and I am convinced that it was a huge help. It helped co-ordinate support internationally, it helped raise money for the defence costs, and it helped provide Louise with the knowledge that for the rest of time there will be proof of her innocence for all to see. I have met some great friends through this campaign (and I've met some total nutters) and I am really pleased to have had the experience.

I am also pleased that for once we can say that the internet actually helped someone, instead of it simply being used for a big company to make money. This was a very personal cause, and it proved that to a certain extent, people could adapt to a new technology, and use it as a tool.

My interaction with Peter demonstrated a number of things for me: that even behind web sites which gave no clues to the identity of their producers there were individuals with biographies, emotions and commitments; that the Internet was indeed perceived as a crucial location in the Louise Woodward case; and that geographic location was still important in the apparently transcendent sphere of the Internet. These points are addressed again in the chapters which follow.

At no point did I consider contacting Louise Woodward herself. It would be very interesting to know her reactions to her portrayal on the Internet, and to investigate her perceptions of the role of the Internet in her trial and release. She has, since returning home, expressed her concerns about the role of the media in her trial: it would be interesting to explore her perceptions of the Internet in this context. However, the interest value of these questions probably does not outweigh the intrusiveness of asking them. This ethnography is about what the Internet made Louise, and what she became as an Internet figure through the activities of web site developers and newsgroup contributors. The aim was never to compare this with a 'real' Louise, or to assess it for the authenticity of its portrayal. In a similar way, Aycock and Buchignani (1995) conducted their ethnographic study of the Fabrikant affair without access to Fabrikant himself. As for their participants, the real Fabrikant for their purposes was the one created through the newsgroup discussions and media portrayals. It seemed to me that to approach Louise, even supposing that she agreed to talk to me, would be unnecessarily intrusive and add little to the primary aim of the research.

The ethnography constituted by my experiences, my materials and the writings which I produce on the topic is definitely incomplete. There were many strategic choices to be made about which sources of information to visit, and which connections to follow. In particular, the ethnography is partial in relation to its choice of particular applications of the Internet to study. I set out to study 'the Internet', without having made a specific decision as to which applications I intended to look at in detail. The WWW and the Usenet newsgroups became the focus, to the exclusion of MUDs, IRC, private emails and other types of bulletin boards. By choosing two contrasting uses of the Internet I was able to use my materials to see differences in the ways in which their users understood them, and the different relationships with time, space and authenticity which were enacted through them. This was a strategic choice, which incorporated what I felt to be an appropriate level of depth in each setting together with the advantages of being able to compare across settings. It is also, however, not incidental that I chose sites to study for which there were readily available search tools. In this, the ethnography is itself thoroughly shaped by the available technology and my understandings of it.

I printed out and saved for later analysis examples of different web sites which were encountered. Some features of sites, such as audio and video or large amounts of information, were not saved but recorded in notes. A set of field notes accompanied the web sites, recording the impressions and emotions which accompanied the web surfing. Field notes recording visits to particular web pages were filed with printouts of the pages themselves, often in different versions as the pages were updated, and kept together with exchanges and interviews with the developers of the web sites. Newsgroup postings were also filed with field notes and with the exchanges between the ethnographer and the authors of postings. Video recordings of television news at key points in the case were transcribed and filed, and newspaper stories relating to the case and the Internet were photocopied and indexed. By the end of this process, the data which had been accumulated took the form of printouts and files of web pages and newsgroups postings, emails to and from informants who had produced web pages and read or contributed to newsgroups, newspapers, video recordings of television news coverage, and field notes recording thoughts and observations which arose during the course of the ethnography.

The very recordability of mediated interactions means that raw data accumulates at an alarming rate. In retrospect, a multimedia hypertext would have been an ideal way to store and index the different sources of data. Field notes could have been connected with the field sites which they described, and web sites could have been linked together in the temporal order in which they were visited, or in the categories which were developed, or in terms of their own interlinkages. Hopefully ethnographers will come to have the tools to organize their multiple sources of data in multiple ways (Howard, 1988; Crane, 1991; Dicks and Mason, 1998; Slack, 1998). Already, packages such as ATLAS-ti, Ethnograph and NUD•IST allow for the computerized storage and organization of qualitative data and may also permit the interlinking and analysis of graphical and web-based data in addition to the more traditional textual data. No doubt these capacities will be extended in the future. However, these packages take time to learn to use effectively and it seemed inadvisable to incorporate the learning of a new package into the already urgent timescale imposed by trying to keep up with developments in the field. In our case, no tool to organize data in this way was close to hand, so a 'low-tech' paper-based solution was adopted. By the end of the writing-up phase I was also suffering sufficiently from excessive keyboard and mouse usage to be quite grateful that my data were accessible on paper as well as on screen.

The analysis of all of these data, as with all ethnographies, was an ongoing process throughout the observation, rather than being a distinct phase. Much of the organization of findings into themes was however retrospective: disengagement from the field allows the time for re-engagement with the theoretical themes and issues which were the starting point for the ethnography as described in Chapter 1. The account which follows in Chapters 5 and 6 is shaped by the particular theoretical concerns which prompted it. It is also necessarily partial (not whole, and not impartial), being shaped by the decisions I took in designing the study, my involvement in data collection, the constructions which I place on the data in my analysis, the technologies which I had available and the understandings which I have of the technologies at my disposal. Like all ethnographies it is unique to both its setting and its author. It is, however, authentic in some key ethnographic senses: the data are born of observation and interaction and the findings have been exposed to being challenged through my interactions with informants and my re-examinations of the data. Throughout, the analysis is illustrated by direct quotations from newsgroup postings, web pages and emails from informants. These have not been corrected for grammar or spelling, in order to preserve some of the feel of the original. The ethnography is divided into two chapters. The first focuses on time, space and technology. It asks how web site designers and newsgroup contributors understood the uses of the technology, and particularly how they conceive of their contributions in time and space. The second chapter focuses on another key dimension of the new technologies, which is the problem of authenticity.

5   Time, Space and Technology

Internet interactions and structure

The aim of this chapter is to take a first look at the social world of the
Internet that emerged through the ethnography described in Chapter 4,
taking the research questions listed in Chapter 1 as a starting point. These
questions were formulated through a review of theories relating to the
Internet, drawing out some key features of social organization that the new
technology was said to enable or enforce. The questions considered in this
chapter are:

- How do the users of the Internet understand its capacities? What
  significance does its use have for them? How do they understand its
  capabilities as a medium of communication, and who do they perceive
  their audience to be?
- How does the Internet affect the organization of social relationships in
  time and space? Is this different to the ways in which 'real life' is
  organized, and if so, how do users reconcile the two?

The next section addresses the first of these sets of questions. In the specifics
of the emergence of Louise Woodward related web sites and newsgroups we
have the basis for exploring the ways in which the use of the Internet
became meaningful to a particular group of people. Lotfalian (1996) discusses the enframing of the technology, meaning how people conceive of it
as a form of communication and in particular how they compare online
settings with face-to-face interaction. Here, though, the concept is expanded
to encompass a broader sense of the social meanings that the technology
has for Internet users. The 'technology as text' metaphor explored in
Chapter 2 suggests that we focus on the ways in which people develop
understandings of what a technology is and what it can do, instead of
deciding in advance what the capacities of the technology are. The capacities of the technology are understood to emerge through the practices
within which the technology is used and represented. An obvious starting
point to examine would be the status of the Internet as a communications
technology. The software that constitutes access to the Internet is seen to
provide different ways of interacting with other people and displaying
information, via MUDs, newsgroups, IRC, WWW and other related possibilities. What is not clear or straightforward is how people interpret the
uses that the technology offers up and whether they all attribute the same

meanings to the technology. It is interesting, then, to focus on the kind of communicative setting which people see as offered up by the Internet, and how this affects the uses to which it is put.

The exploration of practices that make the Internet meaningful to its users sets the scene for a discussion of the temporal and spatial structures that emerged through the ethnography. It has become commonplace to suggest that the Internet lifts social interactions out of spatial and temporal contexts. The Internet 'negates geometry' (Mitchell, 1996: 8), or constitutes the 'death of distance' (Cairncross, 1997). Relationships can be conducted across the globe, irrespective of location and time zone. Temporality becomes disordered, as the apparent intimacy of Internet interactions is combined with asynchronous modes of communication. On the Internet, it is said, you can be intimate with people who are not there any more, or who have yet to arrive.

Much energy has been expended on extrapolating the social consequences of forms of interaction that transcend time and space. Most of this thinking has been conducted on assumptions about the capacities of the Internet without grounds in observations of what the current relationship of Internet interaction with time and space actually is, or by focusing only on the radical possibilities and experimental uses of the technology. Just like the predictions of Chesterton's (1904) 'clever men', there has been a focus on extrapolation from extreme cases. Gillespie and Robins (1989) point out that the new communications technologies are still thoroughly spatial, in the way that they can recreate and intensify existing geographical inequalities. This point deserves an investigation on the micro-level of actual usage.

One nicely nuanced way of thinking about the relationship between the Internet and space–time is provided by Castells (1996a). He introduces two linked concepts, the space of flows and the temporal collage, to discuss the new forms of social relations offered up by developments in transport and communications technologies:

> Localities become disembedded from their cultural, historical, geographic meaning and reintegrated into functional networks, or into image collages, inducing a space of flows that substitutes for the space of places. Time is erased in the new communication system when past, present and future can be programmed to interact with each other in the same message. The space of flows and timeless time are the material foundations of a new culture that transcends and includes the diversity of historically transmitted systems of representation: the culture of real virtuality where make-belief is belief in the making. (Castells, 1996a: 375)

In the space of flows, the emphasis is on connection rather than location. Flows of people, money, objects and communication travel around the world, and connectivity becomes the vital factor that structures inclusion. Much social experience is still tied to place, but the space of flows provides an alternative way of conducting social relations that is increasingly the site of the exercise of power by the elite. Relations between place and flows are possible, but are 'not predetermined' (1996a: 423). The space of flows is connected with the development of timeless time. This is a breaking away from ordered sequences, cycles and rhythms into a disordered temporal collage of jumbled tenses. Again, timeless time does not replace chronological time but coexists with it, providing an alternative way of structuring social relations.

At first sight, the space of flows and the temporal collage offer provocative ways of thinking about the Internet. As a way of connecting distant places, the Internet seems an ideal medium for the space of flows. The anarchic jumble of web sites and newsgroup postings looks like an embodiment of timeless time. For the ethnographer, though, this raises questions. How do people manage the coexistence of flows and places and how do they interpret the temporal collage? How do people negotiate a path through timeless time and the time of place? What kinds of narratives still get told, where, and to whom? How do people interpret their locations, their connections and their histories? Castells's concepts of the space of flows and the temporal collage, when applied with due scepticism, provide a framework for examining the work of web designers and newsgroup contributors. This framework provides a structure for organizing the ethnographic findings discussed in the latter part of this chapter. First, however, it is important to look at understandings of the technology in use, as a backdrop for the formation of temporal and spatial relations. In the next section of this chapter I explore the ways in which first web pages and then, more briefly, newsgroups become meaningful to their users.

Web pages, authors and audiences

The search for web sites related to the Louise Woodward case, and for web site authors who would discuss their sites with me, produced a diverse array of different sites. Some, like Figure 5.1 (Simon), were quite explicitly soliciting support for Louise, while others, like Figure 5.2 (Jim), aimed to provide more neutrally presented information about the case. The most striking feature that united the ways in which the authors talked about their disparate sites was their concern with recognition. Audience, conceived of as actual or potential visitors to the site, was the foremost category in making the production of web sites meaningful for authors. This might seem obvious, but as Scannell and Cardiff (1991) and Williams (1990) show, even for television the idea of the audience emerged and developed over time as programme makers and policy makers came to terms with the technology. The web developers I interviewed are outside professional and institutional frameworks that might reinforce a view of the audience, and yet it was still to them an important category. The narratives that they gave me of developing the site and evaluating its success returned time and again to ideas about whom the audience for the site were.

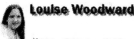 **Louise Woodward**

Home Evidence Opinions Survey

[**Index** (you are here) | Evidence | Opinions | Survey]

- Please also visit the Louise Woodward Campain for Justice (official page).
- And there's the Louise Woodward Boston Support Group
- How to get in touch with Louise
- If you'd like to make a donation, please visit the Campain for Justice page.

Wear a yellow ribbon in support of Louise.

Lastest News: 5 June The pathologist whose evidence helped convict Louise has resigned after it was found that he failed to carry out a proper investigation in another case. The Massachussets Bar Association has called for a review of all the criminal cases he's handled. Read the full story on BBC News

Summary of the site

This site run by ▇▇▇▇ and ▇▇▇▇
Last update: 0359 GMT Sat Jun 6 (▇▇) --- Survey last updated: [Now - thanks to an HTMLScript page]
Note that although this site is hosted in the US, it is run from the UK.

Louise Woodward was convicted of Murder in the second degree. She was sentenced to life in prision, with parole after 15 years. About week later, the judge presiding over the case reduced the conviction to manslaughter, with a charge of time served. Louise is now waiting in the US (the court has her passport) for the outcome of an appeal by the prosecution to have the original conviction reinstated. The date of this appeal is set for March 6th.

But we mustn't forget Matthew Eappen, who died in early February 1997. As the (British) press have shown, there has been much outcry about the way that the supporters of Louise in her home town celebrated her release on that Monday; people have said that Matty has been forgotten. This is not the case. There are those people who support Louise and there are those that don't. But everyone offers symthathy to the Eappens for their loss. It is not something anyone would wish on anyone else.

Innocent. Free her, and let her come home.

Other sites you may like to visit:

- http://orphansoftware.com/Louise/
- Justice for Louise Woodward campain

FIGURE 5.1 *Simon's Louise Woodward support web site as printed out on 8 June 1998*

Updated: **9th June '98** | See '**Latest News**' : **This site is updated regulary....**

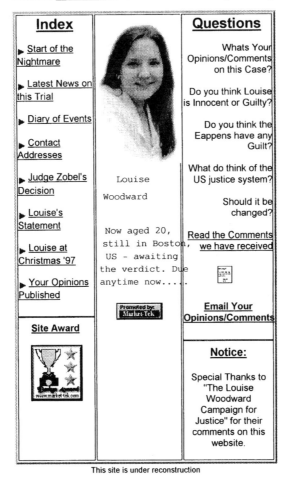

The Louise Woodward Trial

LATEST: <u>Louise fraud</u> : **Verdict to be released by 16th July**

Index

▶ Start of the Nightmare

▶ Latest News on this Trial

▶ Diary of Events

▶ Contact Addresses

▶ Judge Zobel's Decision

▶ Louise's Statement

▶ Louise at Christmas '97

▶ Your Opinions Published

Site Award

Louise

Woodward

Now aged 20, still in Boston, US - awaiting the verdict. Due anytime now....

Questions

Whats Your Opinions/Comments on this Case?

Do you think Louise is Innocent or Guilty?

Do you think the Eappens have any Guilt?

What do think of the US justice system? Should it be changed?

Read the Comments we have received

Email Your Opinions/Comments

Notice:

Special Thanks to "The Louise Woodward Campaign for Justice" for their comments on this website.

This site is under reconstruction

FIGURE 5.2 *Jim's Louise Woodward information web site as printed out on 11 June 1998*

Orientation towards the audience for Louise Woodward pages took several different forms. Authors knew about their audience largely through hit counters and other devices for measuring the number and/or origin (domain name) of visitors to their site. All of the web designers who discussed their sites with me talked of checking their number of visits, and of experiencing pleasure at high numbers of hits and disappointment with low numbers. The hit counter, though, is a very crude measure of the audience, since it gives no information on the assessment that the audience made of the site or often any identifying information beyond the domain name. Hit counters share with television audience ratings many of the interpretive problems discussed by Ang (1996). The audience is largely an imagined construct for web designers, just as it is within mass media production (Espinosa, 1982; Hartley, 1987; Pekurny, 1982; Schlesinger, 1978). This, however, does not prevent designers from orienting quite detailed elements of their practice towards the audience. Many authors spoke of the need to make their pages accessible to audiences on both aesthetic and technical grounds. Sites were designed to convey the nature of the case to the audience, and to provoke suitable reactions. These aesthetic concerns were combined with judgements about what would be easily readable:

> I was quite careful when deciding how my page should look. I chose a white background to give a sense of innocence. I also thought white enhanced the pictures better. The main picture on the page is a large one of Louise smiling. It's own background is white and I thought it went well with a white background. Further through the page I included other pictures. I didn't want to just put any rubbish on so I chose the pictures which would create the best emotional response. Geoff.

Tim mentioned his choice of a black background to convey the 'sombre' nature of the case, and simultaneously to provide a suitable background to make red and white text readable. The decision whether to include images was also often portrayed as a matter of orientation to the audience. Frank used minimal images on his pages, to make them easier to download. Simon said, 'I try to design in a way that is simple, neat and easy to navigate.' The audience is therefore conceived of variously as concerned with the readability and accessibility of a page, but also with its emotional or aesthetic appeal. Authors also considered the audience in terms of their informational requirements. This was mentioned particularly often when I asked whether their site included a link to the Official Louise Woodward Campaign for Justice site. They spoke of the official site as a place to find more comprehensive or more up-to-date information if visitors wanted it. Other authors spoke of the audience's information needs in relation to their decision to create the site:

> The layout is simple but effective and informs people about the latest news concerning the site. I used a marble background to give it a more professional look and easy going on viewing. Jim.

Jim combines a view of the audience as requiring easily accessible and well-presented information with a concern that through his web page the audience will develop a perception of him, which may influence their decision to visit again.

An additional form of orientation to the audience manifested itself as an interest in the ways in which audiences find web sites. The question that I was most often asked by the web authors I contacted was how I came across their site. In some circumstances, a social scientist might find potential subjects asking with suspicion, 'How did you get my name?' This can play out suspicion and hostility, or more sympathetically, indicate that the researcher is asking questions in a way that is not usual for members of that culture. In this setting, the question lacked hostile overtones, being asked in the spirit of monitoring the effectiveness of the various visibility strategies undertaken by the author (and answered in the same spirit). These visibility strategies included submitting the details of a site to search engines, thus enhancing the likelihood of the site being returned by a user entering relevant search terms. Authors also talked about contacting authors of other, related web sites, asking the author to include a link to their page and offering to reciprocate. This strategy is assumed to enhance the visibility of a site by making it more likely that a visitor interested in the Louise Woodward case will stumble across a link to the site. Being linked to by another site is thought of as a success, particularly if the linking site is a highly visible one like the Official Louise Woodward Campaign for Justice site, or a prominent indexing site like Yahoo. Jim's site received a design award, to which he attributed part of the rise in visitors he had noticed. Another strategy for increasing visibility, the web ring, is a mechanism for grouping together web sites on a similar topic and directing visitors between them. There was a Free Louise Woodward web ring at one point, but it had become extinct by the time that I visited. Finally, web site visibility can be enhanced by word of mouth, and its electronic equivalent, by telling friends, posting messages to newsgroups and including the address in an email signature file. None of these strategies are unique to the Louise Woodward sites. However, the authors of these sites showed a high awareness of visitors and visibility strategies that is not necessarily shared by all web authors. This kind of audience awareness requires technical sophistication beyond the basic skills needed to develop a web page.

The audience awareness and visibility strategies displayed by these web authors raise the intriguing prospect that the ethnography may have been skewed: since I found these sites using search engines, there may have been other sites produced by less net-savvy designers, which were not visible to me. The tools used to find and define the field are not neutral, and the choices made here favour the web designer with high visibility. Audience awareness may also have made these web authors more likely to be open to my questions. Their interest in and awareness of the audience may have meant that I was viewed not as an ethnographer but as a particular kind of audience. Ethnographers have to recognize that the informants who are willing to talk to them are often not 'typical cultural members' (as if they existed), but may be marginal, or marked out by particular orientations and experiences that make them more likely than others to collaborate with the ethnographer (Rabinow, 1977). Research on the Internet is no different in this respect, and it needs to be remembered that ethnographic approaches are received differently by different people. Comparative research with other web designers in other contexts, through ethnographies shaped in different ways to this one, will no doubt reveal some quite different interpretations of the WWW and its audience.

The preoccupation with audience showed up in the web pages themselves as well as in the ways their designers talked with me about them. Audiences, in the form of visitors to web pages, were sometimes appropriated for display within the pages themselves. The hit counter is the most basic form of audience appropriation. It denotes the number of unique requests for the information comprising the site. This does not map straightforwardly onto the number of people viewing the site. The hit counter is, however, routinely used to testify to the popularity of a site. The hit count or visitor log can also act in some circumstances like the audience ratings used in television to sell advertising space (Ettema and Whitney, 1994). A particularly popular site, manifested by a high hit count, might be used to persuade an ISP to grant extra free web space. A further twist arose in the use of the hit counter to testify to support for Louise. Ed's hit counter was embedded into a sentence that read 'Your Are Person Number [hit counter] Who Wants to See Louise Freed'. Hits were translated into visitors and then translated again into supporters. Several Louise Woodward support sites also solicited contributions from visitors in the form of email messages or additions to a guest book. When kept private, these messages might be used by the author to gauge opinion, but when posted back on the page they have an additional role in reinforcing the perception that the site is popular and respected.

The concern with audience in the design process and in the continued life of the site bears witness to the importance of recognition to web site designers. The concern with recognition manifests itself in different ways, which depend on the orientation to the Louise Woodward case itself. For Tim, recognition rather than support of Louise was his main motivation for developing a page. He saw the Louise Woodward case as 'the opportunity of creating an up-to-the-minute news web page that would also act as a "gateway" to attract visitors to my main page'. He says of the case, 'I am not for or against Louise – I just like making web pages.' Tim calls himself a 'net junkie'. He tells me that he is off work with depression, and designing web pages and using the Internet more generally is a way of using his time. Tim's orientation to the Louise Woodward case depends on his recognition of its newsworthiness, which he (correctly it seems, from the success of his page) translates into the behaviour of a potential audience: 'When it was announced that the verdict would be given over the net thousands of people were entering "Louise Woodward" into the search engines to hear the latest news.' For him the Louise Woodward pages stand alongside his Clinton/ Lewinsky pages and Princess Diana pages as attractors of visitors to the pages he sees as the core of his web site. This orientation to the Louise Woodward case might be termed opportunistic, since the case is used to attract the audience who are assumed to be searching for information about the case:

> I thrive on the positive feedback from my 'viewers' which makes me keep wanting to make my pages bigger and better. Tim.

Recognition, for Tim, is an end in itself, which makes his web design work meaningful. Several other pages which seemed to fit this category were found through search engines, including sites from religious organizations. While still audience-oriented, the opportunistic sites orient to the imagined searching behaviour of audiences. In some ways, Jim's site too became an opportunistic one. Jim explains the decision to develop his site as a recognition of an unfilled niche: 'This came about after watching most of the trial on Sky Tv, there was not many sites around that actually covered the latest developments.' Jim originally developed what he calls a biased site (presumably in favour of Louise's release). He later decided to make the site less biased, and was pleased to see that his visitor numbers then increased.

For authors whose sites more explicitly solicited support for Louise, the web page stood in for taking action in the case. This could mean fulfilling a need for information, as Frank suggests:

> Because I wanted to collate all the facts available from various places and put them onto one site so that everyone could read it all in one place. Frank.

For others, however, the development of a web page and its presence on the web was a statement in its own right:

> Web pages like this are like the ribbons we wear . . . They are a badge that shows us support also if enough people spend enough time saying the facts they stick. Jeff.

While attracting an audience was not of primary significance here, as it was for the opportunistic sites, recognition was still an important factor in making the page a meaningful action on Louise's behalf. Visitor logs or hit counters affirmed the visibility of the site as a statement of support for Louise.

Recognition, then, was a key element for the web developers in making their work meaningful. At the same time, web design was a pleasurable activity in itself, a craft or skill to be practised, appreciated and displayed:

> I see web design like art. It is a creative process between me and the computer limited only by my knowledge of HTML and the programmes I use. In time I will become masters of these. I don't believe in making complex and fancy web pages (I could!). The advances in HTML, now version 4, and plug-ins take years to

filter down to the majority. Addition of such things inevitably leads to narrowing your market. There's no reason why graphics and text alone can not create a decent webpage. Mike.

This statement was made as part of Mike's self-presentation on his web pages as an aspiring web designer, and could be taken as a reminder to the imagined audience to take the simplicity of design of his pages as a sign of his good taste and consideration rather than lack of ability. Mike's statement also alludes to a learning process. This learning process was made visible in their web pages by several authors. The personal page that Frank's Louise Woodward page led me to contained links to 'my first web page' and 'my second web page', constructing a history of the author's involvement with the web. While this explicit history is unusual, portrayals of the author's engagement with their pages over time are common. Most obvious is the 'under construction' disclaimer. This sign seems both to aim to avert potential audience criticism through its assurance that the author knows it is unfinished, and to promise future developments if those visitors will only return. It also displays the author's orientation to the web site as an ongoing project to which they have a personal commitment and which they hope to improve. Web page development is a learned craft that authors take pleasure in practising. I discovered through my own experiences how satisfying the crafting of a web page can be, and as a teacher I have often observed the pleasure people display at the production of their first web page. Students who learn to make basic web pages become keen to learn how to incorporate features they have seen on other pages into their own work. A large part of learning to produce web pages depends on observations of what is possible through looking at other people's pages: a practice sustained by the opportunity which web browsers offer to look at the HTML source code. In an important sense web page developers are each other's audience. The developers of pages are aware of the context into which their pages will be inserted, manifested in the concern to develop pages that will look good and to justify design decisions on technical or aesthetic grounds lest simplicity be taken for incompetence.

The pleasure in crafting of web pages was closely linked to the importance of incorporating features that the unknown audience would appreciate. Lacking direct feedback, authors used their own preferences to stand in for the unknown audience. Biography was also used to account for preferences:

> I prefer a clean open page with facts clearly listed and sources cited, I've spent most of my life in academia, sciences and tend to structure ally my writing in the formal report style. Jeff.

The web page was spoken of by authors as a project of self-expression in a design sense, as well as in the more explicit sense in which personal home pages provide a picture of the author. The choice of the medium of the web for taking action in the Louise Woodward case was also situated as a product of history and availability. For Geoff, the development of his page is a form of action specific to his circumstances:

> I wanted to do something and had this internet tool at my disposal so I created a web site to add to the publicity of the case. Geoff.

Web pages were seen as expressive of the designers' identities both in the design choices they made and in their use of this tool to take action in the Louise Woodward case.

Thinking of web pages as acts of communication therefore elides a complex array of orientations and imaginings. Web page development is also a craft practice that is pleasurable to designers. They are highly aware of their own skills and of their pages as inserted in a context where they may be compared with other pages. In this sense web design comes across as highly competitive. It is also embedded in the lives of designers as a meaningful project of self-expression or self-improvement, as a skill to be proud of and as an activity that can be fitted into the biographies they tell about their lives. Web page development is made meaningful primarily, however, through orientation to the audience, an imagined category consisting of information seekers and potential aesthetic or technical critics. This practice is comparable with the efforts of media professionals to imagine an audience for their programmes (Espinosa, 1982; Pekurny, 1982; Schlesinger, 1978). Just as these authors found that media professionals often orient to one another as an audience for their products, so too do web page designers. The web designers whom I contacted showed a high awareness of other web pages and design practices, and a keen interest in the web context into which their pages were inserted. Other web designers are therefore a significant element in the imagining of the audience. The idea of audience as manifested in hit counts and visitor logs is, however, the most important feature in understanding web page design as maximizing recognition. Key in promoting the recognition that sustains the web page is an awareness of the visibility strategies that give a web page a presence and attract visitors. Timeliness or up-to-dateness was one key feature by which audiences were assumed to be impressed. The temporal and spatial features of Internet organization discussed later in this chapter and the issues of authenticity and identity discussed in Chapter 6 need to be understood in relation to ideas of audience and the strength of orientation to audience in making web design meaningful.

Web pages have been discussed through the practices that make them socially meaningful. This issue has been addressed in terms of the orientations towards recognition, craft practice and biography which make web development meaningful to its practitioners. Similar questions could be asked of newsgroup contributors: what makes the posting of a message a meaningful thing to do, and how are messages oriented to an audience? The first observation to make is that detailed answers to these questions are likely to vary widely between newsgroups. Newsgroups are highly differentiated social space, as a later section of this chapter will show. While there are shared features between newsgroups, particularly in the structuring features such as message headers, quoting practices and subject threading, there are also marked differences. What makes the posting of a newsgroup message meaningful encompasses both a basic understanding of what the technology is for, and an understanding of what a specific newsgroup is for. Understanding what newsgroups are for enables participation in the social world of a particular newsgroup. Intensive study of a single newsgroup elides the two forms of understanding which newsgroup participation allows. By comparing a topic across newsgroups, there is a possibility of drawing out a common level of shared understanding of the technology, and investigating the ways in which this understanding is developed and reinforced.

The posting of a message to a newsgroup implies an understanding of the online context in which the interaction takes place. This is very different in different newsgroups. One way to explore this difference is in the variation in orientations to the Louise Woodward case in the newsgroups which discussed the topic. In alt.teens the Louise Woodward case became just one topic for practising a particular kind of playfully abusive interaction. By contrast, alt.true-crime embraced the case as one of fundamental concern to the newsgroup, and postings were characterized by detailed discussions of evidential and legal matters. In other newsgroups it was clear that the case was another topic for playing out long-term feuds. The orientation of participants to the newsgroup and the Louise Woodward case therefore varies widely. This can be construed as evidence that each newsgroup constitutes a community, sharing norms and values. My research did not, however, pursue the kind of detailed study of each newsgroup context which would enable this hunch to be substantiated. Rather than conformity to the social norms of a community I take the construction of newsgroup postings to display ideas about who the audience is and what are the appropriate resources for convincing or impressing them. The very structuring of newsgroup postings plays out ideas about the audience. In newsgroups, the use of the > symbol to denote a piece of text quoted from a previous posting performs a number of different things, including: a set of expectations about what the audience should or should not be able to remember from previous postings; moral statements about the ownership and attribution of words; and conversationality, operationalized as turn-taking. Using a newsgroup successfully depends on having a conception of an audience, which is tied up both with ideas of what newsgroups are for and with an idea of what a particular newsgroup is for.

In this section I have shown how both web pages and, more briefly, newsgroup postings arise and are made meaningful through understandings of the technology, the audience and the author. Particular imaginings of technology, audience and context are played out in the interactions which I had with web designers and newsgroup participants, and in the pages and newsgroup postings which they produce. The producers of Internet content have quite specific and detailed ideas about who the audience are and what the capacities are of the communications technology they use. The next chapter looks at the ways in which Internet interactions are portrayed as authentic and the identities which authors perform in their interactions. What follows in this chapter focuses on the performance of relationships in time and space, within the Internet and in the portrayals of it in other media. It will be shown that the audience is imagined as temporally and spatially located, that authors experience themselves as situated in particular temporal and spatial contexts, and that they understand their Internet activities against a backdrop of events which have their own temporal and spatial dimensions. The resulting complex patterns of activity will be considered here within the framework of Castells's (1996a) concepts of the temporal collage and the space of flows.

The temporal collage

A conventional linear narrative usually consists of a set of events which are connected in the order in which they happened. Events can be distinguished by the time at which they occurred and shown to lead to or follow on from one another. Narratives which do not follow this notion of time can be confusing to read: a novel or film which makes use of flashbacks must signal these clearly to avoid confusing readers and viewers who may be expecting to see events portrayed in a linear sequence. The linear chronological narrative is a kind of sorting out of events, a statement about antecedents and consequences. This kind of account assumes a singular absolute chronology, the elapsing of an objective 'time' against which events may be placed and measured. In the previous chapter I gave a linear account of the Louise Woodward case. I described how certain events in the media, on the Internet and in campaigners' lives were linked to the happenings in the courtroom in Boston. The linear account of the case which I gave, however, collapses several different timescales together. Producing this account of the Louise Woodward case depends crucially on cultural competence to interpret complex patterns of temporality. In this section of the chapter I will be considering what those patterns might be, and what cultural competences might be required in order to make sense of them.

The key sequence of events in the Louise Woodward case, on which all others depend, is the happenings in and around the courtroom in Boston. Directly linked to those events were the reactions in Louise's home village. During my ethnography of the Louise Woodward case I was in no doubt that this was the real sequence of events. To me they were unfolding day by day, as a series of linked events where the past was clearly apparent and the future impossible to foretell. This sequence was also used as a reference point by the developers of web sites supporting Louise and by contributors to newsgroups discussing the case. The Louise Woodward case on the Internet has a very obvious real-life referent and everything which occurred on the Internet was somehow related to the real-life events. This is a particular feature of the case which I chose as the focus for the ethnography. I specifically chose an event which had a real-life occurrence and an Internet dimension, being interested as I was in the Internet both as a culture and as a cultural artefact. While in the case I chose the 'real' events were considered the primary reference point by everyone involved, this cannot be taken to be a universal feature of the Internet.

The Louise Woodward case therefore had at its heart the real sequence of events surrounding Louise in Boston. This 'real' chronology, however, was filtered for almost all concerned through another chronology, that of media coverage. The mass media combine multiple voices and discourses to produce narratives which can be followed by viewers (Fairclough, 1995). It is testimony to the power of television coverage to collapse time and space, particularly space, that those who watched the television coverage considered themselves in a position to comment on and evaluate the case. Viewing television coverage, particularly live feeds from the courtroom shown on Court TV or on Sky, counted as having direct access to the real events, as Chapter 6 will show. Television coverage is a specifically timed unfolding of events. News bulletins on the terrestrial television channels occur at set times throughout the day. In the later stages of the case the willingness to disrupt schedules in order to bring news flashes and special programmes on Louise is testimony to the high levels of newsworthiness of the case and the intense public interest which the news reflected and created. Newspapers too have their own specific schedules. A daily newspaper, although it may go through several different editions, is limited by its production schedules. The production schedules of both television and newspapers provide a filter which imposes a temporal structure on the release of information. In the Louise Woodward case, the prospect arose that the medium of the Internet might provide a more instantaneous, less temporally structured medium through which news could break.

The Internet gained prominence in both television and newspaper reporting at the time when Judge Zobel announced his decision to release his ruling on the Internet. Interpretations of this decision in the various media outlets produced highly polarized images of the Internet. On the one hand the decision was seen, despite being technically risky, as a fair and democratic way to ensure wide (global) access to the ruling. On the other hand, the decision was portrayed as bizarre, elitist, high-tech and therefore exclusionary. While polarized in their interpretations, the reports converged on a picture of the Internet as a privileged place to be for instantaneous access to full information. This expectation created the opportunity for any shortfall in instantaneity to be newsworthy. The following week, when the judge's ruling had been released, the role of the Internet was reported in numerous media outlets. Television was not slow to exploit its own relative success in breaking the news. The ITV 'News at Ten' on 10 November 1997 included shots of the Boston campaign group with the commentary: 'The campaign's Internet failed and the news was broken by members of the media.' The camera shot panned across from a group of people sitting intently watching a computer monitor to a television sitting switched on but unheeded in another part of the room. Newspaper headlines too told the story of disappointment at the failure of the Internet to live up to expectations of instantaneity: 'Internet indicted as unreliable witness' (*The Daily Telegraph*, 11 November 1997, p. 3); 'Internet surfers thrown by power failure' (*The Times*, 11 November 1997, p. 2); 'Much-hyped web fails to electrify waiting world as traffic jams and power blunt technology's cutting edge' (*The Guardian*, 11 November 1997, p. 4); 'News is tangled in the web' (*Daily Mail*, 11 November 1997, p. 4); 'Farce on the Internet' (*The Sun*, 11 November 1997, p. 5). It is somewhat ironic that these newspapers appeared on the following day, while the judge's ruling was delayed by only one hour. The success or failure of the Internet was diagnosed according to the expectations which had been set up for it, not by any absolute standards of how fast news should travel.

Media representations of the Internet thus focused on temporal features of the medium, including its potential immediacy and the experienced reality of waiting for information to download. In the large part, this representation was based around the web sites of news organizations with the capacity to react quickly and a considerable commercial stake in getting the news out fast. The same could not be said of the amateur web site developers who formed a large part of this ethnography. These developers could not be said to have the same resources or the same stake in producing up-to-date information as the commercial news organizations. They did, however, share an orientation towards the audience and the importance of recognition. The orientation of web site developers towards the audience which was discussed earlier in this chapter led to a view that web pages should be up-to-date. Audiences were thought of as requiring information which downloaded quickly onto their computers and which gave them the current state of affairs. An examination of web pages shows that this concern translates into the explicit performance of timeliness.

Figure 5.2 is Jim's web site. The central panel locates us in the present – a particular present in which Louise, now aged 20, is still in Boston awaiting the appeal verdict. It also projects us into the near future, with a verdict expected 'anytime now'. The site combines the promise of immediacy with the comprehensive appeal of an archive. Other temporal markers suggest that we can go back in history to see the 'start of the nightmare', or follow the sequence of events in the diary. Back in the present we can read the latest news. But the present is also 9 June 1998, when the page was last updated, or 11 June when I visited the page and printed it out. We are assured that the site is regularly updated, and it again projects itself into the future with the promise that the site is 'under reconstruction'. The site is therefore both up-to-date now and to be altered in the future. The site constructs an audience who want current information and who may be attracted to revisit by the promise of future information. Jim also has an understanding of the timing of visits to his page. He has recently overhauled his page to make it download faster. He speculates that visitors to the site may have increased recently due to media coverage and the impending result of the appeal. He orients to media coverage and its presumed effect on web surfers to make meaningful increases in his hit counter and comments to his opinions page. The external chronology provided by developments in the case reported in the media provided a context for web developers to make variations in visitor traffic over time meaningful. Major events in the case, like the release of the judge's verdict or the Supreme Judicial Court (SJC) final ruling, were commonly seen as increasing visitor interest and hence visitor traffic. As discussed earlier, web site developers envisaged an audience triggered by media events to use search engines to find up-to-date information. They were, of course, correct in my case. As described in Chapter 4, I was one of the people motivated to search the web for information by media coverage of the case.

In the personal section of his web site, Jim offers a commentary on himself and his family. He is 34 years old, disabled with a rare nerve disorder, and has been using computers since acquiring his first Sinclair ZX80 at the age of 16. He gives a narrative on his page of how he came to be using the web. He claims to check his email and browse the web every day, and the speed of his responses in email interactions with me bear this out. I asked Jim how he came to develop the site. He says that he had the idea in October 1997, after watching the trial on Sky TV and finding few sites on the web that covered the latest developments. He updates the site regularly, he says, mostly for news updates or to add the opinions sent in to him, which he claims to add within 24 hours. In his description Jim orients to sequences provided by the events of the trial and their coverage in the media and on web pages. Jim is unusual in that he does not refer to any time constraints in his life which prevent him from updating the site when he would like.

Figure 5.1 is Simon's web site, developed in collaboration with a close friend, printed as viewed by me on 8 June 1998. This is explicitly a support site, which encourages visitors to 'Wear a yellow ribbon in support of Louise'. The site contains a number of temporal markers which locate it in different time frames and sequences. The 'Latest News' of 5 June locates the present by offering us the most recent significant development in the case. The site also tells us when the page was last updated by Simon, shifting the present to a specific time early in the morning of 6 June. The survey page is updated automatically, performing a different present which is defined from the perspective of the visitor. The summary section of the site gives the main sequence of events in the case in the past tense, setting up the background against which the site is to be viewed. Providing the chronology of events which have happened allows the site to act as an evaluation of past events and an exhortation to future action based on that evaluation. The temporal markers on the site therefore have a dual function: they set up a claim for the up-to-dateness of the site and they provide a historical context against which the claims within the site are to be placed.

Looking more closely at Simon's site reveals some inconsistencies in the performance of the present tense. In the site summary we are told that Louise is 'now' awaiting the appeal which is due on 6 March, while the latest news feature implies that the present is some three months later. The inconsistency is unremarked within the site. A variety of resources are available to resolve the apparent reality disjuncture (Pollner, 1987) caused by the conflicting time frames in the web pages. A common sense reading suggests that a mistake was made: the latest news was updated but the author failed to look at the summary to check that it conformed. Common sense stands in for the repair work (Schegloff et al., 1977) that a reader needs to do to make the page meaningful in the face of inconsistencies. When the orderliness of a conversation breaks down, then participants initiate repair work to set the interaction back on track (Garfinkel, 1967). In the case of web surfing, repair work is initiated in the face of apparent inconsistencies, to reinstate the web page as something which makes sense in a context of what is normal and likely. Possible resources for repair strategies include knowing what day it is, having alternative knowledge of the case from other sites and the media, and knowing what web development is like. The updating of web pages is a piecemeal process, and any web developer would know that this site would not have been created afresh at the last update, but would have been altered only in some key respects.

The page presented in Figure 5.1 is frozen in time, as I printed it out. The page was updated as the case progressed. Simon initially told me, 'I *try* to keep it up-to-date. In fact, it needs doing now :) I update it when I get a new opinion to put up, or there's a new development to the story.' Simon expressed the same feeling of responsibility to keep the site reflective of current events as other developers. They shared a feeling that, as Mike said, 'A not updated page looks bad.' The work of updating, however, takes time. On 18 June, Louise arrived back in the UK, and gave a press conference at the airport. That day, a transcript of the press conference appeared on Simon's site. The summary section when I next visited bore a new statement:

> Simon typed like a maniac to get a transcript of the interview at Manchester Airport done before he had to go to work :) Make it worthwhile and <u>see it here</u>.

The summary page also contained an apology to potential disappointed visitors:

> Okay folks, remember that the <u>Opinions</u> section is updated by hand, and has recently gone manic :) So please be patient if I a little behind. thanks. And admittedly the site is perhaps looking a bit out of date (due to exams you see) – I'll be tidying it up and doing a proper update after work tonight (about 10pm BST). Have a nice day.

Simon locates the page for his visitors in the context of his busy life of work and exams, and promises a future time when he will be able to carry out the work of updating the site fully. In an email, I teased him about his busy life. He replied:

> One more exam to go then I'm free. It must be said it takes a lot out of me . . . I'm usually up to 2am if I haven't got school the next day. And I watch Star Trek.

It is clear, then, that web pages take time to produce. Their production competes with other activities and commitments, just as the work of this ethnography did for me. Not having updated a site was seen as grounds for apology or for justification in the light of constraints. When talking about the need to update pages based on developments in the case, the developers of Louise Woodward support sites often referred to events in their own offline lives which took precedence. Geoff talked about the competing demands of school work and the progress of the case:

> The majority of developments have happened recently which has meant, due to exam revision, I haven't had the time to update any of my pages.

On my first contact with Mike he explained:

> I've kinda got a bit lazy updating it recently what with other websites and not having my own computer at home until very recently (last week in fact!).

Mike shared with the other web site developers a belief that web pages should be up-to-date. On his personal web site, the link to his Louise Woodward site states his intention to 'keep this site up even after things have been sorted out as a monument to injustice'. The personal web site acts as a portfolio and expresses Mike's wish to find work in web site design. In this context his Louise Woodward site acquires a meaning as a statement of Mike's web design competence, and a piece of work in a portfolio. The portfolio has a quite different temporal relevance and is oriented to as a record of past achievement and present skill, rather than as an up-to-date source of information.

Far from floating free in time, web pages perform time. They may do it inconsistently, and different pages may perform different times, but still they perform time. As well as performing time, however, web pages take time. Swales (1998) showed that academic writing takes time and is inserted into and has complex relationships with other professional and personal commitments. Similarly, the work of producing web pages has to be fitted in with other commitments and constraints. Web developers have their own chronology through which offline events and their media representations are filtered. The developers of web sites felt a moral imperative to update their sites to reflect events in the case and yet experienced this imperative in ways which were dependent on the demands of their own lifestyles and their exposure to the other media through which they learnt about the case. The interaction between the performance of time and taking time produces the temporal collage. A hypothetical Martian, monitoring the WWW from Mars (but without access to television or newspapers), would indeed experience Castells's temporal collage in all its glory. Depending on where our Martian looked, she might find that Louise was free, still in court, awaiting an appeal verdict, or accused and awaiting trial. Individual web pages perform their own locations in time, construct their own past and future, and portray contextually meaningful sequences. Without reference to the external chronologies of media time and the time of web page development, the temporal collage of the WWW could be a meaningless jumble of tenses. The Martian who is without these external referents and cultural context would be without the cultural competence to read the temporal collage and to make use of the WWW meaningful.

The concept of the temporal collage is therefore to some extent applicable to the WWW, but problematic if applied without an ethnographic context. Newsgroups too can, to some extent, be viewed as a temporal collage. The vagaries of network distribution and time zones can produce some interesting temporal anomalies: replies may be received at a site before the message to which they respond and messages can even be received before they were apparently sent. In this sense, newsgroups have a complex relationship with linear time. Many different topic threads may be going on at any time the newsgroup is accessed, and their beginnings may already be out of sight. Rather than one discussion topic holding the floor at any one time, many different debates are interwoven. Newsgroups (and other forms of Internet communication) might therefore be thought of as distinguished by their simultaneity (Kirshenblatt-Gimblett, 1996). To think of this as indicative of a temporal collage of no coherent time is to disregard the temporal structuring which occurs through the organization of messages into threads, the orientation of message content to external events, and the work of newsgroup readers in structuring the messages they read.

The organization of messages provides some temporal clues. The header of the message gives the time and date when the message was composed. The distribution of messages, too, carries some temporality. Any news feed will not store all messages, due to limited file space, but will store only the most recent messages. The length of time for which messages are stored will vary according to the amount of traffic on the newsgroup and the amount of file space allocated to it, which will in turn depend on a judgement about the relative importance of the newsgroup. Frivolous, high-traffic newsgroups will probably have a fast turnover. The messages available when any one person logs on to any one news feed to read a selected newsgroup might be seen as the present, or what counts as 'now' for the purposes of reading and responding to messages. This present will be subtly different for each instance of logging on. There is, however, a clear sense of the present in newsgroups, which is demarcated by the presence or absence of messages on the news feed. This is not to say that the past is inaccessible.

Archives of newsgroup postings exist, which can be read in sequence, or searched according to keyword. These archives provide a history for each newsgroup, in addition to that provided by the memories of long-term members. There are therefore some grounds for thinking of newsgroups as highly temporal, in that there is a clear (although shifting) demarcation between that which has happened, that which is happening, and that which has yet to happen within the group.

Newsgroup messages are to some extent temporally situated and temporally marked by header information. Some are also, however, positioned in time through the content of the message, explaining why the author chose to send this particular message now. Replies gain their justification by virtue of being responses: their temporal positioning is relative to the message to which they respond and is internal to the newsgroup. New threads, however, often appear to be seen as requiring some justification as to why the author felt it relevant to raise the issue now. It seems that it is important to position a statement as temporally relevant, as a reaction to some external event, rather than an idly expressed passing speculation. Message content, particularly in new threads, was frequently temporally marked in relation to events occurring outside the newsgroup. New discussion threads were often positioned in relation to something which someone had seen on the television, read or heard. New developments such as the overturned murder ruling, Louise's release or her appearance in a 'Panorama' interview were accompanied by marked increases in relevant threads on the newsgroups which had shown an interest in the case.

While in a gross sense discussions in newsgroups can be seen to be related to offline events and a new incident in the case sparks off a new proliferation of threads, the contributions of particular individuals are related as much to having time in their own offline lives as they are to offline events. Web site developers experienced a responsibility to reflect developments in the case on their web pages, but filtered this responsibility through their other commitments. A lack of updates in response to events was seen as an occasion for an apology. By contrast, newsgroup contributors (or potential contributors) do not appear to experience an individual responsibility to respond to events by posting messages. While justifications for messages are common, apologies for absence of messages are rare. Where they occur, they could be taken as an expression of commitment to the forum, or of an expectation that one has had a sufficiently visible presence that one will have been missed. While still oriented to audiences, newsgroup postings are more likely to be construed interactively, for example in terms of correcting misinformation, than they are in terms of a temporal sequencing which prompts a contribution by any particular individual. The link between newsgroup postings and correction of misinformation, particularly apparent in alt.true-crime, is discussed further in Chapter 6.

The final temporal feature in newsgroups is the work of the reader, who can structure the temporality of their reading and can operate a highly developed sensitivity to temporal structuring. Reading a newsgroup as meaningful involves becoming used to the sequencing of messages into threads of conversation. People new to newsgroups often find them difficult to fathom at first. The jumble of simultaneous threads of discussion without beginning or end seems to have no sequence or meaning. Learning to read a newsgroup meaningfully involves resolving this jumble into its separate threads, and understanding messages as part of a present and ongoing interaction. Newsgroup readers and contributors notice when a new thread of interest to them appears, and experience little problem in following its progress. An informant who followed one newsgroup emailed me to let me know when the Louise Woodward discussion had broken out again on the group. To her, newsgroup events did have a temporality which she followed and to which she oriented herself. To view the Internet as an incoherent and structureless temporal collage is to underplay the cultural competence of newsgroup readers to whom it poses little problem.

Castells's (1996a) temporal collage breaks down, therefore, when examined ethnographically. The idea of the temporal collage overlooks the interpretive work which participants do to make sense of conflicting temporal orders, and the cultural competences which they draw on to do so. Adam suggests that 'all time is social time' (1990: 42), to stress that linear, progressive time itself is a social construct, rather than a pre-existing asocial structure upon which other temporal orderings are overlaid. All ideas of temporality are, then, constructs and are the upshot of interpretive practices. The idea of cultural competence to orient to multiple temporalities is not new either, and is not confined to electronic communications. Zerubavel's (1979) 'tempography' of a hospital found that there were many different ways of perceiving time and of controlling activities through time. These multiple temporalities served as a way of dividing and controlling labour and of marking out different subgroups within the hospital. The inhabitants of the hospital showed no problems in navigating a path through diverse and often conflicting temporal structures. Multiple temporalities also figure in the work of Traweek (1988a; 1988b) and the other authors featured by Dubinskas (1988). Here, the operation of different ways of ordering social activities in time, and differing perceptions of time itself, are found as a feature of the organization of work around high technology. Once again, rather than being a meaningless temporal collage, the multiple temporalities are portrayed as both highly ordered and highly meaningful for participants. It is therefore not surprising that, muddled though the temporalities of the Internet might seem, they are also highly meaningful for Internet users.

Space of flows

If temporality is structured in multiple ways on the Internet, then what of space? What is the relationship of the Internet as social space with the other spaces of media coverage and our daily lives? What are the relationships between different Internet spaces and how are their boundaries maintained?

Are all Internet spaces equal, or is there a hierarchy of centrality and marginality? This section focuses on the emergence of space in the course of the Louise Woodward case and on the relationships which form and reform between those places as the case progresses. Spatiality, in a sociological sense, refers to more than physical proximity and distance. Spatiality, via locality and ideas of place (Appadurai, 1996), becomes a way of thinking through the mutual availability and shared coherence of situated practices, interpretations and accounts.

In the eyes of television, radio and newspapers there was little doubt that there were two key central locations on which to focus: Boston, particularly the courtroom where the trial took place; and Elton, the Cheshire village which was the rallying point for the UK campaign for Louise's release. Television coverage returned daily to the steps of the courtroom and the pub 'The Rigger' in Elton to await developments and interview interested parties. The television coverage simultaneously took its viewers to the key locations in the case and constituted those locations as the central ones to be at to gain an eyewitness view. Locations in television coverage are marked for viewers. We may be seeing a sequence of shots showing people gathered in a pub, but the voiceover leaves us in no doubt that this is a particular pub:

> Campaigners who gathered at a local pub in Louise's home town in Cheshire. (BBC1 'News', 9 p.m., 5 November 1997)

Reporters are sent to key locations to offer us their own 'on the spot' observations on the scene and to carry out interviews with those present. Again, the location of the reporter is specifically marked for viewers:

> From the court in Cambridge, Massachusetts our correspondent . . . reports. (BBC1 'News', 9 p.m. 10 November 1997)

> Our correspondent is in Louise's home village of Elton in Cheshire where her supporters have been gathering all day and he joins me live from there. (BBC1 'News', 9 p.m. 10 November 1997)

It is deemed important that we know where these people are. It is also deemed self-evident that we will recognize that these are important places to be. A competent viewer of this coverage would, it seems, have to accept that the news organization was taking them as close to the heart of the action as was practicable to offer direct access to the facts.

Another important location for television news to cover as the case unfolded was the Internet itself. When Judge Hiller Zobel announced his intention to release his ruling on the Internet the television coverage attempted to follow. However, constituting the Internet as a location for television reporting appeared to challenge the ingenuity of the production team. Two devices for rendering the Internet as a location for television reporting were used. The first relied on the already established central physical locations in the case: shots of campaign supporters in Boston or Elton sitting round computer monitors awaiting news were substituted for the earlier views of making yellow ribbons and other campaign activities. This rendering of the Internet focused on the local context of reception and established the centrality of the Internet by means of its prominence in the already established centrality of the physical location. The other device for rendering the Internet as a location decontextualized the machine. Screen shots of web pages filled the television screen, almost as if the television screen and the computer monitor became one and the same. The web page might be scrolled down, providing some movement in an otherwise static shot. Alternatively, the shot might pull back to reveal a person seated at the screen: almost always in back view only, sometimes only a set of fingers typing on a keyboard. This was a general 'computer user' rather than a specific person using the computer.

The Internet was therefore marked out as a significant place in the media coverage. The site most often mentioned in the other media was the *Lawyers Weekly* site which was first nominated by Judge Zobel to carry his ruling. Some news organizations did, however seize the opportunity to advertise their own sites or those with which they had business links, where they had been chosen by the judge to receive independent notification of the ruling. The Official Louise Woodward Campaign for Justice site also received some coverage, particularly when the campaign itself was being discussed. The mass of amateur support and information sites received no coverage that I saw. In marking out the Internet as a space, the media therefore also differentiated that space. Key locations on the Internet emerged through the focus on specific web sites. Television and newspapers therefore provide one version of the spatiality of the web. Another perspective on the spatiality of the WWW is provided by looking at the web itself, and the structures of interlinkages which emerge between sites on related topics.

The WWW has a hypertextual structure. Any word or image can be linked to another image or piece of text. The linked text may be produced by the same author, or it may be produced by someone else, somewhere else, completely unknown to the author. The visitor who clicks the link will not necessarily know in advance to which of these destinations they will be taken. It is this complex interlinking structure, together with the lack of clues to the physical location at which documents were produced and are stored, that has led people to suggest that the web is aspatial. This view, however, deletes the intense awareness which web developers have of the territory of their own web sites, and the spatiality which stems from the differential connectedness of sites. One of the key dimensions of spatiality on the WWW is that of territory. The web developers I interviewed saw sites as their own territory, giving them rights and responsibilities. While the developer of the campaign site recognized his site as the property of the official campaign, other developers had individual (or joint, in the case of

Simon) control over their own sites. These sites, as territories, also had size. They were not infinitesimal points in space, but locations with boundaries and constraints. The amount of web space allocated by different Internet service providers was a topic of interest and concern: too little web space would limit the possibilities of improving sites by providing more information. Additional space was an acquisition to be celebrated, as Geoff showed in his prominent announcement that 10 MB extra web space had been given to him by his Internet service provider, allowing him to plan substantial additions to his site.

The web does have a form of spatiality, although this is defined by connection rather than distance. The high level of audience awareness and strategies of visibility amongst the developers of Louise Woodward support sites manifests itself in the concern for connections. Lacking the direct publicity for their web site addresses through the media which is available to institutionally supported sites, the amateur developers of support sites have to develop their own form of publicity. They hand out their web site addresses to contacts, and carry the web site address in the signature files which end their emails, but this in itself is unlikely to bring high levels of traffic. The developers of these sites feel that they have little chance of attracting large numbers of visitors as an absolute location which people visit by entering the web site address directly into their browser. As a relative location, found through connections from other sites, they may be able to gain visibility. Search engines are seen as key locations through which many visitors may pass, and registering a site with search engines is therefore seen as an important step in acquiring visibility.

During the progress of the trial, we conducted frequent searches for the term 'Louise Woodward', using the same search engine (www.infoseek.com) for comparability. The number of relevant sites which the search engine found grew throughout the trial, climbing from 165 on 5 November to 707 on 11 November. Of the results on 5 November, the Official Louise Woodward Campaign for Justice site came 10th on the list. This site emerged through the progress of the case as the centre of a web of support. The more amateur, less well-connected sites became increasingly marginal. This centrality/marginality is manifested in the different practices of linking which the official site and the amateur support sites employed. The official site was closely linked with that of the Boston support group. The majority of the links within the campaign site were either local, to other pages of information at the same site, or to facilities provided by the Boston supporters. Amateur supporters' sites did receive links from the official site, but these were collected together in an annotated list of other sources of information on a separate page. This contrasts radically with the practice in the amateur support sites, which often featured a link to the official site prominently on the main entry page. Simon's site in Figure 5.1 carries this link near the top of the page and asks visitors to visit it. Many sites referred their visitors to the official site for the authentic support experience. The official campaign site was considered authoritative and up-to-date due to its proximity to the campaigners in Elton, and through them to Louise herself. The counter on the official campaign site told of the many visitors who found their way to the centre.

Anyone could have called their site the official one (in fact some other people did), but the emerging consensus was that the site produced (apparently) by the campaign team in Louise's home village had a justified claim to be called official. Their location at the centre of the web of support was reinforced by their claims to be in a central physical location. The connection between the offline location of the village and the online location of the web site was strongly rendered. It is clear that while space might be expressed as connectivity rather than distance on the WWW, this space is far from homogeneous, and it is not independent of physical, distance-based space. In addition to the key sites from Elton and Boston, officially sanctioned campaign sites were developed for Ireland, France and Australia. The developer of one of these national supporter sites was in no doubt that the Elton and Boston sites remained the main focus for information and involvement. His site was suggested, he said, by the UK campaigners on the basis of information he had placed on his personal web pages. The site declares that it was 'created to provide a [national] focus'. Developments in the case were reported through reviews of the national media coverage, helping to localize the site. The marking of national location in this instance is done with the hope of recruiting and involving a community who might otherwise have felt (geographically) distant from the case. It is unclear how successful this strategy was. Low media coverage may have led to both a lack of local events to cover on the site and a lack of stimulation of interest in potential visitors. The use of the web to promote local involvement is problematic without other stimuli such as media coverage.

Performance of a geographic location can be double-edged. It might promote authenticity, but it might also lead to accusations of bias. While some sites specifically marked themselves as UK based, the majority included no specific statement of location. This could be seen as a response to the prominence of 'national bias' in the case: in erasing national location, these sites may have enhanced their claims to provide neutral commentary on the case. The possibility of erasing national location in web sites depends on the lack of direct linkage between Internet addresses and geographic locations. It is not straightforward to read physical locations from what you see online: as Hoffman (1998) describes, the topological orderings provided by Internet addressing are dynamically enacted and inconsistently linked to geographic space. Domain names gave away national location for only a few sites, addressed as '.co.uk'. I was frequently in some doubt whether the web pages I was reading were produced in the US or the UK. My field notes on visits to Louise Woodward sites record my attempts to make sense of the location of authors. My notes on a visit to Jim's site say:

> Very hard to tell if Jim is UK or US based, although the family page has some UK-based clues.

I was obviously adopting the assumption that being based in the US or the UK was important to the way in which I would interpret sites. I picked up on a mixture of cues to make sense of location. Simon's site was unusual in stating explicitly that it was run from the UK. Frank's site was also unusual, in that it spoke from a specified location, 'here in the UK'. Usually I developed a sense of the author's location by extending my search away from the Louise Woodward sites into the personal pages of the author. There I often found links to local sites, schools, colleges, workplaces and local communities. Not only national locations, but also institutional and local affiliations were being performed. My attention was drawn not to the erasure of locality, but to its performance.

In summary, it is apparent that concepts of space are still meaningful in interpreting the WWW. Links to physical/geographic location are not universally erased, but are expressed in specific contexts. While on a personal page expressions of physical location might be part of the author's identity performance, in other places a statement of location might detract from claims to provide neutral information. The ambiguity inherent in web site addresses allows for play on location as a feature which can be strategically performed in specific situations. The WWW is experienced not as aspatial, but as having complex relationships with space and its own form of spatial organization and differentiation. It is important to recognize that conceptions of space are constructed both by visitors and by web site developers. Developers in particular are thoroughly aware of their sites as territories to which visitors need to be attracted. Whether visitors are attracted is seen as in part depending on the extent to which the site is connected to other key locations. Different levels of connection and different numbers of visitors produce a hierarchy of central and marginal sites. The result is a highly differentiated form of space.

Spatiality also forms a useful concept for interrogating experience of newsgroups. A number of authors, including Kirshenblatt-Gimblett, have pointed out that subject matter rather than physical/geographical location is the key component in carving out space on Usenet:

> Because the topic is the basis for choosing with whom to communicate, topic is of the utmost importance in structuring and navigating the vast electronic net. (1996: 53)

In addition to the maintenance of newsgroups in general as a specific kind of social space, newsgroups are also marked out as different by their addresses and their location within a hierarchy of newsgroups. The name of the newsgroup signals the kind of subject which users can expect to be discussed there. The Usenet hierarchy can operate as a kind of social positioning: its users are expected to know that newsgroups represent places in which certain kinds of thing should be said. Outside the moderated groups, however, no formal filtering is applied to keep newsgroups on-topic.

In my ethnography, I used the search facility provided by dejanews to locate contributions which mentioned Louise Woodward. This highlighted the similarities in style of interaction across newsgroups, such as the practice of quoting parts of previous messages to maintain continuity. It also made starkly apparent the differences between newsgroups, even when they were discussing the same topic. What is sensible and appropriate to say can differ radically between newsgroups. Styles of address and interaction were distinctive to each newsgroup, and messages are made situationally relevant to the newsgroup. Previously, I used the idea of temporal relevance to show how new message threads were positioned as relevant to external events, such as developments in the Louise Woodward case. Situational relevance refers to the way in which developments in the case were rendered as appropriate topics to be raised in a given newsgroup. This uses the symbolic interactionist perspective on situations which Argyle et al. describe: 'situations are not passively there; they are actively perceived and negotiated' (1981: 17). The concept draws on the work of Schutz (1972), Goffman (1971) and Meyrowitz (1985), demonstrating that social interactions can usefully be thought of as performances oriented towards particular understandings of behaviour appropriate to different social spaces. Situational relevance is, however, quite specific to newsgroups and refers to the ways in which postings demonstrate, through both topic and style, that they are relevant to the setting in which they are placed. In so doing, they both enter the setting and contribute to its cumulative construction.

In rec.travel.air, a thread of discussion was started by a message sent shortly after Louise had flown home to the UK. The post was as follows:

I have been following the Louise Woodward story.

I was curious to hear that she had picked up her pasport before travelling home. Surely she did not need it to travel?
She was well known, so the ID is not needed for the airline (BA)
She was accompanied on the flight by Sir/Lord Colin Marshall, so I think he would vouch for her to the airline.
She was a returning UK citizen/subject, flying non-stop BOS-LHR (on BA 212, BTW)
So why did she need her passport?

-Joe
P.S. Aparently even being buddy-buddy with Sir/Lord Colin Marshall cannot get you a seat on the sold-out morning LHR–Manchester shuttle! I'll keep that in mind the next time I can't book a seat on that flight.

This message is made situationally relevant to rec.travel.air. First, and crucially, the Louise Woodward case is raised in an aspect specifically related to air travel: the question is about Louise's flight home. Second, the post displays a general awareness of 'what is normal for air travel' to form a background to raise a specific question. Lastly, the message poster claims that he is a regular air traveller himself, well qualified to be part of the group. Stylistically, this message fits with many discussion threads on the newsgroup, where people exchange experience-based insights into travelling by air. Several of the responses picked up on the air-travel-specific features of the question, and attempted to give answers. Others, however, focused on more general aspects of the case, made value judgements about the outcome or offered tasteless jokes. Increasingly these were accompanied by complaints that the discussion was not appropriate to the newsgroup. The original poster replied to some of these, accepting responsibility for the thread and defending the original message:

> Please read the entire thread.
>
> I started it, so I can tell you it was a question regarding Woodward's wait to get her passport back (hampered by a local Boston holiday) in order to travel. I was curious as to whether she actually needed this passport since she was returning to her home country, probably had other ID, was travelling with the head of British Airways who could vouch for her, etc.
>
> Unfortunately it turned into Woodward's second trial.
>
> Sorry for bringing it up, because I thought that the passport issue would be of interest to this board, since many of us travel internationally.
>
> -Joe

This message received a reply from one of the critics:

> Certainly no need to apologize for bringing the issue up in this context. The ones who need to apologize are those who perpetuated this thing into a political discussion – and a second trial for the woman. THAT is the part that is inappropriate. The passport issue certainly IS of interest AND on topic.
>
> mbd

Situational relevance is reasserted by these two posts, stressing that rec. travel.air is considered by them (and they position themselves to speak for the newsgroup as a whole) as a place for discussions only on air travel, with posts to be valued where they are both relevant and interesting. One reply to the critic suggests that while this position is valid in principle, viewed more practically his reading practices (specifically, his failure to use his killfile) are at fault:

> There are plenty of threads that are not related to air travel and I don't remember seeing you criticizing those posters. The fact is, unfortunately, this is an unmoderated people. Many do drift off. Thus, if I see something I don't like, the most effective means for me is to skip it or put it in my killfile. If you want to be a 'netcop', at least do it more consistently. Many will appreciate you effort if you can really clean up this newsgroup (but I don't think it's an easy task).

This acts as a reminder that the situational relevance of newsgroups is maintained not just through censure of off-topic messages, but also through particular ways of using the technology. Messages that are off-topic can be seen as cluttering up and distracting the newsgroup within one set of reading practices, or as an inevitable and quite trivial irritant catered for by the technology in another. These reading practices entail quite different orientations towards the space of the newsgroup. In the first instance the newsgroup is a topic-oriented domain to be protected from irrelevance, and in the second it is a space of social interaction with which one can selectively engage.

Other newsgroups that showed strong situational relevance in discussing features of the Louise Woodward case particularly relevant to the topic of the newsgroup included alt.astrology (Louise's birth data), soc.culture. indian (ethnicity of Matthew Eappen's father, Sunil), and alt.true-crime (the legal dimensions of the case). Chapter 6 discusses in more detail the styles of argument and substantiation of statements that prevailed across a sample of newsgroups. For now, it is enough to say that newsgroups showed interests in different aspects of the case. The way in which messages were phrased and the content of those messages showed orientation towards the newsgroup as a distinct social space (and simultaneously acted to construct and reinforce that distinct space). The form of situational relevance displayed in rec.travel.air focused both on topic and on style. In other newsgroups the focus on topic was less prominent. In alt.teens, the Louise Woodward case was raised in a relatively casual fashion:

Since no ones bothered to bring this up I thought I would.

I'm sure (I hope) you all know the basics of Woodwards trial so I'll cut right to the chase.

How does everyone feel about Judge Zobel's decision to reduce Louise Woodward's sentence 2nd-degree murder sentence to manslaughter?

I'll add my views when this thread gets going (if it gets going).

Eileen

This message constructs a newsgroup atmosphere in which it is quite normal for the Louise Woodward case to be discussed: its very existence acts as the justification for raising the topic. It also creates an atmosphere in which there will be awareness of the case, and in which discussing one's response is quite appropriate. Some responses were abusive towards either Louise herself or other posters. Most, however, took an approach that sustained an idea of the newsgroup as a social space for the exchange of opinions. In alt.teens, the Louise Woodward case became a site for playing out a particular style of interaction, based not on topic but on a social identity.

The separateness of newsgroup space is maintained by the posting practices of members. Their orientation towards creating situationally relevant messages both responds to and creates the newsgroup as separate space. The separateness might be seen to be enforced by the technology, and indeed it is encouraged by the hierarchy of distinct newsgroups, but it is not inviolable, as cross-posting practices demonstrate. When one cross-posts, the same message is brought to the attention of more than one newsgroup. It can be used by 'spammers', advertisers sending messages to many newsgroups to gain attention, and so irritating readers and consuming resources. Guides to correct use of Usenet (for example Horton et al., 1999) advise against it. Cross-posting is provided for through the technology, but controlled by an array of social sanctions and devices like the Usenet Primer, and thus the separateness of the different newsgroups is maintained. Excessive cross-posting from soc.culture.indian to alt.astrology during discussion of the Louise Woodward case was considered by some members to constitute abuse of the facility, and the cross-posters were reprimanded. Recognition that a message is inappropriate is sometimes accompanied by a suggestion that the discussion be taken elsewhere (another newsgroup). The space of individual newsgroups is maintained through the recognition that they are part of Usenet, and therefore there are general norms as to their use and a context of other newsgroups in which topics could be discussed. Their distinctiveness as social spaces, rather than proceeding automatically from the technology, is continually collaboratively maintained by users.

In contrast to the individually owned territory of web pages, newsgroups are a collectively owned and sustained social space. Each newsgroup could be thought of as providing a distinctive frame of interaction. Goffman (1971) suggests that different frames of interaction are sustained, at least in part by the physical separation of different spaces. The front stage and backstage behaviour of waiters is made possible by the fact that diners in the restaurant cannot see backstage into the kitchen. The boundary according to which performances are organized is for Goffman a perceptual boundary. Meyrowitz (1985) builds on this analysis to suggest that electronic media can help to break down the frontstage/backstage distinction by making performances available across previously impermeable boundaries. In effect, new media can challenge perceptual boundaries. He hypothesizes that it becomes more difficult for adults to maintain frontstage behaviour before children when those children also have adults' backstage performances available to them through television. The experience of newsgroups suggests that this is not universally the case. While there might in principle be no perceptual boundaries between newsgroups (and readers of newsgroups can read also any others that their news feed provides), in practice they are often maintained as separate performative places. The focus in constructing and evaluating messages on situational relevances suggests that it is not perceptual boundaries, in the sense of being able to see, but performative boundaries, as socially constructed and maintained spaces of appropriate action, that are crucial (Cohen, 1985). To attribute social effects to the impact of the medium on perception is to miss the social practices that enable and sustain performative spaces. Cross-posting shows that the situations of newsgroups are mutually visible and accessible to each other and yet still sustained as separate performative spaces.

Having considered the development of a bounded spatiality on Usenet and a connective yet territorially spatialized WWW, it remains briefly to consider relationships between the online spaces of newsgroups and geographic space. The term 'geographic' might appear to suggest an unmediated kind of space that simply exists without human (or technological) intervention. All space can be thought of, however, as in some sense a social achievement as it is interpreted and made meaningful to its inhabitants. One of the most dramatic examples of the social achievement of space is the nation. Nationhood can be thought of as a metaphoric kinship (Erickson, 1997) or an imagined community maintained through circulation of symbols, especially through the mass media (Anderson, 1991). Increased cultural contact (which newsgroups could be seen to encourage) can be seen to create an increase in cultural reflexivity, as people question who they are (Erickson, 1997) or a fragmentation of cultural identity (Featherstone, 1995). Put another way, if the mass media were so implicated in the emergence of the nation in the first place, changes in media such as offered by the Internet provide opportunities for different senses of cultural reflexivity (Lash and Urry, 1994).

National identity was one of the most commented-upon ways in which newsgroup discussions about the Louise Woodward case developed. Louise, as a British subject being tried in the US, became a symbol for national differences between the US and the UK. In some newsgroups, much more explicitly than in web pages, the case was presented as a confrontation between Britain and America. National difference was alluded to more subtly in the mass media, but provoked fierce exchanges on newsgroups. One participant in alt.teens told me:

> I think the louise woodward case became a bit of an anglo-American battle, the yanks wanted her dead, and us Brits being stupidly patriotic, obviously demanded her freedom.

Not only was national identity explicitly expressed on newsgroups, but it also provided a frame through which at least some participants interpreted what went on there. Much of this took the form of the 'crude nationalist invective' and 'acrimonious exchange of ideologies' which Stubbs (1998: 5.4, 5.7) found in soc.culture newsgroups. The case was characterized in newsgroups as exemplifying problems with the American legal system as a whole. Participants expressed their pride or shame in the US and the UK. Louise herself was consistently marked as a British girl being tried in America. Newsgroup discussions explored the potential offered by these characterizations for construing the case as one of national confrontation rather than as an instance of a woman being tried in a court. The Indian dimension noted by soc.culture.indian became a site for playing out the different affiliations that comprised the newsgroup (Mitra, 1997).

What was seen in some of the newsgroups discussing the Louise Woodward case appeared to be not so much a case of cultural homogenization as a polarization or playing out of difference (Preis, 1997), and national identities appeared to be solidified rather than dissolved by the contact. The expression of national identity varies between newsgroups depending on how they are viewed as nationally identified cultural spaces. Performances of national identity are situated. Chapter 6 will show how attributions of bias due to national affiliation were a resource used strategically in newsgroup discussions to undermine accounts. The link between online spaces and offlline geographies was not entirely severed in the Louise Woodward case on the Internet. Neither, however, was this link between online and offline geography and identity universally present. Rather, it was part of a strategic performance which was brought into being as relevant to the social situations which participants understood themselves as being a part of. Recognitions of the Internet as an international yet US-dominated space, and of the Louise Woodward case as a confrontation between nationalities, enhanced the tension between online and offline geographies in this particular instance of Internet usage.

Castells's concept of the space of flows was used here as a device to question whether a different form of spatiality developed through the Internet. Connectivity, as suggested by the space of flows, does turn out to be a major organizing feature of the Internet, particularly the WWW. The understandings which web developers have of the importance of audience and recognition lead them to a concern to maximize connection. Web pages are, however, also viewed as territory, a form of space which stresses boundaries rather than connection. Newsgroups are more straightforwardly rendered as bounded spaces, and rather than a space of flows, the space of place seems to be reasserted online. Offline spaces can be rendered online in strategically situated performances, and in offline settings, such as media representations, the Internet can be portrayed as an important location. It is not fair to say therefore either that the Internet maps straightforwardly on to the space of flows, or that an emphasis on connection automatically transcends concerns about location. As discussed previously in this chapter in relation to time, multiple spatialities coexist but remain meaningful to culturally competent users.

Time, space and technology

Rather than transcending time and space, as some theorists predict, the Internet turns out to have multiple temporal and spatial orderings. These orderings help to make the Internet meaningful in two senses. In the first sense, spatial and temporal orderings help to differentiate areas within the Internet and to make them meaningful as a set of social contexts. In this way the computer becomes, not just one more communication site as Murray (1995) suggests, but a gateway to a diverse array of communication sites. People collaborate to create the temporalities and spatialities which help them to tell when and where they are, when they are on the Internet. In the second sense, the temporality and spatiality of the Internet help to make it a meaningful technology to use, in the local contexts in which content is produced and consumed. Time and space help the users of the Internet to orient themselves towards it and to the other social beings who are construed as inhabiting it. This is particularly apparent in the use of time and space to insert the online world of the Internet into offline contexts, and vice versa. It is through these processes that offline events are portrayed meaningfully on the Internet, and events on the Internet are portrayed offline, for example in the media.

The apparent effects of the Internet on social orderings in time and space are the result of the particular sets of understandings which have been generated around it, and which are interactively available to Internet users through the technology itself. To return to the metaphor of technology as text, we can see that the text is a heterogeneous one, comprising features of both the software and the activities of other users. The users of the Internet read the text in order to develop understandings of the appropriate ways to use the technology. In addition to the activities of other users which they view online, the users of the Internet have a wide array of other resources to draw upon in order to develop their understandings of the technology. Media representations of the Internet help to reinforce the Internet as a unified technology with particular social implications. Materials provided by Internet service providers, guidance from friends, online usage and netiquette guides, and literature on web page design all promote particular sanctioned ways of using the technology.

The observation that the Internet can be seen as a set of diverse social spaces allows us to reflect back on the suggestions considered in Chapter 2 that CMC might have some inherent effects on the ways in which people communicate. The possibility offered by some researchers was that CMC might, because of its narrowing of communication channels, promote decreases in inhibition. This, in turn, might lead to both increases in aggressive behaviour and an equalization in levels of participation in discussion. The problems raised for this explanation by more context-based and ethnographic studies were discussed. On the basis of the multi-sited study described here, it is possible to advance a hypothesis which moves away from positing unidirectional technological influence on online social formations. The hypothesis is as follows: the extent to which particular effects are seen as a result of CMC depends on the perception of the social setting within which the communication occurs. Where CMC is seen as providing a distinct social space separate from offline social spaces, possibilities open up for different kinds of behaviour to become socially sanctioned. Spatial metaphors for understanding CMC, such as cyberspace, promote CMC as a gateway to a different social space. If CMC is seen as a separate space, then it becomes new territory for the formation of behavioural and cultural practices. What appear to be the effects of the technology are rather sets of social practices which have become routinized around the technology.

The Internet (and the offline world) are simultaneously performative spaces and performed spaces. They are performative, in that people try to behave appropriately within them. They are also performed spaces, in that they are shaped and sustained by the social practices through which people interpret and use them. Different practices shape and sustain the WWW and the Usenet newsgroups. To summarize briefly, developers of web pages are oriented to maximizing audience through connectivity within the space of the WWW and through maintenance of pages that are temporally situated as up-to-date in relation to offline events. Web site design is competitive, in that it is aimed at attracting an actual audience from an unknown potential audience, who themselves are differentially distributed across the web. Newsgroup contributors, in contrast, are oriented to producing messages that are situationally and temporally relevant within the space of the newsgroup. Newsgroup use, for active contributors, is collaborative, in that the space of the newsgroup only exists in as far as it is sustained by the posting of appropriate messages. Collaboration and competition entail quite different understandings of the ownership of space and accountability for occupying space. Collaboration suggests that the space is collectively owned, and that one needs to account to the group for one's appropriate occupation of the space. Competition suggests a piece of space that is individually owned and promoted in relation to the territory of others. These two orientations produce the quite different temporal and spatial structures observed in newsgroups and the WWW.

The Internet also provides for ethnography to be differently organized in time and space. The social relations that constitute the ethnography can be forged across greater distances and outside instances of face-to-face communication. They do not, however, lose a grounding in more familiar temporalities and spatialities. Virtual ethnography can exploit mobility to explore the making of spaces and times, and the relationships between them. The mobility of this ethnography across the different social spaces of newsgroups highlighted the ways in which these spaces were sustained in the interactions of participants. I exploited the mobility provided by the dejanews service to explore the differentiation of newsgroup space. This is not to say, however, that the technical mobility provided by dejanews gave me any social mobility. I might have visited the different spaces, as a tourist, but without sustained effort in each space I could not become a participant and fit in. I was, in each newsgroup I visited, quite definitely a stranger. In each new space I had to make an effort to distinguish what features of the Louise Woodward case counted as relevant and what style of interaction the newsgroup routinely practised. There is a ritualized air to newsgroup interactions, and the posting of an appropriately formulated message is a skilled performance (Goffman, 1981). On arrival in each newsgroup I was a stranger, and experienced each time the disorientation of not knowing (socially) where I was.

The ethnography which I conducted oriented towards multiple temporal frames to become meaningful. The first, and most crucial, was finding time for the ethnography, when this had to be fitted in with term times, lecturing schedules, visitors and seminars. Alongside this set of competing pressures, I also experienced a sense of events occurring on the Internet, in tandem with media events, which I needed to catch at the time that they were happening. The framework provided by media events set an expectation that there would be corresponding activity on the Internet, and that not to log on would be to miss something significant. A further temporal structure was provided by waiting for responses from informants, and making sense of the time taken to reply. I found myself being impressed by fast responses, made anxious by delayed ones, and telling myself stories based on what I knew about informants to make sense of an anticipated response not arriving. This reflects the experience which many users also have of using the Internet, and allows for the ethnographer to interpret the experience of other users through a deep sense of the multiple orientations which that experience entails. As Chapter 3 suggested, virtual ethnography is interstitial. I have found it hard to retain this interstitial quality throughout the written ethnography, and have often found myself slipping into the ethnographic present which makes my object of study appear to have an unproblematic ongoing existence (Fabian, 1983). The experience of creating it was far more messy, uncertain and exhilarating.

6 Authenticity and Identity in Internet Contexts

Internet, discourse and authenticity

Chapter 1 gathered together some research questions as foreshadowed problems for the ethnography, which were suggested by a brief literature review. It is now time to consider two more sets of these questions in depth. The questions are as follows:

- What are the implications of the Internet for authenticity and authority? How are identities performed and experienced, and how is authenticity judged?
- Is 'the virtual' experienced as radically different and separate from 'the real'? Is there a boundary between online and offline?

These questions aim to put an ethnographic twist on some features that are commonly attributed to the Internet, namely that it provides new problems in judging what is authentic, and that it provides a virtual sphere of existence separate from the real. The ethnographic angle provides for the application of a form of cultural relativism to the interactions on the Internet. Rather than asking whether Internet interactions are authentic, or whether people really are who they say they are, the ethnographer aims to assess how the culture is organized and experienced on its own terms. The intention is to sidestep questions of what identities really are and whether reality is really there, by shifting to an empirical focus on how, where and when identities and realities are made available on the Internet.

The new technologies of CMC are often said to introduce fundamental problems for judgement of what is and is not authentic. Visual anonymity allows for people deliberately to play with their identities and adopt different personae. There is no guarantee that the identity performances seen in cyberspace will mirror those performed in offline settings. Some people exploit the disjuncture between offline and online identity to explore different roles and personae quite deliberately. MUDs and related role-playing environments can be (although they are not always) explicitly aimed at providing a space for fantasy. The characters that people play on MUDs are 'self-made people' (Reid, 1995: 178). This can be experienced as liberating, providing an environment for trying out new identities or for expressing facets of identity suppressed in offline life (Turkle, 1995; 1996). In many

MUDs, the idea that identities are assumed is routine. The opportunity to play with identity is welcomed, and there is no assumption (if players have acquired appropriate expectations) that people will be offline whom they say they are online. In other circumstances, the realization that roles online may not mirror offline identity can come as a shock. Some more well-known cyberspace stories are about identity play and deceit, such as the story of a male psychiatrist masquerading as a disabled woman on bulletin boards and deceiving her new-made friends and lovers (Van Gelder, 1991; Stone, 1996). The telling of the story serves as a warning to Internet users not to take what they see at (inter)face value. The authenticity of identities on the Internet may be a pleasure or a problem. Whichever it is, some authors see identity play on the Internet as symptomatic of wider cultural shifts, involving the fragmentation of the self (Turkle, 1995; Stone, 1996) or the decentring of the subject (Poster, 1990).

If identity play is as widespread as suggested, this might be expected to have some impact on the extent to which people trust one another, and the ways in which they treat the Internet as a reliable source of information. According to Harrington and Bielby (1995), the conditions for people to trust one another are absent in computer-mediated information exchanges, such as the celebrity gossip forums they studied. They suggest that while in face-to-face settings one uses trust in the person giving out information to assess the quality of the information itself, in computer-mediated settings the conditions for arriving at a relationship of trust are absent. They suggested that this produces a greater emphasis on the attribution of sources as a means to enhance the apparent authenticity of information. There is a tendency to suggest that mediated communication, particularly where it involves visual anonymity, will automatically be accompanied by problems in judging authenticity. Danet is typical in claiming that 'the anonymity and dynamic, playful quality of the medium have a powerful disinhibiting effect on behaviour' (1998: 131) in text-based systems.

The association of the Internet with identity play is not without its critics. On the one hand, some point out that views of identity as performative in all spheres of life predate the Internet and are well established (Wynn and Katz, 1997). Others show that whatever the potential for identity play, many users of the Internet produce quite stable and consistent identity performances. Baym (1998) points out that although there has been an academic fascination with online identity play, the majority of users of the Internet probably do not deliberately construct new identities. In the soap opera discussion group that she studies, participants build up sustained identities that seem consistent with those they sustain offline. Correll (1995) also found high levels of consistency between the identities that her informants performed online and offline. Wynn and Katz (1997) point out that anonymity, far from being ensured by the technology, is largely an illusion sustained through the practices of participants. Tracing statements made on the Internet to real-world referents is not generally impossible. It is not done because of the effort and the resources needed to do the tracing.

To put this another way, the Internet is only a space for identity play as far as the boundary between online and offline is sustained. If this boundary is broken down, the Internet loses its radical potential. Wynn and Katz suggest that the academic (specifically, postmodern) preoccupation with the Internet as a sphere of identity play, fragmentation and virtuality without real referents is not mirrored in the majority of everyday Internet use. The association of the Internet with the authenticity problem is therefore at the least underdetermined (Knorr-Cetina and Mulkay, 1983; Woolgar, 1983) by the technology itself. The conventions are also probably different for different applications: identity play is thought of in relation to MUDs more often than newsgroups.

A further challenge to the notion that inherent features of communications technologies affect their ability to transmit authentic information is posed by Johns (1998). This examination of the history of printing shows that the association of books with stability and reliability is not inherent in the nature of print, but is a cultural achievement. At earlier stages in the history of printing it could not be as readily assumed that each copy of a book would be identical, or that any book would be the product of the named author. This history shows some striking parallels with the current state of concerns about the Internet. It is not always clear that a given statement on the Internet is the product of the person who appears to be the author. This linking of authenticity with identity was raised during the Louise Woodward case, most markedly in the release of Judge Zobel's ruling via the WWW. The problems arose when it became apparent that the judge's ruling, rather than appearing on one web site that would probably become overloaded, would be released by email to several news organizations simultaneously. Suspicions then arose that the process could be sabotaged by someone faking the judge's electronic identity and under that identity sending a message purporting to be the ruling to the news organizations. How then were the news organizations to know whether the ruling they had received was the real one? The problems were debated at length on television and in the newspapers. BBC 'Breakfast News' on 6 November discussed the issue with its expert, the deputy editor of *Internet Magazine*:

> *Interviewer*: So the idea was that news agencies, news organizations would transmit it on their own web sites?
>
> *Expert*: Absolutely. Following this there's I think 12 news agencies approached the judge and said, look, why don't you email, as well as the *Lawyers Weekly*, to all the sites at the same time and so simultaneously it goes to all the network sites?
>
> *Interviewer*: Good idea.
>
> *Expert*: Excellent idea. Bit of a problem though. One of the problems when you send an email, very occasionally people can send maybe an email from me to you with my name on it and I've not actually sent it. It's not very common but you don't want it to happen in cases like this.
>
> *Interviewer*: So the news organizations might get a false email about the judge's decision? They're obviously worried about that.

Expert: They might do. I talked to the head of Reuters and he's trying to coordinate all this and make sure that all the emails come from one source and they run into tremendous technical difficulties and this is nothing to do with the web site, this is just dealing with the email. So now they have this system in place where the judge is going to call each and every one of them an hour before he sends the email to authenticate the fact that it's actually his email. The news agencies then, all of them who are competing for this story, say hang on, that's not fair, such and such may get a call before we do and say look, let's scrap all this and go back to our normal way of working on the courthouse steps, errm, back to paper. So at the moment it's in a state of flux. I talked to them last night.

Interviewer: It doesn't devalue the Internet though, does it?

Expert: It doesn't. It will go through the Internet as well as through the other media.

This interaction plays out the role of the television expert (Fairclough, 1995). The expert, by virtue of experience, qualifications or institutional location (here, the editor of an Internet magazine), is presented as having privileged insight. The authenticity of the report that the expert gives is tied to the authoritative identity performed by and for the expert. The expert is set up by the interviewer as privileged not only to comment on the specific case, but also to interpret the implications of that case for the Internet as a whole. Commentaries such as this one in the mass media serve to establish a unified category, 'the Internet', with particular characteristics and implications. The interview also points to the key role of timeliness for the commercial news organizations using the Internet. For a time, the Internet formed a route via which news organizations might obtain information quickly, thus meeting one of their major preoccupations. The other preoccupation for news organizations, however, is that the information they gather and transmit should be genuine. The Internet, through the judge's email, is marked as a site of potential inauthenticity, where rapid transmission of information is accompanied by the risk that the information might not be true. Authenticity is tied here to the institutionally defined identity of the judge. The only true ruling in this instance was the one that could be trusted as having come from him. To perform the authentic ruling, the email that arrives at the news organization has also authentically to perform the persona of the judge. To verify the authenticity of the message, the news organizations resort to the resources that Wynn and Katz (1997) suggested that ordinary Internet users could, but routinely do not, employ to verify messages. Whether a statement can in principle be verified is different from whether it is in practice verified. The difference depends on the risks associated with trusting the message (or leaving it unchallenged) as well as the levels of trust in the technology and the apparent sender of the message.

This chapter sets out to examine the authenticity problem as manifested (or not) in the Louise Woodward case on the Internet. Building on the ideas of Wynn and Katz (1997), it is taken that both newsgroup postings and web pages are instances of self-presentation which it is hoped will be accepted as appropriate and plausible performances. Discourse analysis (notably the work of Potter, 1996 and Fairclough, 1995) provides some particularly useful resources for developing and maintaining this stance. The techniques of discourse analysis enable us to focus on the ways in which factual accounts are organized to increase impressions of their facticity. Rather than considering whether the accounts that people give one another are true or false, Potter is interested in 'how people themselves manage and understand descriptions and their facticity' (1996: 123). He suggests that there are a range of resources available to people to manage potential challenges to descriptions they produce. Key among potential challenges is that the speaker (or author) is not making a disinterested statement but is saying something biased by their own position, or in some way what they might be expected to say given who they are. The producer of a description might be challenged on the grounds that they have an interest or stake in that description. The question of interest management in descriptions is therefore crucial. It is also crucial that the speaker establishes that they have a right to provide a description, by claiming membership of an appropriate category. This chapter will show that these routine features of the performance of authentic, factual accounts (namely, interest management and category entitlement) are also present in the discussions that occur on the Internet, but are not uniformly distributed.

I made the argument in Chapter 3 that a discourse analytically inflected approach to ethnography might be appropriate to the Internet. The idea was to combine the experientially based knowing of the ethnographer with the detailed attention to interaction that a discourse analyst can apply. Potter's (1996) analysis begins from a point that suggests that descriptions are oriented to produce the impression that they are factual. Whether they are explicitly challenged by interlocutors or not, he suggests that all accounts are produced from an awareness that any account is potentially in competition with alternative versions. This enables him to conduct his analysis of the resources used to maintain the impression of factuality and to defend against potential rebuttals. With the Internet, it is not obvious *a priori* that statements are intended or received as factual. One of the stories told about the Internet focuses quite explicitly on suggestions that truth is no longer a standard to which people aspire. It is important, therefore, to combine the analysis of Internet discourse with an understanding of the context within which that discourse is interpreted (Mulkay et al., 1983). Besides conducting a discourse analysis of the way accounts are organized to display their facticity, it is necessary for me to draw on ethnographic insights to confirm whether indeed the orientation to facticity is a relevant part of Internet use.

Whatever we might think of the position that the authors of web pages or the contributors to newsgroups took up in relation to the Louise Woodward case, there is little doubt that the majority of the traffic related to the case on the Internet consisted of statements about the case and reactions to it, and that these statements become meaningful when viewed as attempts to convince others. Even web sites oriented more towards recognition for the author rather than campaigning or the expression of support were described by their authors as sources of information. This is based on accounts that the web site developers gave to me to justify their activities, and therefore is not immune from the same analytic framework. In their accounts, the web site developers were presenting themselves to me as authentic web site developers. Rather than saying that the production of web sites is really about the provision of information, then, what we can say is that web site developers appear to see it as important that they describe their pages in terms of information provision.

Messages on newsgroups could also be described as oriented towards the production of factual accounts to a large extent. Most of the traffic on newsgroups consists of challenges to statements made by other contributors, for reasons that will be discussed below. With authenticity in mind, I asked several newsgroup contributors what they thought of the quality of information on web sites and newsgroups about the Louise Woodward case and how they assessed the information they got. To one of my informants, Valerie, a regular participant in alt.true-crime, the issue of authenticity in Internet information on the Louise Woodward case was important in making her own contributions meaningful. Here she reflects on the experience of the case, focusing particularly on my question about how information on the net is assessed:

> As I said, I got most of my information from watching the trial. In addition Court tv put up daily summaries on their web site which were objective as much as was possible, I accessed some of the Boston area papers on the net, and I watched a lot of legal commentary shows on TV. There were also some good Woodward web sites to get information from.
>
> . . .
>
> The net is a dangerous place to get information. It travels too fast and wide and anyone says just about anything they want to and people tend to believe what they read without wondering about verifying the source of the information I'ts like a giant gossip and rumor machine.
>
> There were I would say more than 1/2 of the participants on the boards who had not watched the trial and who swallowed any information that was offered in cyberspace that happened to fit in with how they felt about child care, child abuse, people from Britain, working mothers, etc. etc.
>
> The discussions got very heated and resulted in many personal vilifications of the participants. People took sides, not guided by rational thought, but by their emotional reaction to the information, true or not, that they were provided with on the net and on TV.
>
> I almost felt that I was on a mission, and that mission was to make sure that I corrected any misinformation I found on the boards to the best of my ability. It

was really an eye opener as to how many people make their judgements –it was very scary.

One thing that was helpful on the net were the few medical sites that we were able to access to try to put into context some of the medical testimony from the trial.

Valerie makes some clear assessments about the relative merits of different sources of information. For her, the televisation of the trial provided a direct experience of events that positioned her to make assessments of the correctness of other portrayals of the case. She makes a clear distinction between her trusted sources of information and the newsgroups, where she sees her role as being to provide information rather than to consume it. The views of misinformed people are attributed to their reliance on faulty sources: incomplete media information; emotional reactions; and information on newsgroups. In contrast, Valerie portrays herself as competent to find and use credible, objective sources of information and to make reasoned assessments of them. The problem of authenticity, rather than being found in newsgroups *per se*, is located in the individuals who use them. Valerie was an active member of the newsgroup, who had shown a particularly high level of concern with the case and with the attitudes of her fellow newsgroup members towards the case. The willingness to assist in the ethnography revealed features of the situation, and was not neutral. As before, the ethnographer has to take time to look around at their informants in their social setting, to consider in what ways they might be atypical. The informants who discussed their newsgroup involvement with me were often distinctive in their level of concern with the authenticity of what was said in the newsgroup. It cannot be assumed that every participant is similarly concerned. Some might be engaged in the interaction in a more casual way simply for play or the exchange of insults and not to accumulate reliable information at all.

Chapter 5 showed that in the Louise Woodward case on the Internet, temporal and spatial relations played a part in defining what was to count as authentic experience and information. The temporal dimension played on both immediacy and the archival qualities of the Internet. The spatial dimension defined authenticity as being close to the heart of the action, and helped to sustain both the importance of the official campaign site as a privileged source of information and the emerging spatiality of the WWW that grew up around it. Authenticity on the WWW therefore has some ties to temporal and spatial location, which rely on bridging the boundary between online statements and offline events. The rest of this chapter explores other ways in which the accounts of the Louise Woodward case produced by web page authors and newsgroup contributors were organized to increase their apparent factuality. This is not an exhaustive survey of the different resources used, nor is it a systematic mapping of the patterns with which these resources are used. What follows is intended as an evocation of the orientation towards facticity of accounts on the Internet and a demonstration of its diversity. The next two sections of this chapter consider the authenticity problem in relation first to newsgroups and then to web pages. The final section of the chapter then draws together some more general points in relation to virtuality, authenticity and closure.

Newsgroup disagreements

Newsgroups provide a particularly testing ground for the production of factual accounts. Any statement made in a posting can be subsequently challenged by another. Because the setting is construed as interactive, any statement not only in principle is open to challenge, but in practice is often challenged. There is a general practice on newsgroups that agreeing with a posting is not enough to justify posting a message saying that you agree. This avoids the newsgroup being filled with messages that consist of nothing besides 'me too'. It has the effect, however, that the newsgroup can come to seem wholly combative, since disagreeing with a message is seen as a justification for the author to post. Disagreement is often easier than agreeing with the previous poster and also adding something further to the discussion. Chapter 5 established that the newsgroups discussing the Louise Woodward case could be thought of as distinctive spaces. This distinctiveness manifested itself in different topics and styles of discussion that included different ways of framing disagreements. It therefore seems appropriate to consider the organization of discussions in each newsgroup in turn, before considering some more general themes that the comparison of different newsgroups raises. Here I will discuss the issues raised by looking at three of these newsgroups: alt.true-crime, rec.travel.air and alt.teens.

Apart from a few passing references, the discussion of the Louise Woodward case on rec.travel.air was confined to one complex and sprawling thread. This thread, as described in Chapter 5, began when a question was posted relating to Louise's need for a passport on her flight home to the UK. This question generated 58 messages in response. Of these, 19 were concerned with the dispute over whether the thread was related to the newsgroup. The 39 remaining messages referred to some aspect of the case, from specifically air-travel-related aspects to general views on the case itself. Those that referred specifically to air travel were largely posed in a style which stated what was normally the case for travelling by plane and applied it to the case in question. These were unmodalized (Latour and Woolgar, 1986; Potter, 1996) and unattributed statements of fact:

> Because even her face on the front of his morning newspaper won't persuade a UK immigration officer to let her in without a passport. Rules are rules you know!

> The Customs and Immigration computers need to know that the passport number (therefore the individual is out of the country) so that various subsequent scans for overstayers don't 'pick her up' needlessly.

These general statements were rarely disputed, despite the lack of corroborating evidence advanced. Challenges to general statements were often indirect, questioning the relevance of the statement rather than the statement itself. A subsidiary question was asked, concerning how Louise came to be travelling first class rather than economy. One response was as follows:

> It could have got rather out of hand if she was stuck in the middle of economy with all those reporters on board not to mention other curious passengers. Logically it was better for everyone to stick her out of the way in row 1.

A subsequent poster, rather than disputing this reasoning directly, quoted the message above and added the following:

> Her FC tix were paid by some anonymous benefactor – she was not upgraded by the airline.

The juxtaposition serves as a challenge to the previous account. The two messages side by side make sense if we read the second as refuting the first by making it irrelevant.

I received the impression of a stock of group knowledge about air travel that was being creatively applied to the case in question. While the way in which this knowledge was applied might be controversial, the knowledge itself was sufficiently established to be stated without sources or qualification (such as 'I think', 'I believe') and to pass unchallenged. As Fairclough (1995) points out, presuppositions can be used to position the audience as already part of the same world-view as the author. By drawing on facts presented as what everyone knows, the author constructs a community already positioned to agree with what they say. In challenging the presupposition, the readers would be marking themselves as not part of the community. Invoking a presupposition can therefore help to render a statement more robust. The presupposition can also be used to provide for humour. One poster explicitly constructed a sense of what the group knows to support a joke:

> Well, I wonder who assaulted the children on that flight. Instead of being the flight attendants as we usually hear in this group, I wonder if they deferred to our gal Louise, being that she's rather good at it. :-)

In contrast to statements of fact about air travel, statements of fact about the case itself were frequently challenged. An exchange of single-line remarks by two posters (from one, 'Thank God, she's home', with the response 'Yeah, good to hear that that trash is out of the US!'), was treated as an opportunity to make an argument based on statements of facts about the case. This posting can be read as accusing the former poster of making an irrational or unsupported reaction. It makes a direct address to the poster of the previous message and assembles a series of reasons for adopting a different point of view:

> Good to hear you're so tolerant. Did it ever occur to you that there may have been some credence to reports from other au pairs who interviewed for the same position that the mother of the child who died was a 'very scary person'? Given this information and the vindictiveness the parents have shown in filing a civil suit against someone who probably can't afford to pay any judgement, I personally doubt Woodward did it. She's just lucky she got out of the country before she was charged again, and again and again.

Potter (1996) points out that addition of detail can be a mixed blessing for constructing authentic accounts. On the one hand the addition of detail can be seen as contributing to an air of authenticity. On the other, it opens multiple possibilities for the account to be challenged on points of detail. The posting above received two point by point refutations, disputing the interpretation placed on events in the case. Rather than disputing the order or occurrence of events, the interpretation placed upon those events was brought into question. One person replied that it was unfair to cast the 'desire of two bereaved parents to prevent the killer of their child from profiting by it' as a vindictive act. This received the response that 'they didn't seem overly bereaved to me'.

While comments about air travel generally were rarely disputed, except in their relevance, statements about the case and particularly interpretations of motivations often were. This frequently involved direct contradictions, based on what would or would not be a reasonable interpretation or action. While it might be implied that other participants were biased or irrational, this was rarely stated explicitly. Only in one case was the history of a participant in the group drawn upon to construct a picture of her reaction to the Woodward case as biased:

> I believe it was [name of participant] who wrote 'not guilty'. Wasn't it [name of participant] who was recently going on and on about how much she hates kids? Perhaps that is why she would side with the likes of Woodward.

The idea that this participant dislikes children, together with the unappealing behaviour of going 'on and on', does much to undermine any statements this participant might subsequently make about the case.

Very few of the messages referred to sources for the information they gave, whether about the Louise Woodward case or about air travel. The style of statements on rec.travel.air relating to the Louise Woodward case was largely speculative, referring to what one might expect or what might reasonably be thought to be the case. This contrasted with the more assertive style of statements about air travel, cast in a tone of uncontroversial fact. A consideration of other threads of discussion on the same newsgroup suggests that the discussion of the Louise Woodward case could be thought of as rec.travel.air at play. In other threads, statements about air travel might indeed be seen as controversial, and participants called upon to support their statements and provide sources. As well as a specific style of interaction within the newsgroup, there are styles specific to particular threads of discussion.

A very different style of interaction and authenticity performance was seen in alt.true-crime. While rec.travel.air discussed the Louise Woodward case as a form of play, alt.true-crime oriented to discussion of the case as part of its serious business. The relevance of the case for discussion in the group was not a matter of dispute. The Louise Woodward case arose many times over and was discussed at length by the group. Here I will focus on one thread, with the subject line 'Is Louise Woodward guilty or innocent??', which contained 172 messages. The thread began with a message posing a question:

> So what is the story? Is she guilty or innocent? And please verify your claims.

This message sets the tone for what is to follow. Participants are being asked, not for their opinions or reactions, but for their substantiated and reasoned assessments. The majority of participants who responded adhered to this request, which is typical of the style of the newsgroup as a whole. One sequence of messages was triggered off by a response that stated:

> And the babies mom was never around to raise the child. What kind of mom does that but a murderous one?

In some newsgroups the response to this statement might have been a questioning of the interpretation that this places on a set of actions. In alt.true-crime, it led to a sequence of messages that questioned its factual basis:

> [Name of poster] did you watch the complete trial? If you did you would know that Matty's mother (Deborah) only worked part time, not full time and she was around a lot for her children, since she also came home every day for lunch also to breast feed on the days she was working. I personally don't consider working three days a week as not being around for your child. I don't think most do.

This message begins by directly addressing the poster of the previous message, and casting doubt on his ability to speak about the trial. His remarks are positioned as illegitimate since he has the facts wrong, which is taken as suggesting that he cannot have watched the whole trial. Facts are construed as things that emerge directly from the trial and that would speak for themselves if one had heard them. A response to this message transformed the status of the account that the previous poster presented:

I have heard this myth too. That she came home to feed her baby on the days that she worked. Was it just horrible coincidence that she didn't come home on the one day that something seriously bad was happening?

In marking the story as 'myth', the poster renders herself as competent to see through it, and suggests that its adherents are unthinking or credulous. The mythic status of the mother's lunchtime visits was then in turn challenged, and marked as the product of the previous poster's biased inattention to facts:

She did and the baby was perfectly fine at lunch time. You obviously know very little about this case. You apparently don't want any facts intruding on your belief in Ms. Woodward's innocence.

A final response, rather than directly addressing the previous posters or producing reasons for their (mis)interpretations, focuses on the original basis of the disagreement:

I saw the trial a while ago obviously and am beginning to fade on the details but I dont think she came home that day in fact there was a lot made of her supposedly being too busy to even call, which she explained on the stand. Monday was the day she was close enough to come home, the days she was in surgery, This was a Tuesday.

Courttv has a site on America On Line if you can access it where they have a daily summary of the trial.

This message might appear to be undermined by the author's statement that she is relying on her own faulty memory. The amount of detail that she then assembles, however, renders this statement somewhat disingenuous: far from fading, her memory seems very good. The level of detail is far greater than that which the previous posters assembled. It seems that the admission of a potentially faulty memory serves to immunize the account against attack, as 'a little confessed "evil" saves one from acknowledging a lot of hidden evil' (Barthes, 1973: 42). By telling us that she is relying on her memory the poster diffuses any potential claims that the information she gives is faulty, and by not checking her facts although she could, she displays a confidence in her memory which readers are invited to share.

The key category entitlement which participants claim to enable them to make authoritative statements about the case is that of having watched the entire trial or read the evidence. Participants who have only watched parts of the televisation are frequently cast as lacking in the perspective to make a judgement. One participant casts this as promoting a national bias:

IMHO I do think a lot of people in the UK were misinformed about the trial and the evidence. I have one of the people on my mailing list who lives in the UK ([name of informant]) he surprised us by letting us know that they weren't showing the Nanny trial as it was called then in the UK. They finally started showing the trial once the defence started their case, thus a lot of critical evidence wasn't shown to people over there about what happened to Matty, and since they had only seen the defence case, common sense would make them think she wasn't guilty. [Name of informant] did inform us after the trial and the lowering of the decision the papers started reporting the DA's side and people who were thinking she was innocent seemed to change their minds after seeing both sides of the case.

This statement contains several features that help us to reach the conclusion that the author is making a reasoned judgement and is not guilty of a prior prejudice against the people of the UK. While she marks her statement, with the common abbreviation IMHO, as her humble opinion, she then goes on to assemble a considerable array of evidence why we should consider her opinion a valid one. She cites a source who lives in the UK and therefore might be expected to be able to give information about the UK media, and includes additional detail (the 'Nanny trial') to give her account authenticity. That this information is not something she sought or assumed is further provided for by the statement that she was surprised by it. The possibility that she might be prejudiced is further diffused by the presentation of the perceptions of the UK public as quite understandable, given what they were shown. Two clear categories are established: those who have access to the full trial and can therefore make reasoned assessments; and those who have not seen the full trial, and therefore make unfounded (sometimes biased) assessments. The attribution of the second category was frequently used to undermine accounts, as in the following two excerpts:

These two points are merely your *opinions*. You may have to throw in a little about your True Reality next time so everyone can catch the full drift of your *opinions*.

Why can't people look at the testimony in this case, like apparently only the Judge was willing to do????

A further category entitlement that some participants claimed for themselves was that of expert knowledge or experience that gave them a special insight into the case:

I've never in my life heard of a baby being perfectly fine, then all of a sudden presenting with critical brain damage and a swollen face from an old injury. I worked in a hospital for years, saw lots of injuries to children and I don't believe it for a minute.

This account works on contrasts and extremes to make its point: 'perfectly fine', 'all of a sudden', 'for years' and 'lots of injuries'. The claims made in this post were disputed in the following message:

Your personal experience I think cannot be substituted for the opinions of experts who have studied thousands of cases. There was an honest difference of opinion about this particular case but no one, not even the prosecution, was saying what you are here, that it could never happen.

There is much evidence of other cases where it did happen. This was documented at the trial.

I would suggest you find out the facts of this case. Matthew did not have a swollen face. Where did you get that from?

The response disputed both the extent of the claim to expertise (in comparison with 'experts who have studied thousands of cases') and its pertinence to this case. The poster of the previous message is portrayed as mistaken in the extent of her experience, as having reached an extreme conclusion that was not even shared by those who might be expected to have held it, and as having mistaken the factual basis from which she made her inferences. This is a comprehensive attack on the poster's credibility. The only part of the original message that seems to pass undisputed is that the original poster does indeed have the experience of working in a hospital that she claims.

In alt.true-crime, to mark a feature of a posting as an opinion is to undermine its factual status and point to its potential inauthenticity. Participants are involved in interest management, to make their statements seem unbiased. A routine and effective way of undermining someone else's claim is to suggest that they are stating opinion rather than fact. In other words, the presupposition invoked by participants in this instance is that facts exist, and are inherently superior to opinions. To disagree would be to mark oneself as deviant from the group. This approach to opinions is not shared across all newsgroups. In alt.teens, the status of opinions also arose but was approached very differently. It was quite common for participants to mark their contributions as opinion, as the following poster does:

Just for the record, I also believe she is innocent, but I haven't heard all of the trial, so I would know for sure. Like pretty much everyone else, I'm basing my opinion on the 'she couldn't have done it' philosophy, which is really worthless, but powerful nonetheless.

In contrast to alt.true-crime, where facts were considered transportable between contexts, and therefore worthy of being considered seriously within the newsgroup, in alt.teens a clear distinction was drawn between the conclusions drawn by the jury who were there and heard the evidence, and the opinions of those in the newsgroup who were not present and therefore did not have access to the facts. There was a general acknowledgement that contributions could only be opinions, and that this was a valid basis on which to make a contribution. A statement that was unmarked as opinion could be seen as controversial. One such message emphatically asserted Louise's innocence:

She's INNOCENT –
Its just the yanks trying to act like arseholes
(but are they acting?)

Several responses quoted only the 'She's INNOCENT' part of this message. The following response disputes the factual basis of the statement of Louise's innocence, and the depth of the original poster's commitment to her innocence. The impression given is that what was stated as fact is instead to be considered a shallow reaction:

> No, she's free and cleared of all charges it appears now. Let us know when YOU have kids and you hire her as a baby sitter.

Many posts were explicitly oriented to considering the relative status of what happened in the courtroom and what happened on the newsgroup. These were often provoked by direct challenges aimed at the basis for opinions expressed by participants. At these points participants often provided more detailed accounts of how they came to hold the opinions that they expressed. One form referred directly to the factuality of events in the courtroom as a basis for valid opinion:

> How come you know she's innocent? – and don't ask me how come I know she's guilty because I don't but I do have the support of the jury who were actualy in the court room not that that matters if you read most replies on this string.

Another way of buttressing an opinion cast this acceptance of events in the court as naive, and suggested instead that close examination of the evidence was the only sound basis for a conclusion:

> Oh grow up you stupid child, I stated my opinion, if you can't accept that people have different opinions to yourself, then, what can I say, its probably a waste of my time bothering to write this to you. I wouldn't consider the 6 weeks I spent studying this case a waste of time, it was part of my English course at College, and the more one reads into it, the more you see how the little, more ignorant of the population will fall for the media hype, have you actually examined the medical evidence, or are you some stupid kid who has read a few articles in a kiddy magazine.
>
> You claim that just because a jury of 12 found her guilty the they must be right, if you believe the courts are always right, then you're more naive than I thought.

A third way of buttressing an opinion involved explicit acceptance of diversity, such that each opinion would not be construed as a direct challenge to others that differed. This version renders the opinion the property of the individual, and allows for a population of contradictory opinions to coexist:

Look, I was stating MY opinion on the matter, excuse me if I don't fall over crying because its different to yours.

Alt.teens was marked out from alt.true-crime by a very different understanding of the social context in which discussions took place. Discussion for its own sake, based on opinions supported by a variety of resources, was a characteristic of alt.teens. By contrast, alt.true-crime based discussion around the separation of fact from opinion, and the celebration of the former over the latter. Discussion in alt.true-crime provided the greatest emphasis on category entitlement and interest management (Potter, 1996). The first newsgroup considered, rec.travel.air, combined the construction of a sphere of taken-for-granted knowledge about air travel with a speculative assessment of the Louise Woodward case. The reaction of each group to the case enacted a specific and distinctive social space. In each newsgroup, the discussion continued in situationally specific and situationally relevant ways. Orientation to authenticity was a key way in which these social spaces varied. Posters could display themselves as competent members of the group by making the right kinds of authenticity claim and counter-claim.

The three newsgroups, despite their very different orientations towards authenticity and the status of discussions about the case, have one crucial element in common. In none of the discussions that I followed were posters undermining the identity statements of others. Many features of an account might be challenged, but this was never extended to a direct challenge that someone was not who they said they were. Challenges were more frequently oriented to undermining the relevance of someone's experiences or claim to expertise, rather than the claim itself. It might be that without resources to make plausible a suggestion that someone is not who they claim to be, this is simply not a strong rhetorical strategy. The overall impression is of a much more matter-of-fact approach to identity than the theorists of identity play suggest. This is not to suggest that everyone using the newsgroups has a naive view of identity as a transparent portrayal of what a person is. It is simply that discussion goes on as if identities exist, as they do for the practical purposes of the discussion on newsgroups. The status of identity claims is not a normal topic of discussion in these newsgroups. This is not to say, however, that identity is irrelevant. Expressions of identity are often used to buttress claims for the authenticity of accounts, by positioning the author as particularly well placed to know or to judge. These identity statements are also used by other participants to undermine the factual status of accounts, by leading to bias or being irrelevant. Identity statements are a resource in performing and undermining authenticity.

Harrington and Bielby (1995) noted that identity became particularly controversial on the soap opera discussion group they studied when one participant claimed to be an actor who played a part in the soap. While other identity claims were accepted at face value, this one was greeted with derision and suspicion. Harrington and Bielby point out that it is not necessarily that participants trust all other identity claims, but possibly, more mundanely, that most of the time they simply do not care. The status of the identity claim is not pertinent to judgements of the interest value of what someone has to say. With the claimed actor the identity claim was directly relevant to the topic of the newsgroup, and so was accorded more attention than would normally be the case. By analogy, we might expect the appearance of Louise, one of her family or one of the legal team on a newsgroup to have excited considerable interest and suspicion. In none of the newsgroups I visited did this occur (although I did come across several people claiming to be Louise's boyfriend, and receiving no attention at all!). One of the web site developers who talked to me mentioned one bulletin board system that was a particularly good source of information because of the people who were on it:

> There were a lot of people on this BBS who obviously knew a lot about the case. Louise's sister, Vicky, made some brief appearances to defend Louise, but the main person who seemed to be standing up for Louise was someone called 'Sally'. It turns out that Sally is a very close friend of Louise's mum Sue, and she was in phone contact with Sue on every night of the trial, and for months before. This meant that the info we got from Sally on the BBS was direct from Sue and the defence lawyers, i.e. we were getting a different and very accurate viewpoint which was not from the newspapers (one main thing to come out of this case is the terrible pre-trial publicity which Louise received from the Boston newspapers. The BBS allowed Louise's side of the story to be aired without 3rd party intervention).

The informant's close link to the campaign allows him, retrospectively, to interpret someone who appears well informed on the bulletin board as closely linked to the campaign and to Louise's family. The telling situates the author as appropriately trusting of identity on the Internet, not totally suspicious but not naively credulous either. The important and highly relevant identity becomes established over time and with additional sources of information.

It should be clear from the examples given above that many statements made on newsgroups are oriented towards promoting their own authenticity at the expense of competing accounts. This is not obviously the case for all accounts. Apart from the straight contradictions and detailed rebuttals I have discussed so far, there is a separate genre of messages that I have found difficult to incorporate into a discussion of authenticity. Prominent among these are the jokes and insults exchanged between participants. Insults are often short, and directly addressed towards another participant. A typical example was provided by a thread on rec.travel.air that ended with the exchange of the following messages between two participants who had disagreed:

> You're an ignorant shit.

> So are you.

While we might describe these messages as attempts at factual accounts, this hardly seems the richest way to characterize them. Potter (1996) reminds us that statements have more than simply an epistemological dimension: they not only state facts, but are also produced to perform actions. An alternative focus is then to look at insults in context. When I considered where insults occurred in discussions I could see that they were not randomly distributed, but arose more often towards the end of longer threads. Insults are often used during a thread of discussion to signal that, although one still disagrees (violently!) with another participant, one is either going to change the grounds of the debate or stop discussing the matter completely. The insult diffuses the possibility that silence could be taken as agreement. The insult, of course, does not necessarily close the discussion, any more than the strategies for making accounts convincing guarantee that a statement will be taken as factual. Exchanges of insults often follow, as in the example above, as both participants signal that they are not convinced. The use of insults serves as a reminder that on newsgroups silence can often be mistaken for agreement. Given the avoidance of 'me too' messages, a lack of contradiction is the only sign available to the newsgroup that a performance of factuality has been successful. There are circumstances in which participants wish to deflect the possibility that ceasing to discuss a topic will be taken as having been convinced by an opposing point of view. Insults are a 'lack of reconciliation device' (cf. Gilbert and Mulkay, 1984) which can be employed in these circumstances.

A further, important dimension left out by focusing on authenticity is the extent to which newsgroup discussions are pleasing to participants not just as sources of authentic information, but as experiences that are pleasurable and engrossing. Authenticity is not the only standard that operates to judge discussions, and entertainment counts too. Baym's (1995c) discussion of the use of humour in a soap opera discussion group underlines the importance of discussions being enjoyable as well as informative. Clark found that 'trust and "authenticity" are not central to teen chat rooms: "fun" is' (1998: 179). Of the newsgroups discussed here, this seems best to characterize alt.teens. As one participant told me:

> . . . wherever you turned the Woodward case was in your face, all the papers, the television, so it was natural that it came into the newsgroup. But it blew all out of proportion, none of us in alt.teens knew enough about the case to really comment on it. I think we just enjoyed ripping shreads out of people.

When I received this message I thanked the sender for reminding me that authenticity was not the only way of understanding newsgroup postings.

Identity performance and erasure on the web

Having considered the ways in which issues of authenticity are addressed in newsgroup postings, it is now time to look at web pages. This provides for a comparison between the two technologies as they are understood and enacted by their users. Newsgroup postings are, as I mentioned earlier, placed in a context where they are seen as quite likely to receive a direct challenge. Web pages, by contrast, are more isolated from criticism. A direct challenge, even if it were also posted on the WWW, would not have the advantage of juxtaposition that newsgroup rebuttals exploit. A newsgroup rebuttal is produced in the expectation that readers who saw the original message will also be likely to see the rebuttal. The threading of messages (enabled by making sure that the rebuttal uses the same subject line as the original) and the practice of including quotations makes this a reasonable assumption. A challenge to a web page posted on the WWW could not assume that the same visitors who saw the original page would also see the rebuttal. Because web pages are construed as the territory of individual designers, the poster of a rebuttal has no way of inserting a link from the original page to the rebuttal. There is no reason, in principle, why web developers could not alter each other's pages. File permissions could easily be set to allow others the opportunity to alter a web page, but this is not routinely done. On the contrary, the focus is on protecting one's files against unauthorized alteration. It has become self-evident that web pages are the territory of individuals and institutions, and that altering other people's web pages is the work of hackers and other deviants. These practices set the context for pronouncements made on web pages: they are a piece of owned territory in which the developer has the right of free speech, independent of direct challenges. It might be suspected, then, that web pages would not be as focused as newsgroup postings on averting potential challenges to their authenticity. That this is not so depends on the imagining, in their absence, of an audience who are concerned about authenticity. As discussed in Chapter 5, web page development is made meaningful primarily through the imagining of an audience and the seeking of recognition from that audience. The web audience is imagined as consisting of information seekers, making judgements of the authenticity, timeliness and completeness of the information that they find on pages. It is to this imagined audience that web page developers orient their performances of authenticity.

This imagined audience makes performance of authenticity an important part of the activity of web developers. The rest of this section will explore some resources that web developers use in portraying the accounts on their pages as authentic performances. The first set of resources employed to enhance authenticity depends on strategic use of the author's identity. Some sites contained explanations by the author of whom they were and how they came to produce the site. Mike's site contains a detailed account of his orientation towards the making of his site, appearing on a page with his photograph at the bottom:

> I should say now that I don't actually know Louise Woodward, and I've never been to her home town of Elton.

I'm only a few years older than her. We're different sorts of people though, our worlds are those of different stereotypes. But this sort of thing goes beyond those boundaries. It reaches out to all of society.

I think it was a special program on Channel 4 that summarised the details of court proceedings and show the key testimonies. Seeing the theatrics of the lawyers and the calm composure of Louise. Well, she looked so out of place, so certain of her innocence, so beautiful.

And I knew from that moment on she spoke the truth and I knew it in my heart and soul. And then I saw and read the actual facts of the case and there is no way that Louise is guilty of second degree murder and there is an awful lot of people out there who agree with me.

Anyway I felt really sad about what had happened to her and I wanted to something. So here is what I can do and have done. My webpages.

Mike's statement that he has no direct knowledge of Louise might be seen as a potential threat to the authenticity of his page. The account is organized, however, to provide for a different kind of authenticity. On the one hand, the account assures us of the universality of the case, relevant to 'all of society', and Mike's mention of his viewing of a television pro-gramme about the case assures us that he has a direct experience that qualifies him to have an opinion of the case. His description of his response performs the depth of his conviction that she is innocent and renders it an involuntary response compelled by circumstances and not willed by him. Thus, while not relying on direct experience, scientific knowledge or inside information, Mike is using the resources he has to present a performance of authenticity. The colloquial style, direct address and evaluative statements give the air of testimony (Fairclough, 1995). Ethnographers are not alone in using a first-person reporting of their experiences to try to enhance the authority of a text.

It is notable that Mike's account is based wholly around his experience of viewing media coverage of the case. As was seen in newsgroups, viewing the coverage was claimed as producing an entitlement to make authentic statements. In Mike's telling, viewing the media coverage counts as an authentic experience, which gives him something to tell. In his con-sideration of authenticity and the media Scannell (1996) draws on Sacks's suggestion that having an experience is socially recognized as giving someone a story to tell and a right to speak about it. People therefore routinely recount their experiences for other people, telling what they saw and how they felt. This, for Scannell, raises the question of whether things viewed or heard in the media can act as experience in the same way. Scannell considers that mediated experience does confer an entitlement, in as far as what is seen counts as believable. Being believable confers an external reality on a mediated experience that means it can be talked about and used as the basis for the formation of opinions. The proliferation of web pages about Louise Woodward, produced by people who had never met her and had only followed the case through media reports, testifies that to them the experience of viewing the case counted as tellable experience.

A very different kind of authenticity performance is provided by Jim's recognition-oriented site, offering up-to-date news on the case. The Louise Woodward pages contain little clue to the author's identity. The passive 'This site is updated regulary' suggests an almost automatic procedure, and the reference to comments which 'we have received' constructs an anonymous plural authorship. Further pages on the site continue to refer to the authorship as 'we', and present reports on the case in a passive style, for example 'Allegations have been made'. Throughout, the site manages to give the impression that it is the product of a collective rather than an individual, and that no individual authorship was necessary. That other visitors to the site also received this impression is indirectly suggested by the comments sent in by visitors and published on the site. The opinion page seems to have been treated by visitors as a general bulletin board for announcing their perceptions of the case, rather than to address the author of the page. Some messages specifically addressed advice or support to Louise or Judge Zobel. None that I saw were specifically addressed to Jim, or acknowledged that an individual author was receiving their message. Jim's erasure of his identity is limited to the Louise Woodward pages. Amid the logos at the bottom of the main Woodward page is a single link to 'Visit the Author of this site'. Following this link takes us to Jim's personal home page, which is constructed in a very different style. Here Jim tells visitors about himself and his family, with photographs, and shifts into an active and informal style using the first person. It appears that rather than trying to pretend to his audience that he does not exist at all, his identity erasure is situated within his Louise Woodward pages as an appropriate way to perform within that site. On his more personal pages his identity is reinserted as relevant and appropriate.

In the Official Louise Woodward Campaign for Justice web site the erasure of the author's identity was complete. The email address given for contacting the author is the anonymous 'webmaster'. The site contains little clue to its history or its creator. At the point at which I emailed the author asking if he would help me by telling me about the site, I had no idea whom I might be contacting. I had vague ideas that there might be a group of people involved, but had no sense of where they might be other than in a pub in Elton, and I hoped that the email would be read by an individual, rather than discussed by a group. The reply that I received was a highly personal account. I was delighted that someone of whom I knew so little should have trusted me so much. The 'webmaster' acquired a name, an age, a family, a profession, and a set of emotional involvements and reactions to the case. These stood in a stark contrast to the web site. In fact, his description of his involvement in the case and growing conviction that Louise was innocent was very similar to those that some amateur support site developers posted on their web pages or gave to me privately. The erasure of the web site developer's identity allowed the web site to present itself as the voice of the campaign. To have placed emphasis on a web developer as mediator might have dulled this impact, or introduced doubt that the web developer and the campaign were the same.

If Mike's strategy mirrors the ethnographer's use of the first person to denote an authentic subjective experience, then the official campaign site resembles the scientific style of reporting. In the formal scientific paper, the author is absent in the text. The 'ostentatiously neutral' (Knorr-Cetina, 1981) style of the scientific paper helps to present a view of scientific facts as discovered objects which already exist in the natural world independent of the scientist (Woolgar, 1988). This formulation encourages the perception that the findings have emerged alone without human agency. Allowing the facts to speak for Louise's innocence is a significant part of the rhetoric of the campaign site. Knorr-Cetina (1981) points out, however, that the extent to which the portrayal given in a scientific paper is convincing depends not just on the organization of the paper itself, but also on the institutional sanctioning of this way of presenting science. The persuasiveness of the scientific paper depends on the existence of a community of readers who share a set of reading practices. Although we can see similar forms in the web page, it is not yet clear whether the sets of reading practices to accompany these forms are present.

In looking for the identity of the authors of Louise Woodward web pages, it became apparent that performances of identity did not arise at random within the pages. Rather, identity performance was a strategic resource for web developers to draw upon to enhance the apparent authenticity of their pages. In web pages, the two styles of authenticity performance are not as clearly demarcated as in ethnography and the scientific paper. Varying shades between the performance of a present and experienced author and the complete erasure of the author's identity were observed in the amateur Louise Woodward sites. Many authors mingled the two genres in their sites taken as a whole, for example combining an identity-erasing Louise Woodward section with an identity-performing personal section. Amateur web authors are not constrained by institutional factors to present themselves or their topics in particular, institutionally sanctioned ways. They are free to select, from the range of resources available to them, those that appear most appropriate to convince their imagined audience in each (imagined) circumstance.

Thus far I have focused largely on the textual features of web pages. Images, too, have a part to play in the performance of authenticity. The first notable feature here is that pictures of Louise Woodward were present on most web sites about the case that I found. Chapter 5 discussed the ways in which web developers talked about their choice of images as aesthetic and as portraying particular features of the case or qualities of Louise. Choice of image was portrayed as a thoughtful selection process. Given this focus on individual selection, then, it seems surprising that the same image occurs so often on so many different web sites. The image (Figure 6.1) is of Louise turning towards the camera and smiling, in soft focus, within an

FIGURE 6.1 *Portrait of Louise Woodward displayed on a support web site*

oval frame. Individual variations on this adjust or remove the frame, and enlarge or crop the image. Each author adjusts the image to suit their own site. Clearly, many images were obtained by copying them from other web sites, sometimes with permission and sometimes without. The copying of ⁄images is a generally acknowledged practice among web designers, although those who ask permission are in a safer moral (and legal) position. That so many borrowed this particular image seems surprising. I have not been able to trace its origin, although it seems likely that it first came from the official campaign site. For many web developers this image symbolized their support for Louise. They saw it as representing her innocence. The image was however also seen on sites that portrayed the case in ways they considered less biased. This was a negotiable image, which could symbolize the case overall, or could be interpreted as support. Another image frequently present on supporters' web sites was the yellow ribbon symbol (Figure 6.2). This was never found on the sites that promoted themselves as unbiased. This image, used to symbolize someone whose return is awaited, was widely used by the campaigners for Louise Woodward to symbolize their support for her. By including the yellow ribbon symbol on their pages, web designers marked themselves out as true supporters.

Besides images, other kinds of content were clearly circulating between web sites. External sources of information, such as reports from news organizations, were often explicitly attributed to a source that we might assume was intended both to provide due acknowledgement for borrowed material and to attest to the authenticity of the information. Transcripts taken from television programmes were also marked with their origin. Official reports such as the appeal ruling from the SJC were often appropriated by web designers and incorporated into their own sites. It would have been possible simply to link to the official report, rather than making

FIGURE 6.2 *Yellow ribbon image displayed on Louise Woodward support web sites*

a copy of the information. To do this, however, would have risked losing visitors to the (competing) site. By keeping the official ruling in their own file space, the web developer also maximized the chances of keeping a visitor on their own site for longer. In addition, creating their own copy of the official ruling made it possible for the web developer to imprint their own style on the report. Many developers had a distinctive style for their Louise Woodward site, with common colour, logo and menu bars. It would have been possible, then, for the official SJC ruling to be made to look like the rest of the page. Usually, however, this was not done. Even where a logo was applied to the top of a page or a distinctive colour scheme used, commonly the SJC ruling was displayed in the form in which it was first released, and in the same font. This font was often quite distinct from that used in the rest of the site. One interpretation might be that this form displays the status of the official report and marks it out from the rest of the site. The use of a different font is the equivalent of a different voice (an expert, a witness) being employed to construct a narrative in a television programme (Fairclough, 1995). Using a different voice adds authenticity to the account by lending it corroboration. The same could be said of the decision I took to present contributions from informants without correction of spelling or grammar to accompany the analysis in this text.

Another use of the alternative voice was explicitly to mark out the author's voice or opinion from what is left, which is by implication objective reporting. Mike introduced his account of an interview with Louise thus:

Here are some of the things she said (I write this from notes I made) :
My observations are in italics.

Similarly, several sites separated out 'opinion' from 'latest news' or 'the case so far'. Where the author had expressed a link with the case through identity performance, opinions might be considered appropriate, but even in this instance they were often carefully separated out from fact. By including information from respected sources, and by marking these out as different from the voice of the author, the Louise Woodward sites strove to present a robust narrative about the case.

This section has shown that within the general aim of producing plausible sites for audiences, a variety of strategies are available to web site authors. These strategies include the two poles of identity performance and identity erasure. Identity performance situates the author within the page and promotes the page's contents as closely tied to the author's own experiences and expertise. Identity erasure involves presenting information as having an independent existence. Identity performance or erasure aims to set a framework within which the site can be interpreted, either as a considered and sincere response to events, or as an objective portrayal of those events. Beyond identity as a resource to be drawn on for promoting authenticity, other frequently occurring features of web sites perform the authenticity of the information they contain. These include the attribution of external sources for information, the adoption of stylistic features to signal externally sourced content, and the choice of images to convey a desired message or display membership of a community. These resources are in addition to the features of timeliness and connection to key locations seen as crucial in promoting web site recognition (Chapter 5).

Performances of authenticity might be thought of as ways of inducing trust in the information presented among the audience. Authors use the full array of aesthetic and discursive strategies available to them to make their pages convincing. They have little feedback on the success of these strategies other than the hit counters and visitor statistics. Pages might perform authenticity, but this does not guarantee that visitors are convinced. Web authors and ethnographer alike are attempting to predict the reactions of visitors to pages without direct confirmation of the validity of their attempts. As an ethnographer I have developed my own reading practices, and I can feel confident that I am a culturally competent web surfer. This chapter is based both on the analysis of the texts that I found on the Internet and on the skills that I developed to enable me to read and interpret what I found. Given the lack of publicly available displays of assent for web pages, there is no other way within the framework of this ethnography to judge the success of authenticity strategies. To obtain further insights on the success of authenticity strategies it would be necessary to focus on the consumers of web pages rather than the producers upon whom this study has been based. There is still much need for studies that look at how people search for and interpret the information that they find on the Internet.

Virtuality, authenticity and closure

Within this chapter I have relied heavily on a form of ethnography informed by discourse analysis. The techniques of discourse analysis provide a tool for exploring the ways in which accounts are constructed to make them convincing and a resource for the ethnographer to help maintain a sceptical, stranger perspective towards the observed features of text. The robustness of discourse analytic accounts relies upon the analyst being able to present herself as a competent cultural member who can interpret talk and texts as other cultural members would. This provides the grounds for a discourse analysis rooted in the everyday understandings which participants have of their interactions. While discourse analysts of everyday talk can present themselves as already being culturally competent, in less familiar circumstances it is useful to pay attention to the process of becoming a competent cultural member. This helps to make visible features of interactions that are taken for granted.

Using this discourse analytically inflected ethnographic approach, it was possible to see that many, although not all, of the interactions on the Internet referring to the Louise Woodward case were organized to promote authenticity. On newsgroups, the performance of authenticity was a dynamic process, with accounts being presented and undermined by participants in an ongoing interaction. Comparison between newsgroups revealed multiple standards and performances of authenticity, played out differently in different settings. Within web pages the performance of authenticity was no less visible, but here the performance was relatively static. On web pages personal testimony, objective statement and externally attributed sources combined with the choice of images, fonts and layouts to produce a page which web developers hoped their visitors would treat as authentic information about the case. Web developers drew on multiple voices to produce these authentic narratives.

In both newsgroups and web pages, performances of authenticity drew strategically on performances of the author's identity to support their claims. Even in the dynamic forum of newsgroups these identity claims were rarely challenged. While their relevance might be disputed in particular contexts, the validity of the claims was not brought into question. This might suggest that other participants simply do not have the resources to mount a convincing rebuttal of an identity claim. Alternatively, we could say that it is not pertinent to the discussion, for most purposes, whether or not someone is who they say they are. Identity performances are taken as given where trusting does not imply any risk or stake. This is not a naive trust, but a situated trust that depends on what the stakes are in taking a statement of identity at face value. For news organizations, the stakes were high in taking a ruling which was apparently sent by the judge as actually sent by him, and hence a large amount of effort was put into checking the identity of the sender. Higher stake relationships are only likely to be formed where identities have emerged over time or have been validated by multiple sources. The 'strange case of the electronic lover' (Van Gelder, 1991; Stone, 1996) is remarkable because of the investment that the perpetrator made in creating and sustaining an identity, and the resources that were finally invested to undermine that identity. In the majority of Internet interactions that level of investment is absent. For the most part the approach to identity taken in this ethnography mirrors that of participants in newsgroups. I set out not to investigate who people really were, but to interact with the features of their identities with which I came into contact. Identities have been treated as situated performances, and as resources for the undermining of accounts. I have not set out to make definite statements about who people are when they are offline, and thus I have not invested the resources (telephone calls and visits) to undermine online accounts of offline identities. At the outset, the aim of this ethnography was to experience Internet interactions on their own terms, as other users of the Internet might do.

Where authenticity and identities are performed, a link between the offline and the online is also rendered. People speaking about who they are and what is the case are making a statement about a feature of the offline world. Rather than the Internet severing links with the offline, these links are strategic performances. The offline world is rendered as present within the online spaces of interaction. It is not true to say, then, that the virtual automatically transcends the real. The spaces of interaction might be differently configured and differently experienced, but they do not lose all reference to offline realities. The offline world, here the identities and experiences of participants portrayed in relation to the events of the Louise Woodward case, structures and provides reference points for the online interactions. Baym says that 'on-line groups are often woven into the fabric of off-line life rather than set in opposition to it' (1998: 63). In the context discussed here we might reverse this observation and suggest that offline experiences are woven into the fabric of online groups. An offline reality in which the case happened and was available to be experienced by all concerned provided the presumed common ground for discussions to take place and performances to be situated. Rather than playful postmodernism, this looks more like what Stubbs describes as 'the last refuge of a peculiarly modernist discourse and politics' (1998: 6.3).

Although not the focus of the ethnography described here, these interactions also provide fertile ground for considering responses to mass media coverage of events as publicly available experiences. While use of and trust in electronic news sources might be increasing more generally (Jones, 1997b), this was not particularly apparent in the online discussions of the Louise Woodward case. Those discussing the case on the Internet considered that they were enabled to do so by virtue of having watched the case on television. Supplementary information might be gleaned from the WWW, but usually the primary source, or the impetus to search out further information, came from the television coverage. Despite the presence of the Internet, it seems that the role of the mass media in providing for shared experience of distant events is not diminished. Indeed, it could be said that the international nature of Internet interactions depends on events being available cross-nationally. Events covered by television across national borders provide the ground for discussions of those events. Far from replacing the older mass media, the

Internet relies upon them in some settings to structure debate among participants on the grounds of common experience. It is precisely because television is understood to make private experiences into publicly available events, upon which everyone who sees them can feel justified in holding an opinion, that it is such a powerful resource for Internet discussions. The Internet builds on the objectification of experience which television provides (Scannell, 1996). The Internet has become a space where reactions to television viewing, once maybe privately expressed in the living room or between friends and family, become public themselves. Opinions become interactively available and publicly expressible. There are rich grounds for research into the extent to which this interaction might transform the television viewing experience itself.

It is very hard to judge whether ultimately expressions of fact on the Internet are judged as convincing. Whether people believe what they read is not generally made available on the Internet itself. Opportunities for agreement to be expressed are closed off by the focus in newsgroups on expressing dissent, and by the closing of web page territories from visible engagement by readers. Without following the reactions of individual readers, whether they are web surfers, active newsgroup participants or lurkers, it is very difficult to judge the criteria used to interpret Internet information. Some clues are available from the ways in which participants use their own resources as readers to shape their own attempts to convince others. Their understandings of reading practices are incorporated into web pages and newsgroup postings. These observations are, however, limited to understanding the cultural competences of a particular subset of Internet users, the active producers. There is a long way to go in learning about the reading practices of the consumers of Internet content who do not leave traces of their interpretations. Without this, we have little way of telling whether the performances of authenticity and identity of Internet producers are considered convincing. If there is any kind of closure to Internet discussions, it occurs in spaces other than those that this ethnography traversed. Closure is not globally available, but happens in the local spaces of individual Internet users sitting in front of their computer screens. If we look only at newsgroup contexts, discussion 'seems to have a rhizomatic element, for there is no beginning, no end, all happens in the middle' (Lotfalian, 1996: 131). Discussion and closure have come to occupy different social spaces. This is not to say, however, that the closure in the local contexts of use is any more final than the ends of discussions in newsgroups. Gilbert and Mulkay give an important reminder that closure, too, is a 'contextually variable' (1984: 112) discursive phenomenon. In the form of consensus over scientific facts, for them closure is a part of discourse and a rhetorical strategy, rather than being an unproblematic observation of a state of affairs. We would, then, have to look also at the context within which someone declared that they were convinced or not by the truth of something which they read online, and to consider where closure was being performed, to whom, and to what purpose.

It would have been pleasing to have constructed this ethnography in a way that mirrored the ambivalence around closure that it uncovered in the Internet. Concerns about narrowing the readership prevented me from producing one of the 'messy' ethnographic texts in which anxieties about postmodernism and reflexivity are played out on the page (Marcus, 1998). However, it has not been my intention to produce a text that closes down absolutely on the interpretive flexibility of the Internet or the ethnography. I have tried throughout to make clear the contingencies that shaped the ethnography and to make open the possibility of alternative interpretations to the ones I have favoured. At the same time, I have relied upon the traditional ethnographic devices of first-person, experientially based knowledge to bolster the authenticity claims of my text. Had I been more concerned to open the text to interpretation, I might have mirrored the style of the newsgroup and continually undermined my own accounts. I could have used an alternative voice to articulate the confrontational style that characterized some of the newsgroup discussions I studied. There are precedents for ethnographies to be written in this way. The dialogic style is not confined to newsgroups, and has been employed in 'new literary forms' as an attempt to address reflexivity within the text (Ashmore, 1989; Mulkay, 1985; Woolgar, 1988). The second voice is introduced into the text on the reader's behalf, in an attempt to undermine the claims of the author to objective truth. Instead of undermining my own text in this way, I have produced a document which assembles multiple voices in a static text, mirroring the style of a web page that performs the identity of its author to reinforce its own claims to authenticity. The introduction of the voices of my informants into the text promotes my account as an authentic record of experiences. Just as with the web page, the interpretation is up to the reader, but is unlikely to be made available within the text itself. Readers who want to make their interpretations available will need to use other media and other contexts. In that sense, conventional books and web pages are, after all, rather alike.

7   Reflection

Given the remarks made in this book about the practice of extrapolation from extreme examples it hardly seems appropriate to finish by making a counter-claim of the same order about the implications of the Internet. Part of my argument is that understandings of the Internet are, at most, only locally stable phenomena, and the understanding developed in this book stands alongside them rather than pretending to globality (Marcus, 1997). The Internet is a text that is both read and written by its users. It comes into being through the activities of its users, and its capacities are made through the web pages and newsgroup messages they produce and through the multiple representations of what it is and what it can do. I will therefore refrain from using this final chapter to sum up the implications of the Internet, or indeed to tell you how you ought to study it. Instead, I will use this chapter to assemble some reflections on the process of the ethnography and its implications and to point out some of the more obvious areas which this ethnography has left unexplored.

Why do they do it?

The question that I am most frequently asked when I talk about the Louise Woodward support sites that form the material for my ethnography is, 'Why do they do it?' It is generally expected of ethnographers that they will have stories to tell of the strange practices they have encountered in the field, and that while their more formal statements might concentrate on theoretical niceties, in less formal settings they can be persuaded to 'dish the dirt'. The question therefore reveals an assumption that there is more to the ethnography than has been reported in academic form. It also displays a wide cultural distance between my academic audiences and the web authors I describe. The question feels like one which a good ethnographer should be able to answer. In Geertz's sense of 'reducing the puzzlement' (1993: 16) which other people's ways of life can evoke, I should be able to provide an answer which is comprehensible in the cultural world which my audience inhabits. I should be able to tell them something in their own terms about the way of life of the people I studied. And yet I was often stumped for an answer to the question. Its brevity seems to demand a brief, pithy answer, and there was none to give which did justice to the diversity and commitment shown by the web authors I had encountered in the ethnography. I had many detailed observations to make on the organization of web pages in time and space, but my audiences (and I) remained unsatisfied. Finally, at a late stage in the analysis and writing of the ethnography, I feel that I am in a position to give an answer.

'Why they do it' is because they share a set of understandings which render the production of a web page as a form of social action. Without this set of assumptions the production of a web site can seem a bizarre activity to spend large amounts of one's time upon, as my audiences found. The action which the production of the web page represents is different for different authors. For many, the production of a web site in support of Louise's case represented the action of doing something for Louise. Producing a web page can count as a form of 'witnessing' or expressing a reaction to events, as Stubbs (1998) found for newsgroups. Web page production also represented other kinds of social action, such as gaining a reputation as a good web designer, which in turn might lead to benefits in career terms, or in the receipt of more resources from ISPs. The basis then for understanding why they do it is to recognize that the web page, for its designers, represents a social action which has meaning to them and which they consider will have meaning for its recipients. The two purposes of web sites, to stimulate support for Louise and to gain recognition for the web site designer, take different priority depending on the particular designer. Both, however, depend on an ability to construe web site design as social action. This ability to recognize the production of a web page as a form of social action is one part of the cultural competence necessary to make use of the Internet meaningful. This competence involves the conceptualization of the web page as a means of communicating with an audience, the ability to read the temporal collage of the web and to negotiate the space of flows, and the ability to produce appropriate displays of authenticity.

The achievement of web site production as a meaningful kind of social action rests on a particular set of understandings of the technology, the audience and the relations in time and space. Web page designers routinely position their actions against the possible reactions of their audiences, and tailor their pages to maximize the chances of the audience revisiting the site. This includes a concern with incorporating appropriate performances of authenticity into a page. Conceptions of the audience include concerns with the speed of downloading, the concern with up-to-date or complete information, and the provision of a useful set of links. In conceptualizing the audience web page designers make their activities meaningful to themselves. The audience for web pages is not always simply on the web: in other incarnations the audience can include other web designers, potential employers, family and friends, and Internet service providers.

In temporal terms, the web site designers, rather than seeing their pages as free-floating in timeless time, often quite deliberately locate their pages in time. Web page time is linked to the timescales promoted by media reporting of events. Web pages, however, also take time. The interaction of web time and life time (to borrow from Traweek, 1988a) for developers means that experiencing the imperative to produce an up-to-date page does not always translate into the reflection of developments in pages. This complex relationship between web time and life time produces the mixing of tenses and temporal locations that Castells (1996a) refers to as the temporal collage. It is however over-simplistic to treat the temporal collage as a disorienting phenomenon which reduces reliance on linear time. In their practices web designers show themselves as competent in negotiating the temporal collage and relating it to the progress of events in linear time. In practice the temporal collage neither floats free nor is disorienting.

In spatial terms, it is fair to say that conventional understandings of space as relative distance are difficult to apply. The web designers' understandings of space focus on connection rather than on relative distance. The most important task for them is to become visible, and to be found by potential audiences. This understanding of the importance of connection results in a stress on maximizing linkages to a site and on increasing its visibility to search engines. It would be mistaken to treat this as a statement that all spaces in the space of flows are equal. The deep concern which web developers show with maintaining the visibility of their sites reveals an understanding that to be unconnected is to have failed, or that to be connected to by many sites is a measure of success. Web pages, in the links that they contain and the comments that they make, show that other sites are visible to them. Their designers hope that they will become visible to other sites. Space on the web also translates as a concern with having a space in which to display the product of design work. Web pages are not, in the experience of designers, infinitesimal points in an undifferentiated space of flows. The size of a web site is made manifest in the often competing concerns with having enough space to store it in and yet keeping it small enough to download fast. In this sense space and time are firmly tied together on the web, for all the claims that space and time have been once and for all detached from each other as modes of social ordering. Web site developers are concerned with maximizing the use of the space which they have available on servers, and concerned with the allocations of space which different service providers make available to their subscribers.

The space of the Internet is therefore not undifferentiated, nor does it consist of locations without dimension. In the practices of designers it is made as a space where connection and size are crucial in bringing visibility. This space is also not unconnected with physical space. The success of the Official Louise Woodward Campaign for Justice web site in becoming the centre of a network of interconnected sites can be seen as a particularly successful management of the web site as a form of social action. The recognition which the web site received depended also on its unique claim to authenticity, through the closeness which the site declared to Louise and her family. This recognition comes at least in part from the physical proximity of the site's designer with the centre of the campaign for Louise's release. The Boston Support Group similarly built on their physical proximity to the site of the trial to bolster their claims to authenticity.

The 'Why do they do it?' question was asked about newsgroup contributors less frequently. I do not know why the act of contributing to a newsgroup seems less strange or remarkable than the act of producing a web site. It may be that web sites look like highly polished artefacts that must have taken time to produce, while newsgroup contributions, at least on Louise Woodward related topics, often look more like casual contributions to conversation. Viewed in this way, individual postings may not seem to require a major investment of time from their authors, and seem familiar from everyday conversations. The newsgroup contribution seems less of a bizarre phenomenon than the web page on this basis. The idea of meaningful action has relevance to explaining contributions to newsgroups as well as the production of web pages. Here, the key to understanding the posting of messages is that they are meaningful only if the newsgroup is construed as a social setting. Newsgroup messages are viewed not as floating in the ether, but as being the product of individuals with points of view. This kind of forum might be different from face-to-face settings of interaction, but it is routinely seen by participants as sharing the same commitment to viewing utterances as the product of individuals, and of making judgements of the authenticity of statements on conventional grounds. Cultural competences concerning the use of both newsgroups in general and the distinctive space of individual newsgroups sustain the understanding of making a contribution to a newsgroup as a meaningful social action.

There are therefore severe problems with an idea of the Internet as transcending time and space. While that might be convincing in an abstract theoretical sense, it is not made manifest in the lived experience of using and making sense of the Internet. There are also major problems with viewing the Internet as inherently threatening to the provision and consumption of authentic information, or as heralding the end of reality. People still manage to make the complexity meaningful and live relatively simple lives. The Internet might be theoretically baffling, but it is not necessarily experienced as such. As Hasager says 'human beings have the capacity of living sane lives with many different, even conflicting, models or perceptions of the world . . . at the same time' (1997: 185). Complexity can be experienced and lived in simple ways (Friedman, 1997). The multiple and conflicting temporalities, spatialities and authenticities provided by the Internet might be a problem for theorists, but they are not necessarily experienced as such by users. Complexity is combined with the practical expertise to make sense of it (Thompson, 1995: 218).

The interpretive flexibility of the Internet

The term 'closure' is often used to denote the point at which concepts cease to be problematic. In studies of the social shaping of technologies, closure has acquired a specific usage to describe the point at which there has been general agreement on what the technology is and what it is for (Pinch and Bijker, 1987). It has been suggested that while technologies have a certain interpretive flexibility during their development, with the meaning, use and problems associated with the technology differing between social groups, there comes a point when the technology becomes fixed. At this point the technology has reached closure, with general agreement around what it is, such that its design seems a self-evidently optimal solution to a given set of problems. Studies of the social shaping of technologies have used detailed historical reconstructions to display the extent to which technologies such as the bicycle (Pinch and Bijker, 1987) or the refrigerator (Schwartz Cowan, 1987), which might seem to have self-evidently optimal designs, can instead be seen as the upshot of social processes. Woolgar (1991a; 1991c) provides an additional interpretation of apparent closure. He suggests, rather, that technologies are always in principle interpretively flexible, and that it is the sets of social relations that surround their production and use which close down interpretive flexibility and sanction particular uses and interpretations above others. Social relations configure the user to use the technology in the sanctioned ways. What might seem to be a consensus around the technology is only sustained in as far as users can be taught to make sense of the technology in appropriate ways.

The ethnography of the Louise Woodward case on the Internet provides an opportunity to consider the interpretive flexibility of the Internet. It appears, from the observations of online interactions discussed here, that the Internet is both closed and yet still open to interpretation. Around both the WWW and newsgroups, some taken-for-granted uses appear to have stabilized. Newsgroups are seen as a collaboratively occupied and sustained space for social interactions, within which contributions are organized to demonstrate their situational and temporal relevance. These are performative spaces, within which people are encouraged to behave in appropriate ways. Newsgroups are maintained as discrete and distinctive bounded social spaces by the practices of their users and their understandings of what the technology is for. Within the broad category of newsgroups, however, many different kinds of relationships and styles of interaction flourish. Developers of WWW pages also have a commonly shared understanding of the production of a web page as a form of social action, based around ideas of the importance of recognition and the imagining of an audience. Again, this is not to suggest that all web pages are alike. As stated earlier in this chapter, the social action that the production of the web page represents is different for different authors, and for different web sites developed by the same author. Experimentation with the medium and being seen to have a distinctive approach are considered cause for praise among web designers. Nonetheless, a general understanding of web page development as an act of communication remains. There are therefore broadly stable ways of understanding these technologies which suggest appropriate uses and which users learn as part of acquiring cultural competence as Internet users.

The stable understandings of the Internet should not be seen as proceeding directly from the technological capacity. Rather, they are produced in the social relations which support the Internet and occur within it. Social relations which support the development of stable understandings of the Internet include guides, tutorials, etiquette advice and manuals, both online and offline; media coverage; and offline social networks with friends and acquaintances who exchange understandings of what the technology is for. These resources help to promote an understanding that the WWW is about displaying information and maximizing recognition, and that newsgroups are about group communication in bounded spaces. One of the key social influences stabilizing understandings of the Internet is, however, the Internet itself. The common practice among web developers of learning from each other's source code, visiting and assessing each other's sites, and reflexively monitoring their own performance in relation to that of others helps to stabilize understandings of what web pages are for. The prominence given in newsgroups to the need for messages to be relevant to the space within which they are inserted, and the continual reinforcement of this understanding through interaction within those spaces, helps to stabilize notions of newsgroups in general and the distinctive qualities of particular newsgroup places. In effect, the Internet is stabilized as a technology by people using it reflexively to monitor their own use in relation to that of others. Rather than the social relations between users and producers stabilizing the understandings of the technology, as Woolgar (1991c) suggests, here it appears to be the case that users are engaged in configuring one another.

The broad stability described above should not be seen as suggesting that the Internet is without interpretive flexibility. In some key ways, the Internet is still open to interpretation. I have noted in several places that using the Internet meaningfully is about acquiring the cultural competences within which it makes sense. This opens up the possibility for the development of quite different but locally stable understandings. In Chapter 5 it was demonstrated that, far from being aspatial, the Internet can be considered as consisting of a myriad of more or less interlinked spaces. Web sites on the topic of Louise Woodward developed a set of linkages over time which performed spaces for interpretation. Similarly, the different newsgroups in which the Louise Woodward case was discussed formed separate areas whose socially formed boundaries protected specific and distinct ways of knowing about and relating to the world. These observations seem to suggest that rather than thinking of cyberspace, it would be more useful to think of the social environment of the Internet as consisting of more or less linked, more or less strictly bounded social spaces, formed and sustained through social relations. These separately maintained but interlinked social spaces provide for and nurture the interpretive flexibility. At least a part of people's use of the Internet occurs in relation to what they find online, and what is taken to be the sensible thing to do with the technology. What people find is different in the different social spaces they may enter.

   Studies of the use of technologies of the home have demonstrated the ways in which the technology is differently constructed in the different settings into which it is inserted (Silverstone and Hirsch, 1994). The bounded setting of the home allows for the insertion of the technology into a particular set of social relationships which are redefined in the face of the new technology. The interpretive flexibility with which the technology is approached is due at least in part to the bounded nature of the home. Within the boundaries of the domestic context users of the technology are able to develop their own interpretations. By analogy, the development of bounded social spaces on the Internet fosters and facilitates the interpretive flexibility of the technology, and allows quite different versions of what the technology can sensibly be used for to thrive. It can at one and the same time be used for a serious commercial venture, for fantasy and identity play, for support groups and the sharing of common experience, and for abuse, name-calling and graffiti. It is not aspatiality but the development of bounded social space which provides for this possibility. The Internet in use has developed a sense of space which, far from freeing us from the constraints of place, reasserts them in a form that is different, more elusive and more difficult to challenge.

   The Internet tends to be used in isolation or in small groups. By direct inference from studies of technologies in domestic contexts, this isolation may also free up the potential for interpretive flexibility. The reading practices of different users are only made available through the Internet itself to a limited extent. Stable understandings of the meaning of Internet content production are made available through the technology and drawn upon by producers in their reflexive monitoring. Online activity can be seen to enact and make available understandings of the technology. Stable understandings of Internet content consumption are, however, much harder both for the ethnographer and the ordinary users to access. Much of the interpretive work which goes into making sense of Internet content is not made available on the Internet itself. It is therefore likely that both understandings of the technology as manifested in reading or surfing practices, and understandings of content via interpretive practices, are highly unstable. This instability is fostered by the common interpretation of Internet use as a solitary activity. Spatiality and temporality structure the availability of competing accounts of what the technology is for. The diverse and multiple settings in which the Internet is used, often privately in people's homes and offices, seem to separate the users of the Internet from one another and from 'experts' who might teach them conventional ways of understanding it.

   Media statements throughout the Louise Woodward case presented a unified Internet and ascribed qualities to it. The Internet was presented at different moments in the case as a site for instantaneous access to privileged information, as a failed technology for release of legal rulings, and as a site of potential inauthenticity. These stories represented moments of closure in which the Internet was made as an entity. These moments occur not just in media representations but in the talk of Internet users, across the academic literature, and are no doubt still present in this book despite my attempts to eradicate them. These moments of closure reify the Internet as a single phenomenon with given qualities, whether mundane or revolutionary. Looking at the interpretive flexibility of the Internet, however, raises the potential for it to be simultaneously revolutionary and mundane. The conclusion depends on membership of social networks and which network wins out in telling the history. Kirshenblatt-Gimblett and other authors in the volume *Connected: Engagements with Media* (Marcus, 1996) wrestle with the significance of new media, and whether radical changes are occurring. Kirshenblatt-Gimblett herself is unequivocal about the distinctiveness of electronic media:

> electronic communication broadly conceived marks the line between modern and postmodern communication. (1996: 21)

At the same time, Kirshenblatt-Gimblett suggests we turn attention to the everyday uses of the medium. This is what I have done, although I come to somewhat different conclusions about the radical nature of developments in electronic communication. In my view, the Internet is neither inherently revolutionary nor inherently mundane, neither modern nor postmodern at heart. What comes to be seen as self-evidently the way the Internet is, will be the upshot of a long history of negotiations about appropriate use. A more sceptical analytic framework is needed to address the connections between revolutionary claims for new technologies and their everyday uses, although it will be hard to relinquish the habit of associating utopian dreams with the next new technology on the horizon, whatever that may be (Rich, 1998).

Adaptive ethnography

I have argued that an adaptive approach to ethnography will allow it to thrive in the conditions which developments in mediated communication offer. I have adapted ethnography to my own strategic purposes within this study, to produce a partial account of the Internet relevant to a particular set of concerns. A number of significant omissions render this a partial ethnography. The choice of a media event to structure the ethnographic object, the reliance on Internet searching tools for a large part of the making of that object, and the dependence on online interactions at the expense of offline ethnographic engagement, all contributed to the partiality of the ethnography. The themes of time and space, authenticity and identity which I chose to interrogate my ethnographic experiences were those which I found most pertinent to address revolutionary and transcendent claims about the Internet. Other themes, however, arose through the ethnography and would have merited closer consideration than they can be given in this text. In particular, the role of gender in structuring expectations of the

Internet and online interactions would deserve further investigation. These omissions merit deeper exploration in future ethnographies adapted in different ways.

One key area for future studies which I have been unable to address in depth in this book is the ways in which the Internet is interpolated into the concerns of particular local contexts of use. There is much work to be done in understanding the interpretive practices of Internet users. A strategic adaptation of ethnography to the purpose suggests that we could usefully focus on the offline contexts within which the Internet is used, tracking the ways in which the Internet is used in different contexts and the transformations which Internet content goes through as it passes from online to offline contexts. We could study how the particular ways in which institutional networks are set up, accounts allocated and users trained structure the uses which are made of it. Similarly, we could investigate the practices of ISPs, and the ways in which their gateways and services structure understandings of appropriate use. We could consider how people negotiate between the aggregated idea of 'the Internet' and the particularities of their own uses and experiences and the social spaces which they encounter within it. Making the Internet meaningful encompasses both the once and for all transition which people make when they become users, and the ongoing process of making usage meaningful. This suggests a combination of long-term and biographical investigation with detailed studies of the ways in which the technology is produced in the detail of moment by moment activities around its use (Button, 1993).

The role of lurkers has been identified as a major gap in our current understandings of the Internet. This area, again, is likely to benefit from an adaptive approach which focuses on offline contexts of use, accompanying lurkers and web surfers in their activities. Little is known about the ways in which users of the Internet carve out their own social spaces through their reading practices, and how diverse their interpretations are of the activities which they observe online. There is a need to know more about the relevance of concepts of online community to lurkers, and the ways in which lurking relates to other consumption practices like viewing a television programme or reading a book. The ethnography of the Louise Woodward case has suggested an interestingly complex relationship between the Internet and the mass media. It is likely that rather than replacing or transcending the use of traditional media, the experience of Internet use will both transform and be transformed by them.

The projects described above will require methodological innovation, if they are both to locate themselves in offline contexts and to take online contexts into account. The insights which they produce will be limited if they confine themselves to a single idea of the field. Shedding a reliance on holism, face-to-face interaction and dwelling in a bounded location opens up new horizons for ethnography and promises new ways of understanding the Internet. This does not necessarily mean dispensing with the active engagement and experiential knowledge which has been ethnography's strength. Extending and adapting ethnography provides both a site for reflection on what counts as ethnographic experience and a site for reflection on the implications of mediated communication. Virtual ethnography, rather than a finished project, is 'a multi-sited imaginary in the pursuit of ethnography' (Marcus, 1998: 3).

Glossary of Internet Terms

* Used in CMC to denote emphasis, as in 'I *know* this is true', or to display actions as in 'I like this *grins*'.

\> Used in CMC to denote a section of text quoted from a previous message. Often added automatically to the beginning of each quoted line by the newsgroup reading software. Allows users to indicate to which sections of previous messages their comments refer, and therefore helps to maintain continuity in discussions.

Address   A way of indicating to which other computer or user a message sent over the Internet is directed. Email addresses are of the form username@hostcomputer.

Asynchronous communication   Any form of communication in which the parties to the interaction need not be present simultaneously.

Bandwidth   Term used to denote the capacity of a communication channel for information: a narrow bandwidth implies slow or limited communication.

Bit   The basic unit of digital information. Binary, with a value of either one or zero.

Browser   The client program which requests web page information from web servers, displays web pages and allows the user to navigate them. Usually provides a visual display including graphics, but can be text-only or audio-only.

Bulletin Board   A forum accessible over a network, where messages can be placed. Users can access the bulletin board to leave messages or reply to those of other users. The bulletin board can be a discussion forum or information source.

Byte   A group of 8 bits.

Client   A computer or program requesting information from a server over a network, including the Internet.

CMC Computer Mediated Communication   A general term referring to a range of different ways in which people can communicate with one another via a computer network. Includes both synchronous and asynchronous communication, one-to-one and many-to-many interactions, and text-based or video and audio communication.

Computer conferencing   A general term for CMC which allows a group of people to interact.

Cross-posting   The sending of a message to more than one newsgroup at a time. Can be used to draw an ongoing discussion to the attention of more than one group simultaneously, but is controversial and termed 'spam' if over-used.

Cyberspace   The interaction space created by computer networks.

Dejanews   A service which indexes messages posted to newsgroups and allows users to search past messages on the basis of content or header information, to search for forums of interest, and to join forums and post messages.

Domain name   The basis for Internet addresses, domain names indicate a particular host computer to which a message is directed. Domain names have a hierarchical structure, for example brunel.ac.uk is a domain name which indicates the computer of Brunel University, which is within the academic domain, within the UK.

Download   Term for the acquisition of information across a computer network.

Dynamic update   A web page which reflects changes to an underlying source of information, allowing it to display automatically updated, current information.

Electronic mail (email)   The basic form of asynchronous Internet communication, which allows text messages to be sent to specified addresses. In some email packages additional information such as word processor files, images or application programs can be attached to the message to be sent to other users.

Emoticon   A symbol composed of standard keyboard characters which is included in text-based CMC to indicate emotions. Often used emoticons include :-) for smiling, :-(for sadness, and ;-) for winking.

File space   A limited information storage area allocated to a particular user, application or forum.

Flame   An aggressive or hostile message.

Gateway   A service which provides a starting point for accessing the Internet. ISPs often provide a gateway which is the first point of access for their users and which offers a range of different forums and activities for users to try. Directories provided by search engines are also gateways.

Guest book   A feature often added to web pages to allow visitors to leave their own comments to be visible to later visitors and the author of the page. Some automatically display the comments left by visitors, while others are maintained 'by hand' by the author of the page adding each comment as it is received. Authors may also be able to delete offending comments.

Header   Information added to the beginning of an email message or newsgroup posting which shows the source of the message, the recipient, the subject of the message and the time and date the message was sent. More detailed information may also be included on, for example, the route which the message travelled through the Internet. Some features are added automatically, while others can be tailored by the sender of the message.

Hit counter   A device which displays on a web page the number of times that this page has previously been requested from the server. Routinely understood to represent an indication of the popularity of the page, although 'hits' do not translate directly into the number of people who have seen the page.

Home page   A WWW page. Can be used to denote someone's personal page, the starting point for exploring their web site. Home is also the first page which is loaded when a user starts up their browser, which might be their own page or might be the gateway provided by their ISP.

HTML HyperText Markup Language   The language in which web pages are written. This language gives information to the browser on how the page should be displayed, including images and other features to be included together with text. Also specifies the hyperlinks which the page is to include.

Hyperlink   The way in which documents on the WWW are connected to one another. HTML code within the document indicates another document which will be displayed when a user selects the hyperlink, usually by clicking with the mouse on the link.

Hypertext   A way of interlinking documents, which provides for any part of any document to be connected to any part of any other document. The basic form of the WWW.

IMHO   A commonly used abbreviation in text-based CMC, meaning 'in my humble opinion'.

Infoseek   A search engine which indexes web pages, allowing searches by keywords and phrases contained in the pages. The results are listed according to the closeness of the match with the search criteria.

Internet   A network of computer networks all sharing TCP/IP as their communications protocol, which allows messages to be sent across the network to specified addresses.

Internet Service Provider   An organization offering customers access to the Internet, often including an email address, space in which users can store their own web pages, and a gateway to other Internet services.

IRC Internet relay chat   A synchronous text-based form of CMC on the Internet. Discussions are held in real time on channels devoted to particular topics or interest groups.

IRL   Common abbreviation meaning 'in real life', i.e. offline.

ISP   See Internet Service Provider.

Killfile   A feature of newsgroup reading software which allows the user to request that messages posted by a specified user or on a specified topic not be displayed.

Link   See hyperlink.

Logging off, logging out   The act of ending a session using a computer system protected by a password.

Logging on   The act of providing a user name and password in order to gain access to a computer system. This act is necessary to gain access to a secure system or to identify oneself as a particular user. This allows many different users to have secure and separate files stored on one computer, and to adopt distinct online identities.

Lurker   Someone who reads messages posted to a public forum such as a newsgroup but does not respond to the group.

MB   MegaByte. A measure of file space: 1,048,576 (2^{20}) bytes.

Moderated newsgroup   A newsgroup in which one member, the moderator, checks all messages posted for relevance and acceptability before adding them to the newsgroup. Messages can only be posted via the moderator.

MOO Multi-user domain (object-oriented)   A form of multi-user domain.

MUD Multi-user domain (or multi-user dungeon)   A synchronous form of text-based communication which allows users to play self-defined characters, originally used for role-playing games. The MUD includes a description of a physical environment with which users can interact and to which they can add their own features.

Netcop   A term for someone who sets out to identify abuses of the Internet and to reprimand or request sanctions against offenders.

Netiquette   The set of conventions for appropriate and acceptable use of Usenet newsgroups.

News feed   A server storing and providing access to newsgroup messages.

Newsgroup   An asynchronous text-based forum for communication, a form of bulletin board.

Newsgroup hierarchy   The system for organizing Usenet newsgroups into a topic-based hierarchy: for example, rec.travel.air is a recreational group (rec), discussing travel (travel), specifically air travel (air).

Packet   The unit of information which is passed around the Internet. A message will be divided into packets by the computer sending it. Packets of information contain addressing information which allows them to be forwarded from computer to computer until they reach their destination. Packets are then assembled by the recipient computer to constitute the message.

Password   An identifier which, when used to log in, allows a computer to verify the identity of a user.

Plug-in   An additional program which can be downloaded to enable a browser to display information not in HTML format, such as sound or video.

Posts, poster   Messages sent to newsgroups are often called posts and the people sending them posters.

Protocol   A formally agreed standard method.

Quoting   A common practice in text-based CMC which allows a message to include sections of previous messages, enhancing the continuity of discussion. Often denoted by the symbol >.

Search engine   A service which indexes Internet material, allowing users to search for information and services. Sometimes includes a hierarchically arranged directory. Sites are included in search engines either by their authors requesting inclusion, or by programs which search the Internet for newly added sites and add them automatically.

Server   A computer or program providing information over a network, including the Internet.

Signature file A file which is composed by a user to be added automatically to each message they send via email or to a newsgroup. Often contains identifying information and contact details; sometimes used for jokes and quotations or to publicize a web site.

Source code The HTML code which specifies the content of a web page, including layout information and hyperlinks. Web designers often look at the source code to find out how a particular effect has been achieved.

Spam Unwanted messages sent via email or newsgroups, often commercial advertisements.

Spammer A sender of spam is a spammer.

Synchronous communication Any form of communication in which the parties to the interaction need to be present simultaneously.

TCP/IP Transaction Control Protocol/Internet Protocol The agreed standard for assembling and addressing packets of information which allows messages to be sent across the Internet.

Thread A set of messages on a newsgroup on the same subject. When a user replies to a message the subject line of the original message is kept and the newsgroup reading software displays the reply as part of the same thread.

Unmoderated newsgroup A newsgroup to which any subscriber can directly post messages, in contrast to moderated newsgroups.

URL Uniform resource locator A standard way of indicating the location of information on the Internet, particularly used for the World Wide Web. The URL indicates the way the information is stored: for example, in http://www.brunel.ac.uk/~xxctcmh/cmh.htm, 'http://' indicates that this is a WWW document, 'www.brunel.ac.uk' gives the domain name of the computer on which the information is stored, and '/~xxctcmh/ cmh.htm' identifies the directory and file name where the information is stored on that computer.

Usenet The hierarchy of Internet newsgroups.

Video conferencing A visual and audio-based synchronous form of CMC by which two or more users, each with cameras attached to their computers, can both see and be seen.

Virtual environment Any forum for interaction provided across a computer network. Can be used to describe forums in which users control avatars (visual representations of chosen characters) who are moving around an environment graphically represented on screen.

Visitor log A record of the requests made to a server to display a web page. May include information such as the timing of requests, their domain name and the pages from which they came to the site. Allows analysis of the patterns and origins of requests for web page information.

Web page A file in HTML format which can be displayed by a browser. At its most basic, a page of text. This can contain hyperlinks, images, sound, video and interactive elements or dynamic updates.

Web ring A device for linking together related web sites developed by different authors. Members of a web ring include a display on their pages inviting visitors to move on to another site in the ring.

Web server   A repository of web pages which supplies information in response to requests from browsers.

Web site   One or more web pages.

Web surfer   A person who looks for information on the WWW.

WELL Whole Earth 'Lectronic Link   A computer conferencing system, offering a hierarchy of bulletin boards and provision for private email.

World Wide Web   A hypertext-based forum which allows users to develop their own sites and make them available to other users across the Internet.

WWW   See World Wide Web

Yahoo   A directory of WWW sites organized by content categories.

References

Abbate, J. 1998 *Inventing the Internet.* Cambridge, MA: MIT Press.

Abu-Lughod, L. 1997 The interpretation of culture(s) after television. *Representations* 59: 109–134.

Adam, B. 1990 *Time and Social Theory.* Cambridge: Polity.

Allen, C. 1996 What's wrong with the 'Golden Rule'? Conundrums of conducting ethical research in cyberspace. *The Information Society* 12(2): 175–187.

Anderson, B. 1991 *Imagined Communities.* 2nd edn. London: Verso.

Ang, I. 1996 *Living Room Wars: Rethinking Media Audiences for a Postmodern World.* London: Routledge.

Appadurai, A. 1996 *Modernity at Large: Cultural Dimensions of Globalization.* Minneapolis: University of Minnesota Press.

Argyle, K. and Shields, R. 1996 Is there a body in the net? In R. Shields (ed.) *Cultures of Internet: Virtual Spaces, Real Histories, Living Bodies.* London: Sage. pp. 58–69.

Argyle, M., Furnham, A. and Graham, J.A. 1981 *Social Situations.* Cambridge: Cambridge University Press.

Ashmore, M. 1989 *The Reflexive Thesis: Wrighting Sociology of Scientific Knowledge.* Chicago: University of Chicago Press.

Atkinson, P. 1990 *The Ethnographic Imagination: Textual Constructions of Reality.* London: Routledge.

Aycock, A. and Buchignani, N. 1995 The e-mail murders: reflections on 'dead' letters. In S.G. Jones (ed.) *Cybersociety: Computer-Mediated Communication and Community.* Thousand Oaks, CA: Sage. pp. 184–231.

Barthes, R. 1973 *Mythologies.* St Albans: Granada.

Baudrillard, J. 1983 *Simulations.* New York: Semiotext(e).

Bausinger, H. 1984 Media, technology and everyday life. *Media Culture and Society* 6(4): 343–351.

Baym, N.K. 1995a From practice to culture on Usenet. In S.L. Star (ed.) *The Cultures of Computing.* Oxford: Blackwell. pp. 29–52.

Baym, N.K. 1995b The emergence of community in computer-mediated communication. In S.G. Jones (ed.) *Cybersociety: Computer-Mediated Communication and Community.* Thousand Oaks, CA: Sage. pp. 138–163.

Baym, N.K. 1995c The performance of humour in computer-mediated communication. *Journal of Computer Mediated Communication* 1(2). http://shum.huji.ac.il/jcmc/vol1/issue2/baym.html.

Baym, N. 1998 The emergence of on-line community. In S.G. Jones (ed.) *Cybersociety2.0: Revisiting Computer-Mediated Communication and Community.* Thousand Oaks, CA: Sage. pp. 35–68.

Bell, D. 1993 Introduction 1: the context. In D. Bell, P. Caplan and W. Jahan Karim (eds) *Gendered Fields: Women, Men and Ethnography.* London: Routledge. pp. 1–18.

Beniger, J. 1987 Personalization of mass media and the growth of pseudo-community. *Communication Research* 14(3): 352–371.

Berger, P.L. and Luckman, T. 1971 *The Social Construction of Reality: a Treatise in the Sociology of Knowledge.* London: Allen Lane.

Bijker, W.E. 1987 The social construction of Bakelite: toward a theory of invention. In W.E. Bijker, T.P. Hughes and T. Pinch (eds) *The Social Construction of Technological Systems*. Cambridge, MA: MIT Press. pp. 159–187.

Bijker, W.E. 1995 *Of Bicycles, Bakelite and Bulbs: Towards a Theory of Sociotechnical Change*. Cambridge, MA: MIT Press.

Bijker, W.E., Hughes, T.P. and Pinch, T. (eds) 1987 *The Social Construction of Technological Systems*. Cambridge, MA: MIT Press.

Bijker, W.E. and Law, J. 1992 *Shaping Technology/Building Society: Studies in Sociotechnical Change*. Cambridge, MA: MIT Press.

Brettell, C. (ed.) 1993 *When They Read What We Write: the Politics of Ethnography*. Westport, CT: Bergin and Garvey.

Bromberg, H. 1996 Are MUDs communities? Identity, belonging and consciousness in virtual worlds. In R. Shields (ed.) *Cultures of Internet: Virtual Spaces, Real Histories, Living Bodies*. London: Sage. pp. 143–152.

Bruckman, A. 1992 Identity workshop: emergent social and psychological phenomena in text-based virtual reality. http://www.cc.gatech.edu/~asb/papers/index.html.

Burkhalter, B. 1999 Reading race online: discovering racial identity in Usenet discussions. In M.A. Smith and P. Kollock (eds) *Communities in Cyberspace*. London: Routledge. pp. 60–75.

Burnett, R. 1996 A torn page, ghosts on the computer screen, words, images, labyrinths: exploring the frontiers of cyberspace. In G.E. Marcus (ed.) *Connected: Engagements with Media*. Chicago: University of Chicago Press. pp. 67–98.

Button, G. 1993 The curious case of the vanishing technology. In G. Button (ed.) *Technology in Working Order: Studies of Work, Interaction and Technology*. London: Routledge. pp. 10–28.

Cairncross, F. 1997 *The Death of Distance: How the Communications Revolution Will Change Our Lives*. London: Orion.

Castells, M. 1996a *The Rise of the Network Society*. Cambridge, MA: Blackwell.

Castells, M. 1996b The net and the self: working notes for a critical theory of the informational society. *Critique of Anthropology* 16(1): 9–38.

Castells, M. 1997 *The Power of Identity*. Cambridge, MA: Blackwell.

Chesterton, G.K. 1904 *The Napoleon of Notting Hill*. London: Bodley Head.

Clark, L.S. 1998 Dating on the net: teens and the rise of 'pure' relationships. In S.G. Jones (ed.) *Cybersociety 2.0: Revisiting Computer-Mediated Communication and Community*. Thousand Oaks, CA: Sage. pp. 159–183.

Clifford, J. 1992 Travelling cultures. In L. Grossberg, C. Nelson and P.A. Treichler (eds) *Cultural Studies*. London: Routledge. pp. 96–116.

Clifford, J. and Marcus, G.E. 1986 *Writing Culture: the Poetics and Politics of Ethnography*. Berkeley, CA: University of California.

Cohen, A.P. 1985 *The Symbolic Construction of Community*. Milton Keynes: Open University.

Cooper, G. 1998 Simulating difference: ethnography and the social relations of intellectual production. *British Journal of Sociology* 49(1): 20–35.

Cooper, G., Hine, C., Rachel, J. and Woolgar, S. 1995 Ethnography and human-computer interaction. In P. Thomas (ed.) *Social and Interactional Dimensions of Human–Computer Interfaces*. Cambridge: Cambridge University Press. pp. 11–36.

Correll, S. 1995 The ethnography of an electronic bar: the Lesbian Café. *Journal of Contemporary Ethnography* 24(3): 270–298.

Crane, G. 1991 Composing culture: the authority of an electronic text. *Current Anthropology* 32(3): 293–302.

Curtis, P. 1992 Mudding: social phenomena in text-based virtual realities. http://www.cpsr.org/cpsr/sociology/mud_moo/DIAC92.txt. Also available at many other WWW locations.

Danet, B. 1998 Text as mask: gender, play and performance on the Internet. In S.G. Jones (ed.) *Cybersociety 2.0: Revisiting Computer-Mediated Communication and Community.* Thousand Oaks, CA: Sage. pp. 129–158.

Danet, B., Ruedenberg-Wright, L. and Rosenbaum-Tamari, Y. 1997 'Hmmm . . . where's that smoke coming from?' Writing, play and performance on Internet Relay Chat. *Journal of Computer-Mediated Communication* 2(4). http://www.ascusc.org/jcmc/vol2/issue4/danet.html.

Denzin, N.K. 1997 *Interpretive Ethnography: Ethnographic Practices for the 21st Century.* Thousand Oaks, CA: Sage.

Dicks, B. and Mason, B. 1998 Hypermedia and ethnography: reflections on the construction of a research approach. *Sociological Research Online* 3(3). http://www.socresonline.org.uk/socresonline/3/3/3.html.

Dietrich, D. 1997 (Re)-fashioning the techno-erotic woman: gender and textuality in the cybercultural matrix. In S.G. Jones (ed.) *Virtual Culture: Identity and Communication in Cybersociety.* London: Sage. pp. 169–184.

Donath, J.S. 1999 Identity and deception in the virtual community. In M.A. Smith and P. Kollock (eds) *Communities in Cyberspace.* London: Routledge. pp. 29–59.

Dubinskas, F.A. (ed.) 1988 *Making Time: Ethnographies of High-Technology Organizations.* Philadelphia: Temple University Press.

Erickson, T.H. 1997 The nation as a human being – a metaphor in a mid-life crisis? Notes on the imminent collapse of a Norwegian national identity. In K.F. Olwig and K. Hastrup (eds) *Siting Culture: the Shifting Anthropological Object.* London: Routledge. pp. 103–122.

Escobar, A. 1996 Welcome to Cyberia: notes on the anthropology of cyberculture. In Z. Sardar and J.R. Ravetz (eds) *Cyberfutures: Culture and Politics on the Information Superhighway.* London: Pluto. pp. 111–137.

Espinosa, P. 1982 The audience in the text: ethnographic observations of a Hollywood story conference. *Media, Culture and Society* 4(1): 77–86.

Ettema, J.S. and Whitney, D.C. 1994 The money arrow: an introduction to audiencemaking. In J.S. Ettema and D.C. Whitney (eds) *Audiencemaking: How the Media Create the Audience.* Thousand Oaks, CA: Sage. pp. 1–18.

Evans-Pritchard, E.E. 1937 *Witchcraft, Oracles and Magic among the Azande.* Oxford: Clarendon.

Fabian, J. 1983 *Time and the Other: How Anthropology Makes its Object.* New York: Columbia.

Fairclough, N. 1995 *Media Discourse.* London: Edward Arnold.

Featherstone, M. 1995 *Undoing Culture: Globalization, Postmodernism and Identity.* London: Sage.

Ferguson, J. 1997 Paradoxes of sovereignty and independence: 'real' and 'pseudo' nation-states and the depoliticization of poverty. In K.F. Olwig and K. Hastrup (eds) *Siting Culture: the Shifting Anthropological Object.* London: Routledge. pp. 123–141.

Fernback, J. 1997 The individual within the collective: virtual ideology and the realization of collective principles. In S.G. Jones (ed.) *Virtual Culture: Identity and Communication in Cybersociety.* London: Sage. pp. 36–54.

Franco, V., Piirto, R., Hu, H.-Y., Lewenstein, B.V., Underwood, R. and Vidal, N.K. 1995 Anatomy of a flame: conflict and community building on the Internet. *IEEE Technology and Society Magazine* Summer 1995: 12–21.

Franklin, S. 1995 Science as culture, cultures of science. *Annual Review of Anthropology* 24: 163–184.

Freeman, D. 1996 *Margaret Mead and the Heretic.* Ringwood, Victoria, Australia: Penguin.

Friedman, J. 1997 Simplifying complexity: assimilating the global in a small paradise. In K.F. Olwig and K. Hastrup (eds) *Siting Culture: the Shifting Anthropological Object.* London: Routledge. pp. 268–291.

Frissen, V. 1997 ICTs in the rush hour of life. Paper presented to Workshop on Social Shaping of Multimedia, Edinburgh, 27–28 June 1997.

Fulk, J. 1993 Social construction of communication technology. *Academy of Management Journal* 36(5): 921–950.

Fulk, J., Schmitz, J.A. and Schwartz, D. 1992 The dynamics of context–behaviour interactions in computer-mediated communication. In M. Lea (ed.) *Contexts of Computer-Mediated Communication*. New York: Harvester Wheatsheaf. pp. 7–29.

Garfinkel, H. 1967 *Studies in Ethnomethodology*. New Jersey: Prentice-Hall.

Gates, B. 1996 *The Road Ahead*. Revised and updated. London: Penguin.

Geertz, C. 1993 *The Interpretation of Cultures* (1973). London: Fontana.

Giddens, A. 1990 *The Consequences of Modernity*. Cambridge: Polity.

Giddens, A. 1991 *Modernity and Self-Identity: Self and Society in the Late Modern Age*. Cambridge: Polity.

Gilbert, G.N. and Mulkay, M. 1984 *Opening Pandora's Box: a Sociological Analysis of Scientists' Discourse*. Cambridge: Cambridge University Press.

Gill, R. 1993 Ideology, gender and popular radio: a discourse analytic approach. *Innovation* 6(3): 323–339.

Gillespie, A. and Robins, K. 1989 Geographical inequalities: the spatial bias of the new communications technologies. *Journal of Communication* 39(3): 7–18.

Glaser, B.G. and Strauss, A.L. 1964 Awareness contexts and social interaction. *American Sociological Review* 29: 669–679.

Goffman, E. 1971 *The Presentation of Self in Everyday Life* (1956). Harmondsworth: Penguin.

Goffman, E. 1981 *Forms of Talk*. Oxford: Blackwell.

Goodwin, A. and Wolff, J. 1997 Conserving cultural studies. In E. Long (ed.) *From Sociology to Cultural Studies: New Perspectives*. Malden, MA and Oxford: Blackwell. pp. 123–149.

Grint, K. and Woolgar, S. 1992 Computers, guns and roses: what's social about being shot. *Science, Technology and Human Values* 17(3): 366–380.

Grint, K. and Woolgar, S. 1997 *The Machine at Work: Technology, Work and Organization*. Cambridge: Polity.

Gubrium, J. and Holstein, J. 1987 The private image: experiential location and method in family studies. *Journal of Marriage and the Family* 49: 773–786.

Gupta, A. and Ferguson, J. 1992 Beyond 'culture': space, identity and the politics of difference. *Cultural Anthropology* 7(1): 6–23.

Hafner, K. and Lyon, M. 1998 *Where Wizards Stay up Late: the Origins of the Internet*. New York: Touchstone.

Hammersley, M. 1990 What's wrong with ethnography? The myth of theoretical description. *Sociology* 24(4): 597–615.

Hammersley, M. and Atkinson, P. 1995 *Ethnography: Principles in Practice*. 2nd edition. London: Routledge.

Harrington, C. Lee and Bielby, D.D. 1995 Where did you hear that? Technology and the social organization of gossip. *Sociological Quarterly* 36(3): 607–628.

Hartley, J. 1987 Invisible fictions: television audiences, paedocracy, pleasure. *Textual Practice* 1(2): 121–138.

Harvey, D. 1989 *The Condition of Postmodernity: an Enquiry into the Origins of Cultural Change*. Oxford: Blackwell.

Hasager, U. 1997 Localizing the American dream: constructing Hawaiian homelands. In K.F. Olwig and K. Hastrup (eds) *Siting Culture: the Shifting Anthropological Object*. London: Routledge. pp. 165–192.

Hastrup, K. and Olwig, K.F. 1997 Introduction. In K.F. Olwig and K. Hastrup (eds) *Siting Culture: the Shifting Anthropological Object*. London: Routledge. pp. 1–14.

Heath, D. 1998 Locating genetic knowledge: picturing Marfan Syndrome and its travelling constituencies. *Science, Technology and Human Values* 23(1): 71–97.

Herring, S. 1996 Linguistic and critical analysis of computer-mediated communication: some ethical and scholarly considerations. *The Information Society* 12(2): 153–168.

Herz, J. C. 1995 *Surfing on the Internet: a Net-Head's Adventures On-Line*. London: Abacus.

Hiltz, S.R. and Turoff, M. 1993 *The Network Nation: Human Communication via Computer* (1978). Revised edition. Cambridge, MA: MIT Press.

Hine, C. 1995 Representations of information technology in disciplinary development: disappearing plants and invisible networks. *Science, Technology and Human Values* 20(1): 65–87.

Hirsch, E. 1998 Bound and unbound entities: reflections on the ethnographic perspectives of anthropology *vis-à-vis* media and cultural studies. In F. Hughes-Freeland (ed.) *Ritual, Performance, Media*. London: Routledge. pp. 208–228.

Hoffman, J. 1998 Topological orderings in cyberspace. Paper presented at EASST'98 General Conference on Cultures of Science and Technology: Europe and the Global Context, Lisbon, 1–3 October 1998.

Horton, M., Spafford, G. and Moraes, M. 1999 An Official Usenet Primer. ftp://ftp.faqs.org/faqs/usenet/posting-rules/part1.

Howard, A. 1988 Hypermedia and the future of ethnography. *Cultural Anthropology* 3(3): 304–315.

Jackson, A. (ed.) 1987 *Anthropology at Home*. London: Tavistock.

Jackson, M.H. 1997 Assessing the structure of communication on the World Wide Web. *Journal of Computer Mediated Communication*. 3(1). http://www.ascusc.org/jcmc/vol3/issue1/jackson.html.

Johns, A. 1998 *The Nature of the Book: Print and Knowledge in the Making*. Chicago: University of Chicago Press.

Jones, R.A. 1994 The ethics of research in cyberspace. *Internet Research* 4(3): 30–35.

Jones, S.G. 1995 Understanding community in the Information Age. In S.G. Jones (ed.) *Cybersociety: Computer-Mediated Communication and Community*. Thousand Oaks, CA: Sage. pp. 10–35.

Jones, S.G. 1997a The Internet and its social landscape. In S.G. Jones (ed.) *Virtual Culture: Identity and Communication in Cybersociety*. London: Sage. pp. 7–35.

Jones, S.G. 1997b Using the news: an examination of the value and use of news sources in CMC. *Journal of Computer-Mediated Communication* 2(4). http://www.ascusc.org/jcmc/vol2/issue4/jones.html.

Jones, S.G. 1998 Information, Internet and community: notes towards an understanding of community in the Information Age. In S.G. Jones (ed.) *Cybersociety 2.0: Revisiting Computer-Mediated Communication and Community*. Thousand Oaks, CA: Sage. pp. 1–34.

Kern, S. 1983 *The Culture of Time and Space, 1880–1918*. Cambridge, MA: Harvard University Press.

Kiesler, S.L., Siegel, J. and McGuire, T.W. 1984 Social psychological aspects of computer-mediated communication. *American Psychologist* 39(10): 1123–1134.

King, S.A. 1996 Researching Internet communities: proposed ethical guidelines for the reporting of results. *The Information Society* 12(2): 119–127.

Kirshenblatt-Gimblett, B. 1996 The electronic vernacular. In G.E. Marcus (ed.) *Connected: Engagements with Media*. Chicago: University of Chicago Press. pp. 21–65.

Kitchin, R. 1998 *Cyberspace: the World in the Wires*. Chichester: Wiley.

Knorr-Cetina, K.D. 1981 *The Manufacture of Knowledge: an Essay on the Constructivist and Contextual Nature of Science*. Oxford: Pergamon.

Knorr-Cetina, K.D. 1983 The ethnographic study of scientific work: towards a constructivist interpretation of science. In K.D. Knorr-Cetina and M. Mulkay (eds) *Science Observed: Perspectives on the Social Studies of Science*. London: Sage. pp. 115–140.

Knorr-Cetina, K.D. 1992 The couch, the cathedral and the laboratory: on the relationship between experiment and laboratory in science. In A. Pickering (ed.) *Science as Practice and Culture*. Chicago: University of Chicago Press. pp. 113–138.

Knorr-Cetina, K.D. and Mulkay, M. 1983 Introduction: emerging principles in social studies of science. In K.D. Knorr-Cetina and M. Mulkay (eds) *Science Observed: Perspectives on the Social Studies of Science*. London: Sage. pp. 1–18.

Kolko, B. and Reid, E. 1998 Dissolution and fragmentation: problems in on-line communities. In S.G. Jones (ed.) *Cybersociety 2.0: Revisiting Computer-Mediated Communication and Community*. Thousand Oaks, CA: Sage. pp. 212–229.

Kollock, P. 1999 The economies of online cooperation: gifts and public goods in cyberspace. In M.A. Smith and P. Kollock (eds) *Communities in Cyberspace*. London: Routledge. pp. 220–239.

Kollock, P. and Smith, M.A. 1994 Managing the virtual commons: cooperation and conflict in computer communities. http://www.sscnet.ucla.edu/soc/csoc/papers/virtcomm/Virtcomm.htm.

Kollock, P. and Smith, M.A. 1999 Communities in cyberspace. In M.A. Smith and P. Kollock (eds) *Communities in Cyberspace*. London: Routledge. pp. 3–25.

Kuper, A. 1983 *Anthropology and Anthropologists: the Modern British School*. London: Routledge and Kegan Paul.

Lakoff, G. and Johnson, M. 1980 *Metaphors We Live By*. Chicago: University of Chicago Press.

Lash, S. and Urry, J. 1994 *Economies of Signs and Space*. London: Sage.

Latour, B. and Woolgar, S. 1986 *Laboratory Life: the Construction of Scientific Facts*. 2nd edn. Princeton, NJ: Princeton University Press.

Lea, M. and Spears, S. 1991 Computer-mediated communication, de-individuation and group decision-making. *International Journal of Man-Machine Studies* 34: 283–301.

Lembo, R. 1997 Situating television in everyday life: reformulating a cultural studies approach to the study of television use. In E. Long (ed.) *From Sociology to Cultural Studies: New Perspectives*. Malden, MA: Blackwell. pp. 203–233.

Lemos, A. 1996 The labyrinth of Minitel. In R. Shields (ed.) *Cultures of Internet: Virtual Spaces, Real Histories, Living Bodies*. London: Sage. pp. 33–48.

Lindlof, T.R. and Shatzer, M.J. 1998 Media ethnography in virtual space. *Journal of Broadcasting and Electronic Media* 42(2): 170–189.

Livingstone, S. 1998 *Making Sense of Television: the Psychology of Audience Interpretation*. 2nd edn. London: Routledge.

Lotfalian, M. 1996 A tale of an electronic community. In G.E. Marcus (ed.) *Connected: Engagements with Media*. Chicago: University of Chiacago Press.

Low, J. and Woolgar, S. 1993 Managing the social–technical divide: some aspects of the discursive structure of information systems development. In P. Quintas (ed.) *Social Dimensions of Systems Engineering: People, Processes, Policies and Software Development*. New York: Ellis Horwood. pp. 34–59.

Lyotard, J.-F. 1984 *The Postmodern Condition: a Report on Knowledge*. Manchester: Manchester University Press.

McBeth, S. 1993. Myths of objectivity and the collaborative process in life history research. In C. Brettell (ed.) *When They Read What We Write: the Politics of Ethnography*. Westport, CT: Bergin and Garvey. pp. 145–162.

MacKenzie, D. and Wajcman, J. 1985 *The Social Shaping of Technology: How the Refrigerator Got its Hum*. Milton Keynes: Open University Press.

MacKinnon, R.C. 1995 Searching for the Leviathan in Usenet. In S.G. Jones (ed.) *Cybersociety: Computer-Mediated Communication and Community*. Thousand Oaks, CA: Sage. pp. 112–137.

MacKinnon, R.C. 1997 Punishing the persona: correctional strategies for the virtual offender. In S.G. Jones (ed.) *Virtual Culture: Identity and Communication in Cybersociety*. London: Sage. pp. 206–235.

McLaughlin, M.L., Osborne, K.K. and Smith, C.B. 1995 Standards of conduct on Usenet. In S.G. Jones (ed.) *Cybersociety: Computer-Mediated Communication and Community*. Thousand Oaks, CA: Sage. pp. 90–111.

Mantovani, G. 1994 Is computer-mediated communication intrinsically apt to enhance democracy in organizations? *Human Relations* 47(1): 45–62.

Marcus, G.E. 1995 Ethnography in/of the world system: the emergence of multi-sited ethnography. *Annual Review of Anthropology* 24: 95–117.

Marcus, G.E. 1996 *Connected: Engagements with Media*. Chicago: University of Chicago Press.

Marcus, G.E. 1997 Critical cultural studies as one power/knowledge like, among and in engagement with others. In E. Long (ed.) *From Sociology to Cultural Studies: New Perspectives*. Malden, MA: Blackwell. pp. 399–425.

Marcus, G.E. 1998 *Ethnography through Thick and Thin*. Princeton, NJ: Princeton University Press.

Marcus, G.E. and Cushman, D. 1982. Ethnographies as texts. *Annual Review of Anthropology* 11: 25–69.

Markham, A. 1998 *Life Online: Researching Real Experience in Virtual Space*. Walnut Creek, CA: Altamira.

Martin, E. 1994 *Flexible Bodies: the Role of Immunity in American Culture from the Days of Polio to the Age of AIDS*. Boston: Beacon.

Mead, M. 1943 *Coming of Age in Samoa: a Study of Adolescence and Sex in Primitive Societies*. Harmondsworth: Penguin.

Meyrowitz, J. 1985 *No Sense of Place: the Impact of Electronic Media on Social Behavior*. New York: Oxford University Press.

Miller, H. 1995 The presentation of self in everyday life: Goffman on the Internet. Paper presented at Embodied Knowledge and Virtual Space Conference, Goldsmiths' College, University of London, June 1995. http://www.ntu.ac.uk/soc/psych/miller/goffman.htm.

Miller, L. 1995 Women and children first: gender and the settling of the electronic frontier. In J. Brook and I.A. Boal (eds) *Resisting the Virtual Life: the Culture and Politics of Information*. San Francisco: City Lights. pp. 49–57.

Mitchell, W.J. 1996 *City of Bits: Space, Place and the Infobahn*. Cambridge, MA: MIT Press.

Mitra, A. 1997 Virtual commonality: looking for India on the Internet. In S.G. Jones (ed.) *Virtual Culture: Identity and Communication in Cybersociety*. London: Sage. pp. 55–79.

Moerman, M. 1974 Accomplishing ethnicity. In R. Turner (ed.) *Ethnomethodology: Selected Readings*. Harmondsworth: Penguin. pp. 54–68.

Moores, S. 1993 *Interpreting Audiences: the Ethnography of Media Consumption*. London: Sage.

Morley, D. 1980 *The 'Nationwide' Audience*. London: British Film Institute.

Morley, D. 1992 *Television, Audiences and Cultural Studies*. London: Routledge.

Morse, M. 1997 Virtually female: body and code. In J. Terry and M. Calvert (eds) *Processed Lives: Gender and Technology in Everyday Life*. London: Routledge. pp. 23–35.

Mulkay, M. 1985 *The Word and the World: Explorations in the Form of Sociological Analysis*. London: Allen and Unwin.

Mulkay, M., Potter, J. and Yearley, S. 1983 Why an analysis of scientific discourse is needed. In K.D. Knorr-Cetina and M. Mulkay (eds) *Science Observed: Perspectives on the Social Studies of Science*. London: Sage. pp. 171–204.

Murray, D.E. 1995 *Knowledge Machines: Language and Information in a Technological Society*. London: Longman.

Negroponte, N. 1995 *Being Digital*. London: Hodder and Stoughton.

Newhagen, J.E., Cordes, J.W. and Levy, M.R. 1995 Nightly@nbc.com: audience scope and the perception of interactivity in viewer mail on the Internet. *Journal of Communication* 45(3): 164–175.

Nguyen, D.T. and Alexander, J. 1996 The coming of cyberspacetime and the end of the polity. In R. Shields (ed.) *Cultures of Internet: Virtual Spaces, Real Histories, Living Bodies*. London: Sage. pp. 99–124.

NOP 1999 NOP Internet Resarch. http://www.nopres.co.uk/internet_research/images/InternetResearch.pdf.

O'Brien, J. 1999 Writing in the body: gender (re)production in online interaction. In M.A. Smith and P. Kollock (eds) *Communities in Cyberspace*. London: Routledge. pp. 76–104.

Olwig, K.F. and Hastrup, K. (eds) 1997 *Siting Culture: the Shifting Anthropological Object*. London: Routledge.

Paccagnella, L. 1997 Getting the seats of your pants dirty: strategies for ethnographic research on virtual communities. *Journal of Computer Mediated Communication* 3(1). http://www.ascusc.org/jcmc/vol3/issue1/paccagnella.html.

Parks, M.R. and Floyd, K. 1996 Making friends in cyberspace. *Journal of Communication* 46(1): 80–97.

Pekurny, R. 1982 Coping with television production. In J. Ettema and S. Whitney (eds) *Individuals in Mass Media Organizations: Creativity and Constraint*. Beverly Hills, CA: Sage. pp. 131–144.

Phillips, D.J. 1996 Defending the boundaries: identifying and countering threats in a Usenet newsgroup. *The Information Society* 12(1): 39–62.

Pinch, T. and Bijker, W.E. 1987 The social construction of facts and artifacts: or how the sociology of science and the sociology of technology might benefit each other. In W.E. Bijker, T.P. Hughes and T. Pinch (eds) *The Social Construction of Technological Systems*. Cambridge, MA: MIT Press. pp. 17–50.

Pollner, M. 1987 *Mundane Reason: Reality in Everyday and Sociological Discourse*. Cambridge: Cambridge University Press.

Poster, M. 1990 *The Mode of Information*. Cambridge: Polity.

Poster, M. 1995 *The Second Media Age*. Cambridge: Polity.

Poster, M. 1998 Virtual ethnicity: tribal identity in an age of global communication. In S.G. Jones (ed.) *Cybersociety 2.0: Revisiting Computer-Mediated Communication and Community*. Thousand Oaks, CA: Sage. pp. 184–211.

Potter, J. 1996 *Representing Reality: Discourse, Rhetoric and Social Construction*. London: Sage.

Potter, J. and Wetherell, M. 1987 *Discourse and Social Psychology: Beyond Attitudes and Behaviour*. London: Sage.

Pratt, M.L. 1986 Fieldwork in common places. In J. Clifford and G.E. Marcus (eds) *Writing Culture: the Poetics and Politics of Ethnography*. Berkeley, CA: University of California Press. pp. 27–50.

Preis, A.-B.S. 1997 Seeking place: capsized identities and contracted belonging among Sri Lankan Tamil refugees. In K.F. Olwig and K. Hastrup (eds) *Siting Culture: the Shifting Anthropological Object*. London: Routledge. pp. 86–100.

Rabinow, P. 1977 *Reflections on Fieldwork in Morocco*. Berkeley, CA: University of California Press.

Rachel, J. 1996 Ethnography: practical implementation. In J.T.E. Richardson (ed.) *Handbook of Qualitative Research Methods for Psychology and the Social Sciences*. Leicester: BPS Books. pp. 113–124.

Rachel, J. and Woolgar, S. 1995 The discursive structure of the social–technical divide; the example of information systems development. *Sociological Review* 43(2): 251–273.

Radway, J. 1988 Reception study: ethnography and the problems of dispersed audiences and nomadic subjects. *Cultural Studies* 2(3): 359–376.

Rafaeli, S., Sudweeks, F., Konstan, J. and Mabry, E. 1994 ProjectH Technical

Report. Available at http://www.arch.usyd.edu.au/~fay/netplay/techreport.html or via ftp from ftp.arch.su.edu.au/pub/projectH/papers/techreport.txt.

Reid, E. 1995 Virtual worlds: culture and imagination. In S.G. Jones (ed.) *Virtual Culture: Identity and Communication in Cybersociety*. London: Sage. pp. 164–183.

Reid, E. 1996 Informed consent in the study of on-line communities: a reflection of the effects of computer-mediated social research. *The Information Society* 12(2): 169–174.

Reid, E. 1999 Hierarchy and power: social control in cyberspace. In M.A. Smith and P. Kollock (eds) *Communities in Cyberspace*. London: Routledge. pp. 107–133.

Rheingold, H. 1993 *The Virtual Community: Homesteading on the Electronic Frontier*. Reading, MA: Addison-Wesley.

Rice, R.E. and Love, G. 1987 Electronic emotion: socioemotional content in a computer-mediated communication network. *Communication Research* 14(1): 85–108.

Rich, B.R. 1998 The party line: gender and technology in the home. In J. Terry and M. Calvert (eds) *Processed Lives: Gender and Technology in Everyday Life*. London: Routledge. pp. 221–231.

Robins, K. 1995 Cyberspace and the world we live in. In M. Featherstone and R. Burrows (eds) *Cyberspace, Cyberbodies, Cyberpunk: Cultures of Technological Embodiment*. London: Sage. pp. 135–155.

Rosaldo, R. 1989 *Culture and Truth: the Remaking of Social Analysis*. Boston: Beacon.

Rudy, I.A. 1994 A bibliography of organizational computer-mediated communication. http://shum.cc.huji.ac.il/jcmc/rudybib.html.

Rudy, I.A. 1996 A critical review of research on electronic mail. *European Journal of Information Systems* 4: 198–213.

Savicki, V., Lingenfelter, D. and Kelley, M. 1996 Gender language style and group composition in Internet discussion groups. *Journal of Computer Mediated Communication* 2(3). http://www.ascusc.org/jcmc/vol2/issue3/savicki.html.

Scannell, P. 1996 *Radio, Television and Modern Life*. Oxford: Blackwell.

Scannell, P. and Cardiff, D. 1991 *A Social History of British Broadcasting: Serving the Nation, 1923–1939*. Oxford: Blackwell.

Schegloff, E.A., Jefferson, G. and Sacks, H. 1977 The preference for self-correction in the organization of repair in conversation. *Language* 53: 361–382.

Schlesinger, P. 1978 *Putting Reality Together*. London: Constable.

Schmitz, J.A. 1997 Structural relations, electronic media and social change: the Public Electronic Network and the homeless. In S.G. Jones (ed.) *Virtual Culture: Identity and Communication in Cybersociety*. London: Sage. pp. 80–101.

Schmitz, J.A. and Fulk, J. 1991 Organizational colleagues, information richness and electronic mail: a test of the social influence model of technology use. *Communication Research* 18: 487–523.

Schutz, A. 1972 *The Phenomenology of the Social World*. Translated by G. Walsh and F. Lehnert. London: Heinemann.

Schwartz Cowan, R. 1987 How the refrigerator got its hum. In W.E. Bijker, T.P. Hughes and T. Pinch (eds) *The Social Construction of Technological Systems*. Cambridge, MA: MIT Press. pp. 202–218.

Shaw, D.F. 1997 Gay men and computer-communication: a discourse of sex and identity in cyberspace. In S.G. Jones (ed.) *Virtual Culture: Identity and Communication in Cybersociety*. London: Sage. pp. 133–145.

Shields, R. 1996 Introduction: virtual spaces, real histories, living bodies. In R. Shields (ed.) *Cultures of Internet: Virtual Spaces, Real Histories, Living Bodies*. London: Sage. pp. 1–10.

Silverman, D. 1993 *Interpreting Text and Data: Methods for Analysing Talk, Text and Interaction*. London: Sage.

Silverstone, R. 1992 *Television and Everyday Life*. London: Routledge.

Silverstone, R. and Hirsch, E. (eds) 1994 *Consuming Technologies: Media and Information in Domestic Spaces*. London: Routledge.

Slack, R.S. 1998 On the potentialities and problems of a WWW based naturalistic sociology. *Sociological Research Online* 3(2). http://www.socresonline.org.uk/socresonline/3/2/3.html.

Smith, A.D. 1999 Problems of conflict management in virtual communities. In M.A. Smith and P. Kollock (eds) *Communities in Cyberspace*. London: Routledge. pp. 134–163.

Smith, M.A. 1999 Invisible crowds in cyberspace: mapping the social structure of Usenet. In M.A. Smith and P. Kollock (eds) *Communities in Cyberspace*. London: Routledge. pp. 195–219.

Spears, R., Lea, M. and Lee, S. 1990 De-individuation and group polarization in computer-mediated communication. *British Journal of Social Psychology* 29: 121–134.

Sproull, L. and Kiesler, S. 1986 Reducing social context cues: electronic mail in organizational communication. *Management Science* 32(11): 1492–1512.

Sproull, L. and Kiesler, S. 1991 *Connections: New Ways of Working in the Networked Organization*. Cambridge, MA: MIT Press.

Stanley, L. 1990 Doing ethnography, writing ethnography: a comment on Hammersley. *Sociology* 24(4): 617–627.

Star, S.L. and Kanfer, A. 1993 Virtual Gemeinschaft or electronic Gesellschaft? Analyzing an electronic community system for scientists. Paper presented at Annual Meeting of the Society for Social Studies of Science, Purdue University, Indiana, November 1993.

Stefik, M. 1997 *Internet Dreams: Archetypes, Myths and Metaphors*. Cambridge, MA: MIT Press.

Stone, A.R. 1991 Will the real body please stand up? Boundary stories about virtual cultures. In M. Benedikt (ed.) *Cyberspace: First Steps*. Cambridge, MA: MIT Press.

Stone, A.R. 1995 Sex and death among the disembodied: VR, cyberspace, and the nature of academic discourse. In S.L. Star (ed.) *The Cultures of Computing*. Oxford: Blackwell. pp. 243–255.

Stone, A.R. 1996 *The War of Desire and Technology at the Close of the Mechanical Age*. Cambridge, MA: MIT Press.

Strathern, M. 1992 *After Nature: English Kinship in the Late Twentieth Century*. Cambridge: Cambridge University Press.

Strathern, M. 1996 Cutting the Network. *Journal of the Royal Anthropological Institute* 2: 517–535.

Stubbs, P. 1998 Conflict and co-operation in the virtual community: email and the wars of the Yugoslav succession. *Sociological Research Online* 3(3). http://www.socresonline.org.uk/socresonline/3/3/7.html.

Sudweeks, F. and Rafaeli, S. 1996 How do you get a hundred strangers to agree? Computer mediated communication and collaboration. In T.M. Harris and T.D. Stephenson (eds) *Computer Networking and Scholarship in the 21st Century University*. New York: SUNY Press. pp. 115–136.

Swales, J.M. 1998 *Other Floors, Other Voices: a Textography of a Small University Building*. Mahwah, NJ: Lawrence Erlbaum.

Thompson, J.B. 1995 *The Media and Modernity: a Social Theory of the Media*. Cambridge: Polity.

Thomsen, S.R., Straubhaar, J.D. and Bolyard, D.M. 1998 Ethnomethodology and the study of online communities: exploring the cyberstreets. *Information Research* 4(1). http://www.shef.ac.uk/~is/publications/infres/paper50.html.

Thornton, R.J. 1988 The rhetoric of ethnographic holism. *Cultural Anthropology* 3(3): 285–303.

Thrift, N. 1996a *Spatial Formations*. London: Sage.

Thrift, N. 1996b New urban eras and old technological fears: reconfiguring the goodwill of electronic things. *Urban Studies* 33: 1463–1493.

Traweek, S. 1988a *Beamtimes and Lifetimes: the World of High-Energy Physicists*. Cambridge, MA: Harvard University Press.

Traweek, S. 1988b Discovering machines: nature in the age of its mechanical reproduction. In F.A. Dubinskas (ed.) *Making Time: Ethnographies in High-Technology Organizations*. Philadelphia: Temple University Press. pp. 39–91.

Traweek, S. 1992 Border crossings: narrative strategies in science studies and among physicists in Tsukuba Science City, Japan. In A. Pickering (ed.) *Science as Practice and Culture*. Chicago: University of Chicago Press. pp. 429–465.

Trevino, L.K., Lengel, R.H. and Daft, R.L. 1987 Media symbolism, media richness and media choice in organizations. *Communication Research* 14: 553–574.

Turkle, S. 1995 *Life on the Screen: Identity in the Age of the Internet*. London: Weidenfeld and Nicolson.

Turkle, S. 1996 Parallel lives: working on identity in virtual space. In D. Grodin and T.R. Lindlof (eds) *Constructing the Self in a Mediated World*. Thousand Oaks, CA: Sage. pp. 156–175.

Turner, G. 1996 *British Cultural Studies: an Introduction*. 2nd edn. London: Routledge.

Turner, R. 1989 Deconstructing 'the field'. In J. Gubrium and D. Silverman (eds) *The Politics of Field Research: Sociology beyond Enlightenment*. London: Sage. pp. 13–29.

Turner, S. 1980 *Sociological Explanation as Translation*. Cambridge: Cambridge University Press.

Van Gelder, L. 1991 The strange case of the electronic lover. In C. Dunlop and R. Kling (eds) *Computerisation and Controversy: Value Conflicts and Social Choices*. Boston: Academic. pp. 364–375.

Van Maanen, J. 1988 *Tales of the Field: on Writing Ethnography*. Chicago: University of Chicago Press.

Van Maanen, J. 1995 An end to innocence: the ethnography of ethnography. In J. Van Maanen (ed.) *Representation in Ethnography*. Thousand Oaks, CA: Sage. pp. 1–35.

Vehviläinen, M. 1998 Home page subjectivity: women's groups and information technology. Paper presented at EASST'98 General Conference on Cultures of Science and Technology: Europe and the Global Context, Lisbon, 1–3 October 1998.

Wakeford, N. 1997 Networking women and grrrls with information/communication technology: surfing tales of the World Wide Web. In J. Terry and M. Calvert (eds) *Processed Lives: Gender and Technology in Everyday Life*. London: Routledge. pp. 51–66.

Walkerdine, V. 1986 Video replay: families, films and fantasy. In V. Burgin, J. Donald and C. Kaplan (eds) *Formations of Fantasy*. London: Methuen.

Walkerdine, V. 1990 *Schoolgirl Fictions*. London: Verso.

Waskul, D. and Douglass, M. 1996 Considering the electronic participant: some polemical observations on the ethics of on-line research. *The Information Society* 12(2): 129–139.

Watson, N. 1997 Why we argue about virtual community: a case study of the Phish.Net fan community. In S.G. Jones (ed.) *Virtual Culture: Identity and Communication in Cybersociety*. London: Sage. pp. 101–132.

Webster, F. 1995 *Theories of the Information Society*. London: Routledge.

Wellman, B. and Gulia, M. 1999 Virtual communities as communities: net surfers don't ride alone. In M.A. Smith and P. Kollock (eds) *Communities in Cyberspace*. London: Routledge. pp. 167–194.

Williams, R. 1990 *Television: Technology and Cultural Form*. 2nd edn, edited by E. Williams. London: Routledge.

Wolf, M. 1992 *A Thrice-Told Tale: Feminism, Postmodernism and Ethnographic Responsibility*. Stanford, CA: Stanford University Press.

Woolgar, S. 1983 Irony in the social studies of science. In K.D. Knorr-Cetina and M. Mulkay (eds) *Science Observed: Perspectives on the Social Studies of Science*. London: Sage. pp. 239–266.

Woolgar, S. (ed.) 1988 *Knowledge and Reflexivity: New Frontiers in the Sociology of Science*. London: Sage.

Woolgar, S. 1991a The turn to technology in social studies of science. *Science, Technology and Human Values* 16(1): 20–50.

Woolgar, S. 1991b Reflexivity is the ethnographer of the text. In S. Woolgar (ed.) *Knowledge and Reflexivity: New Frontiers in the Sociology of Knowledge*. London: Sage.

Woolgar, 1991c Configuring the user: the case of usability trials. In J. Law (ed.) *A Sociology of Monsters: Essays on Power, Technology and Domination*. London: Routledge.

Woolgar, S. 1996 Technologies as cultural artefacts. In W. Dutton (ed.) *Information and Communication Technologies: Visions and Realities*. Oxford: Oxford University Press. pp. 87–102.

Wynn, E. and Katz, J.E. 1997 Hyperbole over cyberspace: self-presentation and social boundaries in Internet home pages and discourses. *The Information Society* 13: 297–327.

Zerubavel, E. 1979 *Patterns of Time in Hospital Life: a Sociological Perspective*. Chicago: University of Chicago Press.

Zickmund, S. 1997 Approaching the radical other: the discursive culture of cyberhate. In S.G. Jones (ed.) *Virtual Culture: Identity and Communication in Cybersociety*. London: Sage. pp. 185–205.

Index